The Bible Sabbath

Linwood Jackson, Jr.

PUBLISHED BY FIDELI PUBLISHING, INC.

O Sabbath;
Blessed refreshing of the living God;
This is the season that He made for His creation,
Even the appointment of His fame,
Which fame He blessed with His own blessing,
And honored with His own refreshing,
When He Himself partook of what He had sanctified.

O Sabbath;
Blessed remembrance of creation's science;
A time to let be and let lack what should,
That the powers may be rejuvenated,
That the heart may be regenerated,
Until we see you again.
This is that "rest" for His congregation,
Who cease not to examine self,
Who war with their *body* to give it no trouble,
Who through agony learn the fear of His name,
Who willingly pierce self through by faithfulness,
And by faithfulness heal the wound of their doing.
These do understand.

They will destroy the work of the week at the last evening,
That the refreshing that even He Himself was refreshed with,
May fall on them.

O Sabbath;
Blessed pillar of the Creator;
How is your name so sweet?
How do the showers of your fame procure health?
How is your comfort secured to the weary soul?
How is your wonder known among the ignored?
Blessed is this interval of time for your offspring,
And for all that they will endure in the virtue of His wisdom,
Blessed are those that learn to trust in His voice,
That desire to fervently trust in His name's sake.

O Sabbath,
You are blessed and do bless them that bless you.
Your name is excellent; your glory is contagious;
He who did order you is most wonderful in His doing.
In His wisdom He foresaw His faithful's need,
And so He blessed you, and did also kiss you,
He severed you and carefully honored you,
He delighted in your praise and set you as your own,
Ordaining your glory for His face,
That He, every seventh day, would be remembered.

O Sabbath,
Happy is the conversation that keeps you,
Blessed in virtue are they who do not forget you.

© Copyright 2019, Linwood Jackson, Jr.

All Rights Reserved.

No part of this book may be reproduced, stored in a retrieval system, or transmitted by any means, electronic, mechanical, photocopying, recording, or otherwise, without written permission from the author.

ISBN: 978-1-948638-32-6

For more information,
email the author at LinwoodJackson@hotmail.com,
or visit linwoodjacksonjr.com

Published by
Fideli Publishing, Inc.

www.FideliPublishing.com

PRINTED IN THE UNITED STATES OF AMERICA

Contents

	Introduction	vii
1.	Have Entered Into His Rest	1
2.	The Seal Of Love And Blessing	11
3.	The Word Spoken	22
4.	A Perpetual Covenant	31
5.	The Immutable Memorial Of His Righteousness	45
6.	The Israel of God	55
7.	He That Sanctifies	71
8.	The Inward Voice Of The Gospel	85
9.	The Gospel Of The Sabbath	96
10.	The Heritage Of The People Of God	106
11.	The Power And Order Of His Blessing	116
12.	Which Abideth For Ever	120
13.	The Banner Of His Faith	128
14.	Into My Rest	138
15.	The Day Of The Sun	144
16.	Wrath's Assignment	151
17.	From The Beginning	162
18	An Ever-Lasting Commandment	171

19. The Jewish Roman Mystery 181
20. A Risen Appointment 190
21. That Required Offering 202
22. No Sign Given 213
23. That Reasonable Refreshing 223
24. Creation's Body 233
25. An Abolished Ghost 241
26. An Eternal Substitute 253
27. That Alpha And Omega 263
28. Every Jew Of Shu'shan 274
29. One Present Manner 284

Introduction

1. There is great value in understanding the saying, "The Sabbath was made for man, and not man for the Sabbath."[1]

2. If the Sabbath was made for man, this means that no *sabbath* invented of man is that Sabbath of the living God. If the Sabbath was made for man, this means that man had; and still has; no say in the Sabbath made for him, but that the Sabbath made for him is not only above him, but is also an ever-existing institution, whether or not man pays any attention to it. If the Sabbath was made for man, it is evident that whatever Sabbath is made for them belongs to the son and daughter of the One that blessed this Sabbath and created them. If the Sabbath was made for man, then the Sabbath was not made or framed of man for man, for the Sabbath, being created outside of man, is without man's say or judgment, seeing as how "the Sabbath was made for man, and not man for the Sabbath."[2]

3. If man was made for the Sabbath, then man would have every right to either honor that Sabbath made for them, or to invent to themselves a *sabbath*. If man were made for the Sabbath, then man would be the *savior* and *creator* of self's conscience and conversation; if man is made for the Sabbath, then "what is the Almighty, that we should serve him? and what profit should we have, if we pray unto him?"[3] But

---

1 Mark 2:27
2 Mark 2:27
3 Job 21:15

man was not made for the Sabbath; the Sabbath was made for man; we therefore have an established Sabbath of the living God, "for he spake in a certain place of the seventh day on this wise."[4]

4. To hear that that the Sabbath was made for man is to hear that there exists a Sabbath specifically created by One with man in mind, and before the mind of man had the opportunity to take an honest gasp of air. That Sabbath made for man, being already in existence when found on earth, is as Eden was to Adam, for it says, "The LORD God planted a garden eastward in Eden; and there he put the man whom he had formed."[5]

5. As difficult a task as it would be to separate Adam from Eden, it is an equally difficult task to separate man from that Sabbath of Eden's LORD and God, for "the Sabbath was made for man, and not man for the Sabbath."[6] As the living God's Spirit planted Eden, and then led His thinking and feeling creation into that Vineyard, so also the Sabbath of the seventh day was planted by the same Spirit of this same living God, and every creation of His Spirit will find the mind of their conversation led into that Sabbath planted for them, "for the Sabbath was made for man."[7]

6. What is made or planted of the Spirit cannot be altered or disturbed by flesh; its platform is perpetual; especially whatsoever is blessed of the Spirit, which is why His creation says, "He hath blessed; and I cannot reverse it."[8] Why cannot I, or you, or any one, reverse His voice? It is written, "Whatsoever God doeth, it shall be for ever: nothing can be put to it, nor any thing taken from it."[9]

7. Now, if we believe some thing can be put to His voice, then we call the living God a liar and His counsel no word at all, making it foolish to hear how it is said, "Thy word is true from the beginning."[10]

---

4 Hebrews 4:4
5 Genesis 2:8
6 Mark 2:27
7 Mark 2:27
8 Numbers 23:20
9 Ecclesiastes 3:14
10 Psalm 119:160

8. The Sabbath is a commandment existing from the beginning: if we take what exists from the beginning to not be true, then what is after the beginning, and also what is at the end of that beginning, is also not true; the entire God of the Bible is then become a sham no better than any of the other gods and superstitions of various tribes and cults. In such a case; by our failure to count the living God's Word as true from the beginning; man may now take all things for himself, even a handcrafted *sabbath* devoted to the *righteousness* of self. But "the Spirit is truth,"[11] and "in the beginning was the Word, and the Word was with God, and the Word was God."[12] This same Word conformed to His Christ's conversation is that same Spirit from the beginning, and when any man rejects any thing of this beginning Word, it is "because he believeth not the record that God gave of his Son."[13]

9. "Whosoever transgresseth, and abideth not in the doctrine of Christ, hath not God,"[14] and this is important to know. In the beginning, the Word was God, and today, the Word of the living God is still that God of His assembly. Because the Word is that Spirit proceeding from the living God's throne, every one born of His mind will return to His throne.

10. At this throne, there are ten laws of creation for the member of His heavenly Sanctuary, for "we do know that we know him, if we keep his commandments. He that saith, I know him, and keepeth not his commandments, is a liar, and the truth is not in him."[15]

11. Thus, it is well to know that, since "the Spirit is truth,"[16] and since "the Spirit of life"[17] is "the Word of life,"[18] if we fail to know the doctrine of the Word, we will fail to know the commandments of this same Word, which Word, in the beginning, was that God of creation, seeing as how "all things were made by him; and without him was not

---

11 1 John 5:6
12 John 1:1
13 1 John 5:10
14 2 John 1:9
15 1 John 2:3,4
16 1 John 5:6
17 Revelation 11:11
18 1 John 1:1

any thing made that was made";[19] for "the Word was God."[20] Therefore, it may say, "God blessed the seventh day, and sanctified it,"[21] but, in reality, it is that the Word blessed and sanctified the seventh day, and if we do transgress this Word's present Faith, we will maintain a conversation without the Spirit of this Word, having no mind for this doctrine's character to hear, do, and love this Spirit's commandments, "and this is love, that we walk after hiscommandments."[22]

12. If we are not of that class honoring that Sabbath made for them from the beginning, it is because we are violators of that Sabbath's present spiritual understanding, for what person, possessing a conversation without the living God's will and wisdom, can think to honor the voice of that instruction?

13. Any thing contrary to His voice is "sin" against that commandment, "and the strength of sin is the law."[23] The "law" mentioned by Paul as "sin" is "the handwriting of ordinances"[24] fashioned by the pen of priests and elders, and the living God's man, "having abolished in his flesh the enmity, even the law of commandments contained in ordinances";[25] and "not only in this world, but also in that which is to come";[26] has blatantly defined "sin" for us, "and the strength of sin is the law."[27]

14. This Word's man on the tree means the absolute and perpetual condemnation of the philosophy of the religious law from His God and Father's religious character, making it a violation of that doctrine to treat what is abolished as though it is not. The flesh of this man passed away on the tree is a figurative illustration of a religious spirit and philosophy blotted out of the living God's higher education, which is why the intention of this man's sacrifice was "to redeem them that

---

19 John 1.3
20 John 1:1
21 Genesis 2:3
22 2 John 1:6
23 1 Corinthians 15:56
24 Colossians 2:14
25 Ephesians 2:15
26 Ephesians 1:21
27 1 Corinthians 15:56

were under the law,"²⁸ for this "Christ hath redeemed us from the curse of the law."²⁹ Therefore, when we observe a *Christ* pick up what the Word acknowledges as "sin" against His name; which "sin" is "the handwriting of ordinances";³⁰ we may know that we are in the presence of an erroneous spirit and philosophy.

15. Now, "if I build again the things which I destroyed, I make myself a transgressor,"³¹ therefore to observe a *Christ* inventing to his self a creed, a ceremony, a baptism, a *sabbath*, is to observe a *Christ* of spiritual error. Today; and ever since His man said, "It is finished";³² it is religious negligence to invent, adopt, and forward religious laws and commandments. His "Christ hath redeemed us from the curse of the law, being made a curse for us: for it is written, Cursed is every one that hangeth on a tree."³³

16. We are become "the enemies of the cross of Christ"³⁴ when failing to soberly discern the illustration of the living God's man on the tree, for with the light now shed on spiritual falsehood, it is that "his own self bare our sins in his own body on the tree, that we, being dead to sins, should live unto righteousness."³⁵ And now that we know "the strength of sin is the law,"³⁶ it is that, where we understand our conversation to be ruled by the pen and judgment of flesh, we turn our mind from that spiritual wrong; why should we have to hear, "How turn ye again to the weak and beggarly elements, whereunto ye desire again to be in bondage?"³⁷ The Spirit's man purged his God's spiritual wisdom from the order and elements of the religious world, which system is built upon the foundation of "philosophy and vain deceit, after the tradition of men."³⁸

---

28 Galatians 4:5
29 Galatians 3:13
30 Colossians 2:14
31 Galatians 2:18
32 John 19:30
33 Galatians 3:13
34 Philippians 3:18
35 1 Peter 2:24
36 1 Corinthians 15:56
37 Galatians 4:9
38 Colossians 2:8

17. Today, we are to be "written not with ink, but with the Spirit of the living God."³⁹ What is of ink is of men and ministers, but to be written of the living God's Spirit, this is the aim of *life* when under the instruction of His course of learning. To hear that the Sabbath was made for man is to hear that the Sabbath is not of ink, but is of the living God's Spirit for the spirit of His creation's mind. All transgression against heaven's new covenant law is understood by that handwritten rule of priests and elders, for His intention is a personal matter, which is why He promises, "A new heart also will I give you, and a new spirit will I put within you,"⁴⁰ and, "I will put my law in their inward parts, and write it in their hearts; and will be their God, and they shall be my people."⁴¹

18. Creation is the Godhead's will for man's inwards, which is why His doctrine's "circumcision is that of the heart, in the spirit, and not in the letter; whose praise is not of men, but of God."⁴² There is no ink or tradition of flesh with this fellowship, seeing as how it is a "circumcision made without hands."⁴³ The conversation of priests and elders is *blessed* by hands in carnal doctrines and sensual baptisms, but that of the living God is higher than flesh, which is why it says, "That which is born of the Spirit is spirit,"⁴⁴ and, "By his knowledge shall my righteous servant justify many."⁴⁵

19. Right baptism is by the mind's edification, which is why we are counseled, "Be renewed in the spirit of your mind."⁴⁶ This means that, according to salvation's science, only the Spirit's words forward creation, and this newness occurring only within the conversation's inwards, as it says, "Thou desirest truth in the inward parts: and in the hidden part thou shalt make me to know wisdom."⁴⁷ By taking in His

---

39   2 Corinthians 3:3
40   Ezekiel 36:26
41   Jeremiah 31:33
42   Romans 2:29
43   Colossians 2:11
44   John 3:6
45   Isaiah 53:11
46   Ephesians 4:23
47   Psalm 51:6

Spirit's voice; as it says, "Be ye transformed by the renewing of your mind";[48] knowledge of His ministry's goodness will move the heart to confess, "The law of the Spirit of life in Christ Jesus hath made me free from the law of sin and death."[49]

20. Liberty of the conscience from the chain of priest and elder is the new covenant's intention, which is why it is well to "know that ye were not redeemed with corruptible things, as silver and gold, from your vain conversation received by tradition from your fathers,"[50] for it says, "Ye are clean through the word which I have spoken,"[51] and, "Through knowledge shall the just be delivered."[52] Because it is this Spirit's intention to "purge your conscience from dead works to serve the living God,"[53] it is our assignment to personally comprehend His voice for our own self, even as His faithful says, "I will meditate in thy precepts, and have respect unto thy ways."[54]

21. If we deviate from His commandment in any way, or if we are ignorant of His voice, it is because that will and law of His Spirit's intention is not within our conversation's conscience. Until that Word of newness and creation is become our faith's personal Savior and Governor, we will continue to violate the living God's throne, and to think that it is lawful to do so. We may therefore understand that our conversation fails of that newness and creation when we are of that class fulfilling the saying, "Full well ye reject the commandment of God, that ye may keep your own tradition."[55]

20. Now, if it is written, "In the beginning was the Word, and the Word was with God, and the Word was God,"[56] and, "God blessed the seventh day, and sanctified it,"[57] then any thing more or less than

---

48 Romans 12:2
49 Romans 8:2
50 1 Peter 1:18
51 John 15:3
52 Proverbs 11:9
53 Hebrews 9:14
54 Psalm 119:15
55 Mark 7:9
56 John 1:1
57 Genesis 2:3

this confession of the Word and His seventh day is plain traditional religious error. Such erroneous tradition falls under the category of "the law of commandments contained in ordinances,"[58] categorizing it as "sin" against the living God's will and wisdom, seeing as how "the strength of sin is the law."[59] Thus, whosoever is *born* under the religious law and tradition of a *sabbath*; or of any charge; contrary to that of creation's Word and Father, is born a "sinner" against creation's Father and Spirit, and is therefore conceived in transgression against heaven's will and intention, for the religious law blatantly reveals its hardheartedness against the Godhead's science.

21. This is a true saying, for the Jew and the Christian, who are naturally "in bondage under the elements of the world,"[60] are naturally violent towards creation's wisdom. But since His "Christ hath redeemed us from the curse of the law,"[61] we show our affection for his mission and ministry by abstaining from what his flesh pronounces as "sin," and, "having abolished in his flesh the enmity, even the law of commandments contained in ordinances,"[62] it is an eternal and indisputable fact that "the strength of sin is the law."[63]

22. Where we find our conversation governed by a *Christ* exalting the religious law; that is, for example, inventing and claiming a contrary *sabbath* for his name above that Sabbath of creation's former, present, and ever lasting Word; it is well for us to quit that counterfeit spirit to personally know the face of the living God's religious character. Such a spirit of error is not of the living God's Faith, but is of that philosophy persuading its hearer to believe that what the living God curses is not cursed, and that what He blesses is not blessed. For when it says, "He that is hanged is accursed of God,"[64] it is counsel pointing to His man suspended between heaven and earth while on the tree. What is accursed of the Word is not the man, but rather the flesh of the

---

58 Ephesians 2:15
59 1 Corinthians 15:56
60 Galatians 4:3
61 Galatians 3:13
62 Ephesians 2:15
63 1 Corinthians 15:56
64 Deuteronomy 21:23

man, which flesh is a figurative illustration of a religious conversation ruled by "the handwriting of ordinances."[65] Thus, with the pen of flesh blotted out of the Spirit's Faith, all that remains to do is "fear God, and keep his commandments."[66]

23. The Spirit's commandments are not the commandments of men, for Moses, concerning heaven's commandments, says, "I stood between the LORD and you at that time, to shew you the word of the LORD."[67] Now, if it is written, "The word of the Lord endureth for ever,"[68] then that God saying, "The seventh day is the Sabbath,"[69] is that same Word saying, "God blessed the seventh day, and sanctified it."[70] The Word of the living God's Ten Commandments is the same Word of creation, and if our conversation is contrary to this Word, and if the *Christ* we profess is contrary to that man born "to redeem them that were under the law,"[71] then our conversation is fallen to a *Christ* of no living value.

24. At the heart of the living God's spiritual understanding is the revelation of His throne's religious character, which revelation states the reason for blessing His name, even as it says, "In six days the LORD made heaven and earth, the sea, and all that in them is, and rested the seventh day: wherefore the LORD blessed the Sabbath day, and hallowed it."[72]

25. The Sabbath was made for man because of creation's assignment. The one examining and proving His doctrine's law and judgment will know the refreshing held to His seventh day, for it is that Sabbath celebrating creation's present wisdom and learning. This Sabbath was blessed to Eden's host, but after Eden's priest violated heaven's will, religious error passed to every man of his line. But with His man purging the spirit and course of religious error from Eden's

---

65 Colossians 2:14
66 Ecclesiastes 12:13
67 Deuteronomy 5:5
68 1 Peter 1:25
69 Exodus 20:10
70 Genesis 2:3
71 Galatians 4:5
72 Exodus 20:11

Faith, only the living God's character remains within that commandment, along with that seventh day refreshing greatly magnifying His person.

1

Have Entered Into His Rest

1. Here is the counsel of the living God, "Hear ye him,"[73] and, "Believe on the name of the Son of God,"[74] for it is written, "We which have believed do enter into rest."[75]

2. To soberly believe on His man's name is to possess the "rest" of his God, even "the rest of the holy Sabbath,"[76] that is, that refreshing of "the seventh day, which is the Sabbath."[77] Before the Ten Commandments were ever given, the LORD tried to administer Sabbath reform to the ones under His care, for the Sabbath was a precept originating not at Si'nai, but rather after all things had been created in the beginning. "For he spake in a certain place of the seventh day on this wise,

---

73 Matthew 17:5
74 1 John 5:13
75 Hebrews 4:3
76 Exodus 16:23
77 Exodus 16:26

And God did rest the seventh day from all his works. And in this place again, If they shall enter into my rest."[78] If there is an honest soul professing the Faith of this Word's Christ, they will know the rest of his Father, "For we which have believed do enter into rest,"[79] confirms the apostle.

3. As it was of old, so too is it even now, that with the Spirit's voice comes the Spirit's "rest." Thus, "If ye will hear his voice, harden not your hearts, as in the provocation."[80]

4. Now, we "are not come unto the mount that might be touched,"[81] but are rather joined to the living God "by a greater and more perfect tabernacle, not made with hands,"[82] "for Christ is not entered into the holy places made with hands, which are the figures of the true."[83] No longer is the Christian compelled to keep, by a fleshy service, that which came from "the midst of heaven, with darkness, clouds, and thick darkness,"[84] but rather, "Refuse not him that speaketh,"[85] even "Jesus the mediator of the new covenant,"[86] for it says, "Hear ye him,"[87] seeing as how the conversation's conscience is to be "renewed in knowledge."[88]

5. The former manner *blessed* its servant through acts and deeds that failed to reach the heart, rendering the conversation *perfect* by the performance of commandments, yet, under heaven's current will, our conversation is to be "perfect, as pertaining to the conscience."[89] As they anciently heard Moses, so today our mind is to personally learn of and do the voice of His Son, seeing as how, by all things, "unto us was the gospel preached, as well as unto them,"[90] and it is yet the respon-

---

78 Hebrews 4:4,5
79 Hebrews 4:3
80 Hebrews 3:7
81 Hebrews 12:18
82 Hebrews 9:11
83 Hebrews 9:24
84 Deuteronomy 4:11
85 Hebrews 12:25
86 Hebrews 12:24
87 Matthew 17:5
88 Colossians 3:10
89 Hebrews 9:9
90 Hebrews 4:2,3

sibility of the professor to examine that which was anciently given and passed over.

6. "There remaineth therefore a rest to the people of God,"[91] and "it remaineth that some must enter therein."[92] The Sabbath is the name of the living God declaring the creative power of His Spirit's Word, for it is known, "He spake, and it was done."[93] Therefore, "upon the Israel of God"[94] comes the Spirit's Word, saying, "The children of Israel shall keep the Sabbath, to observe the Sabbath throughout their generations, for a perpetual covenant."[95]

7. So "let us worship and bow down: let us kneel before the LORD our maker,"[96] for only such who confess the Word as their Maker may receive entrance into His refreshing, even as the believing conversation says, "The Spirit of God hath made me."[97] This is that same Spirit who, in the beginning, was God, for "the Word was God."[98] We cannot therefore ignore the fact that "the Spirit of life"[99] is "the Word of life,"[100] for if this Word of creation is that God of creation; and He is; then every spirit created by this same Spirit will understand the Sabbath of His benevolence, seeing as how they rightly understand that "all things were made by him; and without him was not any thing made that was made."[101]

8. Because creation is today forwarded by the heavenly mediation of this same Spirit's counsel, service to the Father and Word of creation is an eternal fact, and through this same counsel "in whom we have redemption,"[102] for which cause he says, "Why call ye me, Lord, Lord, and do not the things which I say?"[103]

---

91   Hebrews 4:9
92   Hebrews 4:6
93   Psalms 33:9
94   Galatians 6:16
95   Exodus 31:16
96   Psalms 95:6
97   Job 33:4
98   John 1:1
99   Revelation 11:11
100   1 John 1: 1
101   John 1:1
102   Ephesians 1:7
103   Luke 6:46

9. What gives off a louder sound: the voice or the actions? Isn't it that "God speaketh once, yea twice, yet man perceiveth it not"?[104] This Spirit did not simply utter His Sabbath, but He also "rested on the seventh day,"[105] and His man, whose ministry remained "both in the land of the Jews, and in Jerusalem,"[106] "as his custom was, he went into the synagogue on the Sabbath day."[107] This man's Sabbath; seeing as how "the Word was made flesh";[108] is the same Sabbath as that Word of creation. To find him in the Jewish temple on the Sabbath is to observe him reverencing the Sabbath of the LORD his Father, and seeing as how both He and his LORD blessed the seventh day, must we do contrary to them? "Do we provoke the Lord to jealousy? are we stronger than he?"[109]

10. Do we not know that to associate the LORD's man to a *sabbath* contrary to that of his LORD's Word is to "blaspheme his name, and his tabernacle, and them that dwell in heaven"?[110] Have we no real knowledge of redemption's science? Concerning the definition of "redemption," we read how it says, "Concerning redeeming and concerning changing."[111] To "redeem" is to "change," and if it is the new covenant's will to "purge your conscience from dead works to serve the living God";[112] and it is; then it is that the conscience of the conversation is to find its heart changed into the image of the Spirit's Son, wherefore it is well to know that our conversation is "changed into the same image from glory to glory, even as by the Spirit of the Lord."[113] We understand our course is without this Spirit when we have no knowledge of the redemption forwarded by this Spirit, and we know that this Word is

---

104 Job 33:14
105 Genesis 2.2
106 Acts 10:39
107 Luke 4:16
108 John 1:14
109 1 Corinthians 10:22
110 Revelation 13:6
111 Ruth 4:7
112 Hebrews 9:14
113 2 Corinthians 3:18

not that law of our confidence when we have no knowledge that "God blessed the seventh day, and sanctified it."[114]

11. Heaven's Faith was preached to them of old as it is to us, for it was told them, "At even ye shall eat flesh, and in the morning ye shall be filled with bread."[115] Even, or "eveningtide,"[116] is that time "before the morning."[117] "Even, at the going down of the sun,"[118] is as "darkness and the shadow,"[119] and we do know that the time of Moses was as "a shadow of things to come; but the body is of Christ."[120] Therefore after the shadow did pass, in the morning the dew lay, for He had said, "My doctrine shall drop as the rain, my speech shall distil as the dew."[121] "For the law having a shadow of good things to come, and not the very image of the things, can never with those sacrifices which they offered year by year continually make the comers thereunto perfect,"[122] which is why it is written, "Labour not for the meat which perisheth."[123] "My Father giveth you the true bread from heaven,"[124] says our High Priest, "believe on him whom he hath sent."[125]

12. And "we which have believed do enter into rest,"[126] for if we actively learn of and trust on His Christ's Faith, we know how it says, "Him hath God the Father sealed,"[127] for his students will bear "his Father's name in their foreheads,"[128] even as He prays, "Holy Father, keep through thine own name those whom thou hast given me."[129]

---

114   Genesis 2:3
115   Exodus 16:12
116   Isaiah 17:14
117   Isaiah 17:14
118   Deuteronomy 16:6
119   Job 3:5
120   Colossians 2:17
121   Deuteronomy 32:2
122   Hebrews 10:1
123   John 6:27
124   John 6:32
125   John 6:29
126   Hebrews 4:3
127   John 6:27
128   Revelation 14:1
129   John 17:11

13. Who are they that refuse the day of the LORD's Word but them that "believeth not the record that God gave of his Son"?[130] "I receive not honour from men,"[131] His man says, for "all men should honour the Son, even as they honour the Father,"[132] yet "he is an'tichrist, that denieth the Father and the Son."[133] "Hereby know we that we dwell in him, and he in us, because he hath given us of his Spirit";[134] "if any man have not the Spirit of Christ, he is none of his."[135] So then, is it not written, "To whom sware he that they should not enter into his rest, but to them that believed not?"[136]

14. "There remaineth therefore a rest to the people of God,"[137] even a refreshing for them of whom it is promised, "I will dwell in them, and walk in them; and I will be their God, and they shall be my people."[138] They that do not hear the Spirit's voice cannot know the appointment of His Faith's regeneration, for by failing to learn of and do "the law of the Spirit of life,"[139] it is evident that we do not have, within our heart, "the law of Christ"[140] to know that the Word is today still God, and that this God "blessed the seventh day."[141]

15. None can say, "It is he that hath made us, and not we ourselves,"[142] unless they experience the doctrine of heaven's Word, to the end they may suffer self to trust His counsel "as unto a faithful Creator."[143] The creation and the fall of man take the mind to the redemption ratified through the tree, and to the glorification of man's inwards by that accomplished on the tree. "The beginning of the

---

130   1 John 5:11
131   John 5:41
132   John 5:23
133   1 John 2:22
134   1 John 4:13
135   Romans 8:9
136   Hebrews 3:18
137   Hebrews 4:9
138   2 Corinthians 6:16
139   Romans 8:2
140   Galatians 6:2
141   Genesis 2:3
142   Psalm 100:3
143   1 Peter 4:19

creation of God"[144] "hath abolished death, and hath brought life and immortality to light through the gospel,"[145] and since "the sting of death is sin; and the strength of sin is the law";[146] it is today "sin" to invent and forward religious laws and traditions, and seeing as how "the seventh day is the Sabbath,"[147] any other *sabbath* is understood as "sin" encouraging "death" to its subject.

16. As of old, when they were in the wilderness, in the evening flesh was to be consumed, even that meat that was to perish; for it says, "He taketh away the first, that he may establish the second";[148] it is that in the morning, in the one who did "come unto us as the rain,"[149] he was to declare, "This is the bread which cometh down from heaven, that a man may eat thereof, and not die."[150] As it was told them, "To morrow is the rest of the holy Sabbath...bake that which ye will bake to day,"[151] and, "To day is a Sabbath unto the LORD,"[152] so too he says, "I am the bread which came down from heaven,"[153] and, "If a man keep my sayings, he shall never see death,"[154] even as when the Israelites obeyed for a time and the bread "did not stink, neither was there any worm therein."[155] "Death's" sting is "sin," and the wisdom of "sin" is the religious law, wherefore we understand that our conversation is built up on "death" when religious laws contrary to the living God's religious character rule our heart.

17. Connected to the Spirit's voice is the Sabbath of His LORD, for anciently the test was to obey the voice of commandments concerning the man'na, and presently the same charge concerning that *bread* from the heavenly Sanctuary is not changed or altered. After they disobeyed

---

144 Revelation 3:14
145 2 Timothy 1:10
146 1 Corinthians 15:56
147 Exodus 20:10
148 Hebrews 10:9
149 Hosea 6:3
150 John 6:50
151 Exodus 16:23
152 Exodus 16:25
153 John 6:41
154 John 8:51
155 Exodus 16:24

the Spirit's voice, the living God said, "How long refuse ye to keep my commandments and my laws,"[156] for there was not yet given those ten precepts of God, but rather the commandment to obey His voice concerning His Sabbath law. Yet today the Spirit says, "I will put my laws into their hearts, and in their minds will I write them,"[157] and this "signifieth the removing of those things that are shaken, as of things that are made, that those things which cannot be shaken may remain."[158] For this cause it is said, "If that which is done away was glorious, much more that which remaineth is glorious,"[159] for with this LORD's man "blotting out the handwriting of ordinances,"[160] what remains is love to his LORD and Father, "and this is love, that we walk after his commandments."[161]

18. Therefore God "hath called us unto his eternal glory by Christ,"[162] to the end that all things after a flesh-based routine may cease, that is, that are "after the commandments and doctrines of men."[163] The Spirit's voice is now "the eternal purpose which he purposed in Christ"[164] "through the redemption that is in"[165] his name. The Word's Sabbath is not changed or done away with, for then God would be a liar and the gift of *life* by the works of the flesh. With redemption preaching the "putting off the body of the sins of the flesh,"[166] it is that the doer of creation's law reports, "The law of the Spirit of life in Christ Jesus hath made me free from the law of sin and death."[167]

19. We then praise the name of the LORD God by the name of His Son, by whom "there remaineth therefore a rest to the people of

---

156 Exodus 16:28
157 Hebrews 10:16
158 Hebrews 12:27
159 2 Corinthians 3:11
160 Colossians 2:14
161 2 John 1:6
162 1 Peter 5:10
163 Colossian 2:22
164 Ephesians 3:11
165 Romans 3:24
166 Colossians 2:11
167 Romans 8:2

God,"[168] which is why it says, "To day if ye will his voice, harden not your hearts,"[169] for it should rather be said, "Ye have obeyed from the heart."[170]

20. The doctrine of this LORD's man is yet joined to the name of the Father, even as it was of old expressed through "the example and shadow of heavenly things."[171] To refuse knowledge of the day of the glorious Memorial of the Word is to know neither this God nor His Christ, for His man himself says, "The Son of man is Lord (absolute ruler, master, director, governor) even of the Sabbath day."[172] Thus, "we which have believed do enter into rest,"[173] for the Spirit's voice yet sounds from heaven, saying, "Here are they that keep the commandments of God, and the faith of Jesus."[174]

21. Seeing that "unto us was the gospel preached, as well as unto them";[175] them "with whom he was grieved forty years";[176] "they to whom it was first preached entered not in because of unbelief";[177] as it says, "They do alway err in their heart";[178] let none bear "an evil heart of unbelief, in departing from the living God."[179] The Christian is to know "the only true God, and Jesus Christ,"[180] within their conversation through the Spirit and Counsel of the heavenly Sanctuary. There is no one professing the confidence of the Spirit's Temple without the name of that Temple's Father, and there is no revelation of the Father without the name of His Christ, "for he whom God hath sent speaketh the words of God,"[181] and to profess the words of His man without the

---

168   Hebrews 4:9
169   Hebrews 3:7
170   Romans 7:17
171   Hebrews 8:5
172   Matthew 12:8
173   Hebrews 4:3
174   Revelation 14:12
175   Hebrews 4:2
176   Hebrews 3:17
177   Hebrews 4:5
178   Hebrews 3:10
179   Hebrews 3:12
180   John 17:3
181   John 3:34

Spirit of his Father is to faithlessly confess, "Shew us the Father, and it sufficeth us."[182]

22. So do we know Him? Who reverences the Word without His Spirit and claims to honor Him "that is passed into the heavens"?[183] We are become liars who should know how it says, "We which have believed do enter into rest."[184]

---

182 John 14:8
183 Hebrews 4:14
184 Hebrews 4:3

2

The Seal Of Love And Blessing

1. "And on the seventh day God ended his work which he had made; and he rested on the seventh day from all his work which he had made."[185]

2. Marriage and the Sabbath were two key institutions existing since the beginning, even as it says, "God blessed them,"[186] and, "God blessed the seventh day."[187]

3. Before man needed an image of a perfect personal and devotional character, the Spirit's blessing dwelt within the mind of His creation. Blessing was to rest in marriage and in His Sabbath, for concerning the Sabbath, "the Sabbath was made for man, and not man for the Sabbath."[188] This day of refreshing is a day of mental and

---

185 Genesis 2:2
186 Genesis 1:28
187 Genesis 2:3
188 Mark 2:27

spiritual cessation from the labor of suppressing self for knowledge to live by. Thus, "Whosoever doeth any work therein, that soul shall be cut off,"[189] says the Spirit blessing this institution, and His language is important.

4. Not the physical life, not the literal breath of the individual, but rather the soul of the one maintaining a stubborn and superficial spirit against His Sabbath will perish from before His Faith's face. The soul of the one yet willing to labor for *righteousness* when the seventh day's appointment calls for an end of self-regulated *righteousness* will fulfill the saying, "For this cause God shall send them strong delusion, that they should believe a lie."[190]

5. "In six days the LORD made heaven and earth, and on the seventh day he rested, and was refreshed,"[191] says Scripture, for this "God ended his work."[192] Nothing continued to be created by His Spirit on the eighth day, or rather again on the next first day, but rather "God saw every thing that he had made, and, behold, it was very good,"[193] for the work was suffered to remain in the condition that it then was.

6. Even after the fall of man, and after God Himself had reported, "It repenteth me that I have made them";[194] for by their disobedience "it repented the LORD that he had made man on the earth";[195] the LORD did not again pick up the work of creation to immediately undo the error that had been made, but rather the literal work of creation had ceased days before, and the Spirit let remain the work which He saw to be good. Though He did not undo the error of "sin," but allowed that which was ended to continue by that which was falsehood, the living God declared, "I will put enmity,"[196] creating a new work that was to return man to that which was good.

---

189 Exodus 31:14
190 2 Thessalonians 2:11
191 Exodus 31:17
192 Genesis 2:2
193 Genesis 1:31
194 Genesis 6:7
195 Genesis 6:6
196 Genesis 3:15

7. The living God's example is for us who believe on His name, and for us who labor during the week in a work of righteousness for the cleansing of our soul temple, even for them that "labour therefore to enter into that rest."[197] The works of His Spirit ended on the seventh day, the work of His mind and the labor of His heart ceased to exist upon entering the seventh day, for in that day the Spirit put down His instruction for a moment of spiritual relief and remembrance, which is why He counsels, "In returning and rest shall ye be saved; in quietness and in confidence shall be your strength."[198]

8. The Sabbath is an event that is made for man; that is, for one who acknowledges, "Man is born unto trouble,"[199] and, "Man that is born of a woman is of few days, and full of trouble";[200] because man is born as that same living soul to Adam's fraudulent heart. For as we are naturally born of man in to *heavenly things*, it is that we all do confess, "I covered my transgressions as Adam, by hiding mine iniquity in my bosom,"[201] and, "My temptation which was in my flesh."[202]

9. The Sabbath is made for man, that is, is made for "a man that is a sinner"[203] who cares to confess, from observing the living God's religious character, "Christ Jesus came into the world to save sinners; of whom I am chief."[204] The Sabbath is made for Adam the sinner, and to those who throughout the week are "made sorry after a godly manner,"[205] "bringing into captivity every thought to the obedience of Christ."[206] The Sabbath is therefore a blessed occasion; in that day God ended His work, and so too His student temporarily ceases the work of the charge, "Ye shall afflict your souls."[207]

---

197 Hebrews 4:11
198 Isaiah 30:15
199 Job 5:7
200 Job 14:1
201 Job 31:33
202 Galatians 4:14
203 John 9:16
204 1 Timothy 1:15
205 2 Corinthians 7:9
206 2 Corinthians 10:5
207 Leviticus 23:32

10. After creation, the Spirit suffered what would prosper to prosper and what would fail to faint, for He did not go back to creating after the Sabbath of His "rest," but He did work after the Sabbath to bring health to what was wrongfully done to His labor the previous week. The works were done, the endeavor completed, and what did lack would lack, for on the seventh day His spirit rested. Yet after that day, the living God began to work again, not changing, for gratification, the error of the previous week in the week then present, but "forgetting those things which are behind, and reaching forth unto those things which are before,"[208] this Spirit built without discouragement.

11. If the eye is willing to behold the depth of the living God's will and wisdom, it will declare, "God hath called us to peace."[209] Active or conscious labor for His pleasure is to cease on the seventh day, for "six days may work be done,"[210] and if the Scripture were to be held only to a literal platform, wherein is the mind of the power of God?

12. "We know that the law is spiritual,"[211] therefore the Sabbath law is a precept ultimately blessing the spirit and soul of man. The servants of the living God; those who desire to fear His name for understanding what the will of His Spirit is; these are them that will enter into His doctrine's "rest" from previously suffering their mind to learn of that regeneration within "the law of the Spirit of life."[212] The Sabbath is made for that mind touched by His Faith's offering and ashamed of its heritage in Adam, for that heritage speaks against the things of His mind.

13. Our work for six days is a work of soul affliction. It is a work of self-surrender and of humiliation through self-regulation with mental taxation to know the Godhead's science. It is for this reason that the living God instituted the Sabbath for His thinking and feeling creation, for this daily labor needs a moment of relief.

---

208 Philippians 3:13
209 1 Corinthians 7:15
210 Exodus 31:15
211 Romans 7:14
212 Romans 8:2

14. The work of reformation is not attractive, and to naturally love the Bible's spiritual understanding is even less attractive, but to the one touched by the work of His Spirit through the tree, that soul surrendered to the Creator will suffer anguish of heart to know the refreshing of His voice. The greatest miracle is indeed a mind made to feel and acknowledge "sin" against the living God's name to then boldly hold on to His man's name by faith, that through obedience they may be even as his conversation yet is, as it says, "He liveth unto God."[213]

15. The work of soul reformation and character reparation by living God's spiritual understanding therefore needs a season of refreshing for the human being. The Sabbath is that appointment for the afflicted conscience to learn how to cease the torpid and dissonant mind of the week. The hours of the seventh day are for the doer of creation's new covenant law to rest in the spirit of heaven's intercession so that the spirit of their mind may find comfort in its spiritual course.

16. As the living God ended His work and rested, so too "the work of righteousness"[214] is put off so that the understanding of the believer may find their thoughts and feelings refreshed. It is herein well to know that the "comfort" of the Spirit is in all spiritual learning, even as it says concerning the word "comfort," "All may learn, and all may be comforted."[215]

17. For this cause, the Sabbath is that sign of true allegiance to the knowledge of the living God's science, for the Sabbath was given, He says, "That ye may know that I am the LORD that doth sanctify you,"[216] even as it says, "The very God of peace sanctify you wholly."[217] It is that "your whole spirit and soul and body be preserved"[218] through His wisdom's sanctification, for the soul of man would be bowed down within him, and in a most bitter state, if there was not a period of inward

---

213   Romans 6:10
214   Isaiah 32:17
215   1 Corinthians 14:31
216   Exodus 31:13
217   1 Thessalonians 5:23
218   1 Thessalonians 5:23

refreshing for his heart and mind, therefore "God blessed the seventh day, and sanctified it."[219]

18. The Sabbath is blessed and set apart of God for those who would care to follow the example of His conversation. "For peace I had great bitterness,"[220] says the one who throughout the week examines self, for the ground of Adam is cursed; "In sorrow shalt thou eat of it,"[221] says the Spirit. "The first man Adam was made a living soul; the last Adam was made a quickening spirit";[222] and the work of transformation to become a spirit quickened of this Spirit through His will and wisdom involves a bitter work of inward taxation. This is why His doctrine counsels, "The words that I speak unto you, they are spirit."[223] It is therefore well to know that "that which is born of the Spirit is spirit"[224] because "it is the spirit that quickeneth,"[225] for "the spirit giveth life."[226]

19. The Christian is to come by His Spirit's wisdom for the health of the spirit of their mind to regulate the mind of their faith's "body"; which "body" is in Scripture called, "The flesh"; and this daily work is most difficult, distressing, depressing, perplexing, and internally painful. Without the counsel of heaven's Mediator, the flesh will alone produce a religion most suitable to its shame, leading to an emotional acceptance of heaven's Faith with presumptuous works, which in turn will thin the soul and depress the intended experience. But "the flesh profiteth nothing,"[227] it says, for the living God's refreshing is intended to revive the heart that the mind may be encouraged to reform the conversation.

20. This daily work of aggravating self, of suppressing and re-educating the thoughts and the appetite of both hereditary and cultivated religious error, to then say within the mind, "I count all things but

---

219 Genesis 2:3
220 Isaiah 38:17
221 Genesis 3:17
222 1 Corinthians 15:45
223 John 6:63
224 John 3:6
225 John 6:63
226 2 Corinthians 3:6
227 John 6:63

loss for the excellency of the knowledge of Christ,"[228] needs a break; this assignment needs a moment of stillness for mental and spiritual rejuvenation.

21. Only those who exasperate self for the six days allotted to do so may say, "I am thy servant, and the son of thine handmaid: thou hast loosed my bonds."[229] Only those who are not content in a man made religion, or in a self-professed spiritual indulgence, can appreciate His Sabbath. It is therefore simple: the Sabbath was made for man by the Creator, and any qualms against this period of refreshing while professing *the name* of *the Creator* is a confession rejecting how it is written, "The LORD he is God: it is he that hath made us, and not we ourselves."[230]

22. What then is the *wisdom* of that inherited nature of man? It states, "Ye shall be as gods,"[231] and, "Ye are gods."[232]

23. As we are born of Adam, it is that we believe, without compelling argument, that we are our own creation, yet the soul aware of its error against the living God's religious character, and desiring to escape that error through His Spirit's voice, will confess, "Let us worship and bow down: let us kneel before the LORD our maker."[233] This is why the Spirit says of His Sabbath, "Israel shall keep the Sabbath, to observe the Sabbath throughout their generation, for a perpetual covenant. It is a sign between me and the children of Israel,"[234] for the seed of Israel will do as their father, in that "as a prince hast thou power with God and with men, and hast prevailed."[235]

24. The Spirit says, "Israel, whom I have chosen";[236] "that made thee, and formed thee from the womb";[237] "thou, Israel, art my servant,

---

228 Philippians 3:8
229 Psalms 116:16
230 Psalms 100:3
231 Genesis 3:5
232 Psalms 82:6
233 Psalms 95:6
234 Exodus 31:16,17
235 Genesis 32:28
236 Isaiah 44:1
237 Isaiah 44:2

Jacob whom I have chosen, the seed of Abraham my friend."[238] They of the seed of Israel are born of the seed of Abraham, for His man also "took on him the seed of Abraham"[239] and "was made of the seed of David."[240] David did not hesitate to confess, "I was shapen in iniquity; and in sin did my mother conceive me,"[241] for as the soul is, by His understanding, brought low and convinced of personal and devotional error, it is that, "through the righteousness of faith,"[242] the spirit will be made better, even while continuing "as seeing him who is invisible."[243]

25. But what is the birthmark of the children of Israel? It says, "He halted upon his thigh,"[244] therefore of these people it is promised, "I will make her that halted a remnant, and her that was cast far off a strong nation."[245]

26. The Sabbath is a perpetual covenant of edification between the touched and willing and sorrowful soul, and their Creator. "Those that have made a covenant with me by sacrifice,"[246] says this Spirit, these will be "blessed with faithful Abraham."[247] So then who is that faithful witness but that conversation fearing this Spirit's Word above "philosophy and vein deceit, after the tradition of men,"[248] which is why it says, "Fear God, and give glory to him,"[249] and, "Worship him that made."[250]

27. It was God "who created all things by Jesus Christ,"[251] and it is His doctrine's will to have our conversation edified through "the adoption of children by Jesus Christ to himself,"[252] so wherein is it

---

238 Isaiah 41:8
239 Hebrews 2:16
240 Romans 1:3
241 Psalms 51:5
242 Romans 4:13
243 Hebrews 11:27
244 Genesis 32:31
245 Micah 4:7
246 Psalm 50:5
247 Galatians 3:9
248 Colossians 2:8
249 Revelation 14:7
250 Revelation 14:7
251 Ephesians 3:9
252 Ephesians 1:5

justified to refuse righteousness' sure labor for receiving His wisdom's blessed refreshing? Who professes this Spirit's wisdom and yet has no knowledge of the power of His mediation? Who honors the Creator but is left out of His Sabbath? Who serves the Spirit of creation but refuses to hear, "Why call ye me, Lord, Lord, and do not the things which I say?"[253] "Who is among you that feareth the LORD, that obeyeth the voice of his servant, that walketh in darkness, and hath no light? let him trust in the name of the LORD, and stay upon his God."[254]

28. Because there is not knowledge of the living God's name, or simply a willing effort to allow the heart to be touched by His Spirit, it is that "the desire of the slothful killeth him; for his hands refuse to labour."[255] "There remaineth therefore a rest to the people of God";[256] "peace be on them, and mercy, and upon the Israel of God";[257] "for we which have believed";[258] believed "that Jesus is the Christ"[259] and do "confess that Jesus is the Son of God";[260] "do enter into rest."[261]

29. Before Israel and Abraham and David, before Moses and any of the covenants of promise, before those ten precepts were written on stone and then blessed by His man's blood for the purpose of obedience through exercising faith on his conversation, before there was a Christian or a Hebrew, it was, "God blessed the seventh day, and sanctified it."[262]

30. Before any division of religious practices, before any creed or institution of ministers, the living God created the *earth's* confidence in likeness to that practice within His heavenly Sanctuary. By this one commandment of the seventh day, man may not forget that it is not self that does bless the inwards, nor is it the inwards that maintain life and

---

253 Luke 6:46
254 Isaiah 46:10
255 Proverbs 21:25
256 Hebrews 4:9
257 Galatians 6:16
258 Hebrews 4:3
259 1 John 5:1
260 1 John 4:15
261 Hebrews 4:3
262 Genesis 2:3

health within self, but that by efforts to cooperate with creation's new covenant science, man may forever remember, "We should not trust in ourselves,"[263] and, "Our sufficiency is of God."[264]

31. The seventh day is the highlight of the week for the reforming Christian. This day is the only day where the mind may rest from its work, receiving health through inward stillness. In the beginning there was made of God a law that was not to be limited to race, denomination, creed, institution, geographical location, spiritual perception, and such like, for all naturally "sin" against His name, and all are of that religious error moving the person to act out the presumptuous ignorance of the heart. "But after that the kindness and love of God our Saviour toward man appeared,"[265] the heart will stop and acknowledge the name of the living God, only to endure the work of righteousness for Sabbath blessings that last for ever.

32. All common religious things cease during the hours of this day. It is pure and unadulterated love for the name of the living God's spiritual wisdom, and an acceptance of that love's work and doctrine within the conversation's conscience, that will bring the soul into the bond of covenant with His will and wisdom, for then His Sabbath will be a delight.

33. Empty the heart of its stout philosophical nature. How long must the heart go untouched? How long must the conscience remain violated? How long must the body dictate a religious profession that, in reality, causes alienation from creation's new covenant science?

34. "Wherefore do ye spend money for that which is not bread? and your labour for that which satisfieth not?"[266] "My people have committed two evils,"[267] says the Spirit, "they have forsaken me the fountain of living waters, and hewed them out cisterns, broken cisterns, that can hold no water."[268] But what is the counsel? "He that dwelleth

---

263 2 Corinthians 1:9
264 2 Corinthians 3:5
265 Titus 3:4
266 Isaiah 55:2
267 Jeremiah 2:13
268 Jeremiah 2:13

in love dwelleth in God,"[269] because "whether there be knowledge, it shall vanish away,"[270] but the mark of the law of "charity (of heaven-appointed self-sacrificing love) never faileth."[271]

35. As God ended His work on the seventh day, so too the religious world's reformer is to enter into the seventh day for the purpose of receiving a refreshed mind of devotion for the new week. This period of time is for experiencing that kindness bearing the living God's name and blessing, and within it the love of the believer will be revitalized for the betterment of their spirit. Through the wisdom added by the seventh day's "rest," newness of heart will allow the tasks of the week to bear a sweet fragrance, rather than a vile.

---

269 1 John 4:16
270 1 Corinthians 13:8
271 1 Corinthians 13:8

3

The Word Spoken

1. "If we confess our sins, he is faithful and just to forgive us our sins, and to cleanse us from all unrighteousness."[272]

2. It is written, "He that covereth his sins shall not prosper: but whoso confesseth and forsaketh them shall have mercy."[273] This is written so that we may actively believe on the living God's will of being "justified freely by his grace through the redemption that is in Christ."[274]

3. "The Son of man is not come to destroy men's lives, but to save them,"[275] for it was that at a certain time He said, "Maid, arise. And her spirit came again, and she arose."[276] Again, it was confessed

---

[272] 1 John 1:9
[273] Proverbs 28:13
[274] Romans 3:24
[275] Luke 9:56
[276] Luke 8:54,55

by one who had heard of the Spirit's man, "Say in a word, and my servant shall be healed,"[277] for, that same man of faith was similar to her that lost her only son, for to her son he said, "Young man, I say unto thee, Arise. And he that was dead sat up, and began to speak,"[278] and also of the servant for that man of faith, "returning to the house, found the servant whole that had been sick."[279]

4. These were justified or sanctified by their faith on the living God's counsel; the ones who had confidence in His voice and the ones for whom their supplication was made; for as he said and it was done just so as they had hoped, so was it perfected through their faith's exercise, making them whole by their experimental faith on the voice of the living God's man.

5. The Spirit's servant tells us that "he is faithful and just to forgive us our sins,"[280] so why should his counsel exist as though it is not fact? That commandment born of this Spirit's voice does come to pass, for His words are life and power, therefore hear Him say, "The Son of man hath power upon earth to forgive sins."[281]

6. The Spirit has said it first Himself, and not the apostle, for what is the testimony of John? He says, "That which we have seen and heard declare we unto you."[282] No thing can exist unless it is first spoken by the living God's Spirit, for of old "he spake, and it was done,"[283] and even now He says, "Thy sins be forgiven thee."[284] That word, "be," should rather mean, "exist." Forgiveness of sins exists within the voice of the living God's counsel, or else the psalmist is a liar, who says, "There is forgiveness with thee."[285] Yet the one of faith

---

277   Luke 7:7
278   Luke 7:14,15
279   Luke 7:10
280   1 John 1:3,9
281   Luke 5:24
282   1 John 1:3
283   Psalms 33:9
284   Mark 2:9
285   Psalms 130:4

knows how it is said, "God is not a man, that he should lie,"[286] and, "God, that cannot lie."[287]

7. Hear the magnitude of creation's science from the living God's own mouth: "The word is gone out of my mouth in righteousness, and shall not return."[288] And now hear the prominence of His wisdom's Spirit: "Because he could swear by no greater, he sware by himself."[289]

8. Now, why is it that when on earth, many approached His man as if He was God? Why did many ask of His man that which they asked of God, and indeed carried the same faith of God in his voice for that which they asked? Many "sought to touch him: for there went virtue out of him, and healed them all";[290] why? Why would a Roman stranger say to him, "Say in a word,"[291] and why should a woman do for him as it is written, "And began to wash his feet with tears, and did wipe them with the hairs of her head"?[292] These things are recorded that we may know the advice of creation's chief messenger is our faith's power and wisdom, even as it says, "Christ the power of God, and the wisdom of God."[293]

9. What is written? It says, "The life was manifested,"[294] even "that eternal life, which was with the Father."[295] His man says, "Believe me that I am in the Father, and the Father in me,"[296] for he also says, "If a man keep my saying, he shall never taste of death."[297]

---

286 Numbers 23:19
287 Titus 1:2
288 Isaiah 45:23
289 Hebrews 6:13
290 Luke 6:19
291 Luke 7:7
292 Luke 7:38
293 1 Corinthians 1:24
294 1 John 1:2
295 1 John 1:2
296 John 14:11
297 John 8:52

Is it not written, "He that was dead sat up"?[298] How was he raised? It is written, "And he";[299] he the living God's man; "And he said."[300]

10. He that spoke with power executed that wisdom because he had, within the flesh of he conversation, the name or impression of His Father, and it is this same power that in the beginning said, "And God said,"[301] for it is known that it was "God, who created all things by Jesus Christ."[302] Many treated His man's doctrine as that Word of the living God because his speech is of the living LORD's Word. For "God was in Christ,"[303] and of his knowledge on heavenly things, he says, "As the Father hath life in himself; so hath he given to the Son to have life in himself,"[304] for which cause it is written, "He that hath the Son hath life,"[305] because "the Spirit is life."[306]

11. Man's redemption is blessed of the Spirit to send the heart to His creation in the beginning, for He that made all things, and then instituted Adam's refreshing, is the same Spirit that spoke on earth and among priests and elders. Therefore hear him who bears within his name "the fullness of the Godhead,"[307] "Thy faith hath made thee whole."[308] Again, we here have the Spirit's spoken Word, therefore what we have before us is the fact of wholeness established "by the law of faith."[309]

12. His man says that our living faith in his name will make our inwards whole, and from none other source is it said, therefore from his mediation there is today power given to this precept, making this charge the hope of the *life* of our spirit. So now hear the apostle: "These are written, that ye might believe that Jesus is the Christ,

---

298 Luke 7:15
299 Luke 7:14
300 Luke 7:14
301 Genesis 1:3
302 Ephesians 3:9
303 2 Corinthians 5:19
304 John 5:26
305 1 John 5:13
306 Romans 8:10
307 Colossians 2:9
308 Luke 8:48
309 Romans 3:27

the Son of God; and that believing ye might have life through his name."[310]

13. Faith begins with active examination and belief on the name of His man, and from this faith we will receive understanding for the "death" that consumes the heart of our conversation. Therefore if we have confidence in this man's doctrine, we should know the fact of his spiritual understanding being made available for our convenience.

14. What is the counsel of the apostle? "I have written unto you that believe on the name of the Son of God; that ye may know that ye have eternal life,"[311] he says. Is it not said, "This is the promise that he hath promised us, even eternal life"?[312] Again, did this man not say, "I send the promise of my Father upon you"?[313] What promise is it that would come and leave them "endured with power from on high"?[314] Is it not written by the same author, "They were all filled with the Holy Ghost"?[315] Is not this Holy Ghost that God he spoke of when saying, "I will send unto you from the Father, even the Spirit of truth, which proceedeth from the Father"?[316] Is not this Spirit "that holy Spirit of promise"[317] which the living God "shed on us abundantly through Jesus"?[318]

15. The same "life" or conversation existing in His man is in the same conversation within the living God's religious character; His Christ is made "after the power of an endless life,"[319] and in his conversation's doctrine rests "eternal redemption"[320] "through the eternal Spirit,"[321] which Spirit is of "that eternal life, which was

---

310 John 20:32
311 1 John 5:13
312 1 John 2:25
313 Luke 24:49
314 Luke 24:49
315 Acts 2:4
316 John 15:26
317 Ephesians 1:13
318 Titus 3:6
319 Hebrews 7:16
320 Hebrews 9:12
321 Hebrews 9:14

with the Father."³²² That which is therefore spoken by His man has no choice but to exist, "for it pleased the Father that in him should all fullness dwell,"³²³ and being filled with that living Word of the LORD's Spirit, his name or charge is "equal with God."³²⁴

16. Therefore he or she refusing any commandment of God does not refuse to hear Paul or Malachi, but rather the One who speaks, even as it says, "He therefore that despiseth, despiseth not man, but God."³²⁵ Should any one profess the doctrine of His man without entering into controversy with self to settle the conscience under the wisdom of his voice, they profess the wind. They that lack confidence in the authority of what is and has been written for their learning to soberly advance in the application of faith in that counsel "is a liar, and the truth is not in him."³²⁶

17. This is the reason why it should be noticed that he who spoke and it was done on earth is of the same Spirit that, in the beginning, spoke and it was done. This same Spirit is that same God of creation, and it was because His people should not lose sight of His name that He ordained a Sabbath of refreshing for that name. It was this Spirit that declared, "Know that I am the LORD that doth sanctify you,"³²⁷ and this sanctification justly arranged by He Himself, for "God blessed the seventh day, and sanctified it."³²⁸

18. Again, the Spirit's Word is here made into a fact because the Sabbath was not simply instituted without a reason, but for the purpose of mental and spiritual relief and purification, thereby making it sure that there can be no other day to call the memorial of this Word when it was this Spirit who spoke the day in to existence and sanctified it, separating it to be in remembrance for all of man-kind. This we can say because, in the beginning, Adam was

---

322   1 John 1:2
323   Colossians 1:19
324   Philippians 2:6
325   1 Thessalonians 4:8
326   1 John 2:4
327   Exodus 31:13
328   Genesis 2.2

neither Jew nor Christian, but it says, "Adam, which was the son of God."[329]

19. "There remaineth therefore a rest to the people of God,"[330] "for we which have believed do enter into rest."[331]

20. Is it not this same man that said, "Hear all weary and full of anxiety, and I will give you rest?"[332] Again, did he not confess, "The Son of man is Lord also of the Sabbath?"[333] The living God's man spoke this! He spoke these words, therefore the one professing His name's understanding should not be void of this counsel, seeing as how his counsel is an ever living force, even like as the instruction of that Spirit confessing to "the immutability of his counsel."[334]

21. There is hope to learn of and do every word of creation's heavenly mediation if we actively believe on the force of its office. Herein is why it is written, "The Holy Ghost, whom God hath given to them that obey him,"[335] for which cause it is said, "Hereby we know that he abideth in us, by the Spirit which he hath given us,"[336] and, "He that keepeth his commandments dwelleth in him, and he in him."[337]

22. Maybe we haven't heard how His man says, "Why call ye me, Lord, Lord, and do not the things which I say?"[338] The purpose of the Spirit's gift when doing the Spirit's wisdom is to bring our conversation into a living experience with His will. How may we then know this doctrine's "rest" if we will not hear, "The Spirit of the LORD caused him to rest"?[339] How may we know that there is no other form of sanctification except through the name and course of creation's present counsel? And how may we know the power of that sancti-

---

329 Luke 3:38
330 Hebrews 4:9
331 Hebrews 4:3
332 Matthew 11:28
333 Mark 2:28
334 Hebrews 6:17
335 Acts 5:32
336 1 John 3:24
337 1 John 3:24
338 Luke 6:46
339 Isaiah 63:14

fication if we fail to remember the Sabbath of that name's wisdom? The living God's Spirit has spoken all of this, yet what is our duty? It is written, "Without faith it is impossible to please him: for he that cometh to God must believe that he is."[340]

23. It is a living fact that our conversation is made righteous by faith on the virtue of the confidence of heaven's doctrine, and through faith our conversation's conscience will be made whole to grow up as a son or daughter of creation. John writes that our faith's intellect will be cleansed of all unrighteousness, and he says so only because His wisdom says, "Their sins and their iniquities will I remember no more,"[341] and, "I will receive you";[342] this is what "God hath said."[343]

24. Again, the Spirit has spoken these things! It is now a living fact that if we would consider His love, to study after His doctrine to fulfill His will, "whatsoever we ask, we know that we have the petitions that we desired of him."[344] It is then a fact that if we are cleansed of "unrighteousness," this means that in the very moment of our supplication, we are then without self-righteousness and unrighteousness, thereby leaving us naked before God, for, "all unrighteousness is sin."[345] In being "naked," consciously remorseful for our spiritual negligence, there now arises an opportunity for His wisdom to clothe us in its good care, "even the righteousness of God which is by faith of Jesus."[346]

25. We will be cleansed from all spiritual ignorance because He has said so! The Father has given the penitent the privilege of learning His man's benevolence for their "remission of sins"[347] "through faith in his blood."[348] The LORD God Himself has said that He will do this, so "wherefore do I take my flesh in my teeth, and put my life

---

340   Hebrews 11:6
341   Hebrews 8:12
342   2 Corinthians 6:17
343   2 Corinthians 6:16
344   1 John 5:15
345   1 John 5:17
346   Romans 3:22
347   Romans 3:25
348   Romans 3:25

in mine hand?"[349] As the reformer acknowledges the intercession of creation's understanding, its mind of devotion is then given to purify the soul's temple, for even Abel "obtained witness that he was righteous,"[350] "whereof the Holy Ghost also is witness to us."[351]

26. The LORD has spoken the word. All the reformer needs to do is examine and do that instruction, for isn't it written, "He is in the way of life that keepeth instruction"?[352] We are become just or righteous by an experimental faith on the Spirit's voice, and by no thing else. It is herein well to remember that complete obedience through whatever circumstance "yieldeth the peaceable fruits of righteousness unto them which are exercised thereby."[353]

27. So then "exercise thyself rather unto godliness."[354] "Whosoever will lose his life for my sake, the same shall save it,"[355] says the new covenant's messenger, for to lose self is to gain self, and to gain self is to love self, and in love we die to *life* to live courageously to heaven's will and doctrine, that by exercising faith in every word from this Spirit, we may comfortably know why he says, "I am in the Father, and the Father in me,"[356] and, "He that believeth on me, believeth not on me, but on him that sent me. And he that seeth me seeth him that sent me."[357]

---

349 Job 13:14
350 Hebrews 11:4
351 Hebrews 10:15
352 Proverbs 10:17
353 Hebrews 12:11
354 1 Timothy 4:7
355 Luke 9:24
356 John 14:10
357 John 12:44,45

4

A Perpetual Covenant

1. "Keep the Sabbath day to sanctify it, as the LORD thy God hath commanded thee."[358] "Remember that thou wast a servant in the land of Egypt, and that the LORD thy God brought thee out thence through a mighty hand and by a stretched out arm: therefore the LORD thy God commanded thee to keep the Sabbath day."[359]

2. The Sabbath day; as opposed to "the sabbath days" allotted to and invented by the Jews "in respect of an holyday";[360] is the appointed Sabbath of the living God's Word and Wisdom. The Sabbath is that appointment ordained by His Spirit at the creation as "a perpetual covenant"[361] for His Israel, that is, for "the children of Jacob, whom he

---

358   Deuteronomy 5:12
359   Deuteronomy 5:15
360   Colossians 2:16
361   Exodus 31:16

named Israel."³⁶² The sabbaths; plural; or rather, "the new moons and sabbaths, the calling of assemblies";³⁶³ these were ordained only for the Jews under the old covenant by the pen of Moses through their *God*, and it was with them that He Himself would end them, even as He says, "I will also cause all her mirth to cease, her feast days, her new moons, and her sabbaths, and all her solemn feasts."³⁶⁴ Therefore hear the counsel of the apostle against them that violate the Spirit's name: "Ye observe days, and months, and times, and years. I am afraid of you."³⁶⁵

3. Listen to how they once told the living God's man, "If thou be the king of the Jews, save thyself."³⁶⁶ Why may not this saying have disturbed God's chief messenger?

4. He could have quit the tree; the Spirit's chief minister knew within himself, "Thinkest thou that I cannot now pray to my Father, and he shall presently give me more than twelve legions of angels?"³⁶⁷ Should he have let his lower nature reign, he would have maintained his prayer, "Remove this cup from me,"³⁶⁸ but instead, "for the joy that was set before him endured the cross, despising the shame."³⁶⁹

5. Should he have delivered his self to the wishes of men, not one soul would have had the opportunity to receive a covering for their inherited nature's religious error. Yet he "his own self bare our sins in his own body on the tree,"³⁷⁰ and this saying, "If he be the King of the Israel,"³⁷¹ could not, nor could it ever, move him.

6. Why should this man have not moved at this provocation? It is written that, at one time, "when Jesus therefore perceived that they would come and take him by force, to make him a king, he departed."³⁷²

---

362 2 Kings 17:34
363 Isaiah 1:13
364 Hosea 2:11
365 Galatians 4:10,11
366 Luke 23:37
367 Matthew 26:53
368 Luke 22:42
369 Hebrews 12:2
370 1 Peter 2:24
371 Matthew 27:42
372 John 6:15

7. He did not forward his ministry as that king or high priest of creation,[373] for it was known among many that "this is of a truth that prophet."[374] This man came as the voice of his Father's royal religion, and as many were "looking upon Jesus as he walked,"[375] they heard his doctrine saying, "I am among you as he that serveth."[376]

8. The man said to him, "If thou be,"[377] for was he not that prophesied King, the Messiah and Christ, of the Jews? Hear him: "My kingdom is not of this world."[378] Who then was that *king* of the Jews? Listen to the Jews: "We have no king but Caesar."[379] Why is this fact of rule or governorship significant? Listen again: "The LORD the King of Israel, and his redeemer,"[380] and, "I am the LORD, your Holy One, the creator of Israel, your King."[381]

9. This living God's man is not that *king* of the Jews, for his name or doctrine does magnify the only King and Creator of Israel, even "the LORD, the God of heaven, and the God of the earth."[382]

10. To "the Israel of God,"[383] he is "first being by interpretation King of righteousness, and after that also King of Sa'lem, which is, King of peace."[384] Thus, "Christ is not entered into the holy places made with hands, which are the figures of the true; but into heaven itself."[385] By this man's doctrine, his name's reformer is joined "to the general assembly and church of the firstborn, which are written in heaven,"[386] for he "is the beginning, the firstborn from the dead,"[387] and all who

---

373 A "king" is another term for a priest, as it says, "And hath made us kings and priests unto God and his Father," Revelation 1:6.
374 John 6:14
375 John 1:36
376 Luke 22:27
377 Luke 23:37
378 John 18:36
379 John 19:15
380 Isaiah 44:6
381 Isaiah 43:15
382 Genesis 24:3
383 Galatians 6:16
384 Hebrews 7:2
385 Hebrews 9:24
386 Hebrews 12:23
387 Colossians 1:18

would be joined to his speech must know his name's commandment, how it says, "Have continued with me in my temptations,"[388] that is, "Being put to death in the flesh."[389]

11. There is no earthy denomination restricted to his Spirit's Faith, for she who did enter into bond with this spiritual understanding is yet "the habitation of devils,"[390] even as it says, "How is the faithful city become an harlot!"[391] Therefore the mind and the experience must look beyond the general realm of *earth* "unto the city of the living God,"[392] "which is the mother of us all."[393]

12. The living God's man cannot be that *king* of the Jews because he, from a basic understanding, did not bless one small fraction of the human race. Herein it is well to understand just what is meant by the phrase "Christ," seeing as how "henceforth know we no man after the flesh: yea, though we have known Christ after the flesh, yet now henceforth know we him no more."[394] This allows us to understand that "Christ," as it is used by the Bible, is no reference to a man, and it is no reference to a man, but is rather a moniker or appellation of the living God's new covenant wisdom, which wisdom is called, "The Lord Jesus Christ our Saviour,"[395] which "Lord" and "Savior" is "the commandment of God our Saviour."[396] This man could not quit the tree because the commandment of his ministry was not his own to claim, which is why he says, "The Father which sent me, he gave me a commandment, what I should say, and what I should speak."[397]

13. To quit the tree would mean to invent and forward a religious law devoted to worshipping his own person. "Christ hath redeemed us from the curse of the law,"[398] "for it is written, Cursed is every one

---

388 Luke 22:28
389 1 Peter 3:18
390 Revelation 18:2
391 Isaiah 1:21
392 Hebrews 12:22
393 Galatians 4:26
394 2 Corinthians 5:16
395 Titus 1:4
396 Titus 1:3
397 John 12:49
398 Galatians 3:13

that hangeth on a tree,"[399] wherefore to find a *Christ* without the tree is to find a *Christ* speaking against the ministry of the living God's man, which ministry is ordained "to redeem them that were under the law."[400]

14. If this man was that King of the Jews, he would have quit the tree, inventing to himself laws of a religious tradition to adhere to, but since he suffered the tree, and nailed "unrighteousness" to that tree, since "all unrighteousness is sin,"[401] this man has made it clear that "the strength of sin is the law."[402] With him on the tree, creation's new covenant law is become a reality for the conversation's conscience "that we should serve in newness of spirit, and not in the oldness of the letter,"[403] that is, not "through the law, but through the righteousness of faith."[404]

15. It was the LORD's Spirit who declared the end of His bond to the Jewish religion, saying, "I will wipe Jerusalem as a man wipeth a dish, wiping it, and turning it upside down,"[405] for which cause He promised, "I will overturn, overturn, overturn, it: and it shall be no more, until he come whose right it is; and I will give it him."[406] Who is this *one* whose right it is? It says, "Till the seed should come to whom the promise was made,"[407] and, "To thy seed, which is Christ."[408]

16. The reign of the Jewish economy in heaven's light, along with the standard of their devotion, was to cease when the Spirit's man should say, "It is finished."[409] He "abolished in his flesh the enmity, even the law of commandments"[410] which taught to "observe days, and months, and times, and years."[411] For him to quit the tree, it would be for him to establish, around his own person, what he abolished by

---

399 Galatians 3:13
400 Galatians 4:5
401 1 John 5:17
402 1 Corinthians 15:56
403 Romans 7:6
404 Romans 4:13
405 2 Kings 21:13
406 Ezekiel 21:27
407 Galatians 3:19
408 Galatians 3:16
409 John 19:30
410 Ephesians 2:15
411 Galatians 4:10

his flesh, making *him* that *king* of the Jews, but since he suffered the tree, we may know that this man is that man of the Spirit's will and commandment because He "hath redeemed us from the curse of the law."[412]

17. So then why resort "to the weak and beggarly elements, where unto ye desire again to be in bondage? Ye observe days."[413] The Word's man "abolished in his flesh the enmity, even the law of commandments"[414] "which was against us, which was contrary to us, and took it out of the way, nailing it to his cross."[415] But wait, who are we? Who is the "us" spoken of by the apostle? Surely it is we who "are the circumcision, which worship God in the spirit, and rejoice in Christ Jesus, and have no confidence in the flesh."[416]

18. They of the Spirit's commandment do not maintain the carnal laws and ordinances administered by man or Moses; why? Simply put, "whatsoever is not of faith is sin,"[417] "and the law is not of faith."[418]

19. The Word's kingdom is today a present reality, and only through the eye of faith will the heart remain uplifted to its course of learning. The appointed holy days of old by the pen of flesh; and every other after their fashion; ceased the moment blood and water came from out of the pierced side of this man and fell onto the earth. Therefore whosoever would refuse the Spirit's Sabbath to maintain the *sabbaths* of men, "how dwelleth the love of God in him?"[419]

20. Today, there is no bond outside of that which says, "He is a Jew, which is one inwardly; and circumcision is that of the heart, in the spirit."[420] "For they are not all Israel, which are of Israel";[421] not all born of the Spirit's house on *earth* bear the name and semblance of that Israel

---

412 Galatians 3:13
413 Galatians 4:9,10
414 Ephesians 2:15
415 Colossians 2:14
416 Philippians 3:3
417 Romans 14:23
418 Galatians 3:12
419 1 John 3:17
420 Romans 2:29
421 Romans 9:6

within the heavenly Sanctuary; "but the children of the promise are counted for the seed."[422]

21. The Word's Israel does as Paul has confessed, they serve the Spirit's name in the spirit of their mind and rejoice in His doctrine by the same manner; "here are they that keep the commandments of God, and the faith of Jesus."[423] The Spirit's Faith being that Creator of *Israel* should encourage the mind to remember that "God formed man,"[424] and in doing so, the mind must also look towards the fact of how He did "make in himself of twain one new man"[425] "that he might reconcile both unto God in one body by the cross, having slain the enmity thereby."[426]

22. He who originally created man gave His Spirit to create man again, and this time more "perfect, as pertaining to the conscience."[427] This is that Spirit who will today bless them that learn of and do the name of Abraham, for there was one sure law of God maintained by His faithful until they were under Egyptian bondage, and that commandment was as it says, "Abraham obeyed my voice."[428]

23. What then is the voice that Abraham obeyed? The Ten Commandments were not then etched in stone; there was no strange thing done of the flesh for virtue within the assembly; the Jewish customs and rites were not yet prescribed; there was no baptism for a Christian; there was no Jew or Christian, but rather it was said, "Abram the Hebrew."[429]

24. Do we today possess this Hebrew spirit? Abraham received one charge of the living God as a sign of his faith, and that was circumcision, but what was that Faith he kept to receive the reward of his faith? Hear

---

422 Romans 9:8
423 Revelation 14:12
424 Genesis 2:7
425 Ephesians 2:15
426 Ephesians 2:16
427 Hebrews 9:9
428 Genesis 26:5
429 Genesis 14:13

the word that was passed down to Abraham: "I heard thy voice in the garden."[430]

25. That which was established in the sinless state of man and written for our observation contains the very voice of God for us to live by. That one law which was given for our observation, which law is joined to the other immutable precepts found at creation and in Eden, is as it is written, "God blessed the seventh day, and sanctified it."[431] Nine of the Ten Commandments are new, in that they did not clearly or officially exist before sin, but rather unofficially. But it is the fourth commandment, and reverence to this judgment, that will procure mental sanctification to maintain obedience to the other nine through an advancing confidence in the wisdom of his man's *blood*.

26. This law has existed from before the beginning; from before the time man had a thought to remove his conversation from the LORD's Word. If established for man in a sinless spiritual state, how much more for man in sinful state? Can this Sabbath of creation be against us if the Word of this Sabbath has proven His Spirit to be for us?

27. Abraham honored the Spirit's Sabbath, for he knew the voice of his God. Until Moses, the Word's voice was that Faith issuing from the garden of Eden, or else it would not say, "Did ever a people hear the voice of God speaking out of the midst of the fire, as thou hast heard, and live?"[432]

His people have ever heard His voice, and that which was from the beginning preaches the voice of heaven's wisdom, for that voice spoken out of the fire would again maintain a new dispensation, wherefore it is said, "Refuse not him that speaketh. For if they escaped not who refused him that spake on earth, much more shall not we escape, if we turn away from him that speaketh from heaven."[433] That covenant made with the literal Jews ceased to exist the moment his man's blood

---

430 Genesis 3:10
431 Genesis 2:3
432 Deuteronomy 4:33
433 Hebrews 12:25

met the air, for it says, "He taketh away the first, that he may establish the second,"[434] and, "In that he saith, A new covenant."[435]

28. As this new covenant Faith is that Redeemer and Creator of *Israel*, and the conversation of his man that chief priest of this blessing, it then emphasizes the fact that "the children of Israel shall keep the Sabbath, to observe the Sabbath throughout their generations, for a perpetual covenant."[436] Before, "sabbaths" were be plural, yet now the Sabbath is singular, but the word "generation"; as it says, "Throughout their generations";[437] is plural; why?

29. If the generations of the Jews are ended, and God Himself said that it would be His Spirit who personally ends them, how then can more generations come of God if He has caused an end? It is said, "Ye are come unto mount Si'on, and unto the city of the living God,"[438] to "a greater and more perfect tabernacle, not made with hands."[439] His man declared his kingdom not of this *earth*, therefore "our conversation is in heaven,"[440] and the generations of Israel maintained through obedience to His mediation's instruction, which instruction says, "If any man will do his will,"[441] and, "If any man hear my voice, and open."[442]

30. He who created man would not abandon that precept He Himself spoke to ensure the condition of that man. Who then is the Sabbath made for? We read: "The Sabbath was made for man, and not man for the Sabbath."[443]

31. Indeed this is fact, but which man is the Sabbath made for? Is it for all men? "All men have not faith."[444] So then to whom is the Spirit's remembrance reserved? It is written, "To make in himself of twain

---

434 Hebrews 10:9
435 Hebrews 8:13
436 Exodus 31:16
437 Exodus 31:16
438 Hebrews 12:22
439 Hebrews 8:11
440 Philippians 3:20
441 John 7:17
442 Revelation 3:20
443 Mark 2:27
444 2 Thessalonians 3:2

one new man,"[445] that is, "the new man, which after God is created in righteousness and true holiness,"[446] even that conversation "renewed in knowledge after the image of him that created him."[447]

32. The Sabbath was made for man-kind as a whole, but consider how that the Spirit's Faith "is the Saviour of all men, specially of those that believe,"[448] for "whosoever believeth that Jesus is the Christ is born of God."[449] He who is the Spirit's creation is the Word's man, and as to Adam there was a Sabbath of rest, to the generations that should continue in the second Adam's doctrine by faith of its intended refreshing, even in that wisdom of the heavenly Sanctuary, to them would the same Sabbath follow to add sanctification and needed understanding for the toil of the heart.

33. The Spirit formed man in the beginning, and the illustration given is to provide room to consider creation's perfect fulfillment, as it says, "O Jacob and Israel; for thou art my servant: I have formed thee."[450] "The kindness and love of God our Saviour towards man"[451] is to send the believing man and woman back to creation, for the power that spoke all things in to existence is the same wisdom that is to now revive our conversation's conscience into the image of the living God's religious character.

34. "O the depth of the riches both of the wisdom and knowledge of God!"[452] As the breath of life was given to Adam, so shall the living God's doctrine "quicken your mortal bodied by his Spirit,"[453] thereby recovering our mind of devotion from that natural breath of *life* to more perfectly confess, "Renew a right spirit within me."[454] Our inherited breath receives correction through an experimental faith in "the

---

445 Ephesians 2:15
446 Ephesians 4:24
447 Colossians 3:10
448 1 Timothy 4:10
449 1 John 5:1
450 Isaiah 44:21
451 Titus 3:4
452 Romans 11:33
453 Romans 8:11
454 Psalms 51:10

law of the Spirit of life,"[455] wherefore remember that "without faith it is impossible to please him."[456]

35. All things were given to the Jews; both literal and spiritual; yet what is their record? It says, "Of the Rock that begat thee thou art unmindful, and hast forgotten God that formed thee,"[457] and, "They are a very froward generation, children in whom is no faith."[458]

36. But I thought that faith was only established after His man's endeavor? Why is faith an ordinance in these times of old? Faith's higher learning for the Word's manner of righteousness is a precept of Eden, for it says, "They were both naked and were not ashamed."[459] "That Rock was Christ,"[460] and as "Christ" was that Rock, so it was this Faith that led them through the desert and wrought victory against Pharaoh, therefore to His established nation He said, concerning His Sabbath, "Remember that thou wast a servant in the land of Egypt, and that the LORD thy God brought thee out...therefore the LORD thy God commanded thee to keep the Sabbath day."[461]

37. It was after the sixth day that the Spirit rested from creation, that is, after He had created man He ordained the Sabbath. Again, after the Word had purchased and redeemed a people, He brought them into the wilderness "that I,"[462] he says, "may prove them, whether they will walk in my law, or no."[463] What law was this that these people were tested on? Moses said, "This is that which the LORD hath said, To morrow is the rest of the holy Sabbath unto the LORD."[464]

38. After they failed to obey the Spirit's voice, He then said, "How long refuse ye to keep my commandments and my laws?"[465] What commandments and laws did they fail to keep? They failed to properly

---

455 Romans 8:2
456 Hebrews 11:6
457 Deuteronomy 32:18
458 Deuteronomy 32:20
459 Genesis 2:25
460 1 Corinthians 10:4
461 Deuteronomy 5:15
462 Exodus 16:4
463 Exodus 16:4
464 Exodus 16:23
465 Exodus 16:28

honor righteousness by faith on His voice, and the commandment of His Sabbath. These two things would follow down to His man when, at the time of his passing, his disciples "rested the Sabbath day according to the commandment."[466] When speaking of the work done for him by Mary, this man said, "She did it for my burial,"[467] for he knew the hours that would surround his death, and also the desire of his disciples, therefore he acknowledged the fact of his care beforehand, for he would not have the Sabbath disturbed.

39. The living God's man rested the entire Sabbath in the grave, and then it was that after the Sabbath his Father's Spirit brought him up, leaving us an example of the import of the seventh day's Sabbath, and to whom it should now be given.

40. To us who are of this man's name and doctrine, it is that "the first man Adam was made a living soul; the last Adam was made a quickening spirit."[468] After every established creation of heaven's wisdom, the Sabbath is further magnified. As this man rested on the Sabbath, so too the one exercising confidence on his doctrine will receive a mind to know the acceptable rest of his Spirit and mediation, and that "the Son of man is Lord also of the Sabbath."[469] All born of this wisdom will not refuse creation's present voice, for "if any man have not the Spirit of Christ, he is none of his."[470]

41. The *life* breathed into the lungs of Adam is, since His man suffered the tree, exchanged for the Spirit of *life* within creation's new covenant commandment, therefore it is said, "Be filled with the Spirit,"[471] that is, "Be filled with all the fullness of God."[472] The *life* in this wisdom is indeed "that eternal life, which was with the Father,"[473] and if this *life* is that which was with the Father and is now joined to heaven's ministry; in that he says, "So hath he given to the Son to have

---

466 Luke 23:56
467 Matthew 26:12
468 1 Corinthians 15:45
469 Luke 6:5
470 Romans 8:9
471 Ephesians 5:18
472 Ephesians 3:19
473 1 John 1:2

life in himself";[474] it is that this "life" is that power which of old spoke and created, therefore "God, who created all things by Jesus Christ,"[475] "hath given to us eternal life, and this life is in his Son."[476]

42. The Spirit's new man is given this life by faith on creation's law, for that obedient conscience will "receive abundance of grace and of the gift of righteousness"[477] that it may continue to prolong its conversation in heaven's will. Through the creative power of grace, man's inwards are to be created into the image of the living God's religious character, and if indeed it is the Word who is creating, then it is by faith that He will allow the soul of such an individual to know the "rest" that He has given for their sanctification.

43. They who are not the Spirit's creation will not at once know the refreshing of His operation, for it is said of them, "Their eyes were holden that they should not know him."[478] Why are they refused knowledge on the one law that is to add comfort to their spiritual understanding? It is written, "Mine enemies, which would not that I should reign over them."[479]

44. Such as refuse to be governed by creation's doctrine; who are contrary to "men that have hazarded their lives for the name of our Lord Jesus Christ";[480] these will not, and cannot, become new creatures in the Spirit's law, for he spoke when in judgment that it would so be, saying, "If I tell you, ye will not believe: and if I also ask you, ye will not answer me."[481] Such are them "that walk after the flesh in the lust of uncleanness, and despise government. Presumptuous are they, self-willed."[482] These are the "murmurers, complainers, walking after their

---

474 John 5:26
475 Ephesians 3:19
476 1 John 5:11
477 Romans 5:17
478 Luke 24:16
479 Luke 19:27
480 Acts 15:26
481 Luke 22:67,68
482 2 Peter 2:10

own lusts; and their mouth speaketh great swelling words, having men's persons in admiration."[483]

45. It is sadly forgotten that His man "loved us, and washed us from our sins in his own blood,"[484] yet "will a man leave the snow of Leb'anon which cometh from the rock of the field?"[485] That "sin" removed from our conversation by the offering of the LORD's man is stout and stubborn adherence to "the law of commandments contained in ordinances,"[486] but if we fail to learn of and do creation's course, must we think to understand that our desire to reverence the pen of flesh over the Spirit's instruction is religious error? The Spirit will therefore secure within His creation the seventh day Memorial of His name. His "rest" is for them touched at, and immersed within, the operation of His man concerning the redemption of their conversation's conscience.

---

483   Jude 1:16
484   Revelation 1:5
485   Jeremiah 18:14
486   Ephesians 2:15

5

The Immutable Memorial Of His Righteousness

1. "I have sworn by myself, the word is gone out of my mouth in righteousness,"[487] says the living God, "and shall not return."[488]

2. What is the word? It says, "God blessed the seventh day, and sanctified it,"[489] therefore He said, "It is a sign between me and you throughout your generations; that ye may know that I am the LORD that doth sanctify you,"[490] and, "That ye may know that I am the LORD your God."[491]

---

487 Isaiah 45:23
488 Isaiah 45:23
489 Genesis 2:3
490 Exodus 31:13
491 Ezekiel 20:20

3. At the end of His creation, the LORD God spoke the word of His day of "rest"; He has not tarnished that word. He Himself has said that the word flowing from His mouth will not return to Him, so wherein is one justified to violate that which not even He Himself would dare defile?

4. "Why call ye me, Lord, Lord, and do not the things which I say?"[492] says his man. For who was it that created all things? It was "God, who created all things by Jesus Christ."[493] His man's doctrine and conversation became "the image of the invisible God,"[494] and when once passed away on the tree, "all things were created by him, and for him,"[495] and after that his doctrine ascended to the living God's throne, it is still that his name "is before all things, and by him all things consist."[496]

5. Who is it that is rejected when the Spirit's Sabbath is denied? Who is hurt when His Memorial is set aside? Surely the Word is not hurt; "if we believe not, yet he abideth faithful: he cannot deny himself";[497] but rather it is the soul and mind of the conversation that suffers, for there is no day separated by the Spirit for sanctification other than His seventh.

6. How then may the one professing the Creator's will and wisdom reject His Memorial for creation? The Word is the one who, in the beginning, created and spoke; He is the one who ordained and blessed; and yet what is His counsel? It says, "If a man love me, he will keep my words."[498]

7. Who spoke at the beginning but the LORD's Spirit, and who sacrificed His mind and conversation for the spiritually erroneous but the same Spirit of the same LORD God? To reject creation's Memorial is to reject the One who spoke the commandment, died for it, and revived for its perpetual justification, for He has confessed, "The word

---

492 Luke 6:46
493 Ephesians 3:9
494 Colossians 1:15
495 Colossians 1:16
496 Colossians 1:17
497 2 Timothy 2:13
498 John 14:23

is gone out of my mouth in righteousness, and shall not return,"[499] and there can be no word of the Spirit returned to Himself or altered by man, for "the word of our God shall stand for ever."[500]

8. His speech is an everlasting counsel mingled with everlasting strength, and by faith and acceptance of "the immutability of his counsel,"[501] all will "excel in strength, that do his commandments, hearkening unto the voice of his word."[502] "Hereby we do know that we know him, if we keep his commandments,"[503] for by allowing the heart to become touched at the Spirit's doctrine of ransoming and elevating the conversation's mind, He promises, "Ye may know that I am the LORD your God."[504] It is that the living God would have us know His name as our personal spiritual confidence, for the Spirit of the Creator of all things "gave himself for our sins, that he might deliver us from this present evil world,"[505] therefore it is said, "He shall abide before God for ever,"[506] and, "According to the greatness of thy power preserve thou those that are appointed to die."[507]

9. The Spirit's man, "to deliver their soul from death,"[508] gave his course of faith for the Spirit's students. This he did that it may be fulfilled, "Let thy lovingkindness and thy truth continually preserve me,"[509] or rather, as the living God says, "I will cure them, and will reveal unto them the abundance of peace and truth."[510]

10. Concerning "truth," we read, "All thy commandments are truth,"[511] and, "All thy commandments are righteousness."[512] As lovin-

---

499   Isaiah 45:23
500   Isaiah 40:8
501   Hebrews 6:17
502   Psalms 103:20
503   1 John 2:3
504   Ezekiel 20:20
505   Galatians 1:4
506   Psalms 61:7
507   Psalms 79:11
508   Psalms 33:19
509   Psalms 40:11
510   Jeremiah 33:6
511   Psalm 119:151
512   Psalm 119:172

gkindness is the abundance of His peace, it is that "they which receive abundance of grace and of the gift of righteousness shall reign"[513] in creation's science, for "grace and truth came by Jesus Christ."[514] As the commandments of the Spirit are for His righteousness, it is that the LORD of this Spirit says, "My righteousness shall not be abolished,"[515] for the word spoken is that which will never be annihilated, eradicated, extinguished, prohibited, repudiated; "but the word of our God shall stand for ever."[516]

11. The same immutable voice that called all things to be in righteousness spoke those things in the power of his wisdom, for it is by His voice that all things yet remain, and it is now "according to his glorious power"[517] "that Christ may dwell in your hearts by faith."[518] He who commanded, and by that command brought all things to be, is the same whose voice, when once obeyed, will usher in that same sanctifying power to cleanse the temple of the soul.

12. "The law of the Spirit of life"[519] is become "the author of eternal salvation unto all them that obey him,"[520] but obey what of it? It is written, "Taking vengeance on them that know not God, and that obey not the gospel of our Lord."[521]

13. That which teaches, "God was in Christ, reconciling the world unto himself,"[522] is the word of concern for the sincere and humble soul. This wisdom "is gone into heaven, and is on the right hand of God; angels and authorities and powers being made subject unto him,"[523] and it is only by "the fullness of the blessing of the gospel of

---

513 Romans 5:17
514 John 1:17
515 Isaiah 51:6
516 Isaiah 51:8
517 Colossians 1:11
518 Ephesians 3:17
519 Romans 8:2
520 Hebrews 5:9
521 2 Thessalonians 1:8
522 2 Corinthians 5:19
523 1 Peter 3:22

Christ"[524] that we may know the Word as that Lord and God of our conversation, and that "we which have believed do enter into rest."[525]

14. "The rest of the holy Sabbath unto the LORD,"[526] and "the word of the Lord Jesus,"[527] which is "the word of God,"[528] cannot be separated. From examining and doing heaven's doctrine, His "rest," and the appointment of that refreshing, will be given to the doer. It is from obeying redemption's wisdom that the mind will know its Creator, and from knowing its Creator will be known of His counsel to enter into the knowledge of His will and refreshing.

15. There is only blessing in the word of God, and His man has confessed of his mediation's confidence, "The Son of man is Lord also of the Sabbath."[529] Why, then, is it easier to hear, "The Son of man hath power on earth to forgive sins,"[530] than to hear, "God blessed the seventh day"?[531] Is it of no relevance that he is that "Son, which is in the bosom of the Father"?[532] God the Father is in the spirit of His man's commandment, for it is said that "God was manifested in the flesh,"[533] and that "the life was manifested,"[534] even "that eternal life, which was with the Father,"[535] and of course we know that "the Spirit is life,"[536] for His man says, "God is a Spirit."[537]

16. Even though His man reveals the knowledge of the living God's will, He says, "Hear what the Spirit saith,"[538] for it is that word which "God gave unto him, to shew unto his servants,"[539] which is why

---

524 Romans 15:29
525 Hebrews 4:3
526 Exodus 16:23
527 Acts 19:10
528 Acts 19:20
529 Luke 6:5
530 Matthew 9:6
531 Genesis 2:3
532 John 1:18
533 1 Timothy 3:16
534 1 John 1:2
535 1 John 1:2
536 Romans 8:10
537 John 4:24
538 Revelation 2:7
539 Revelation 1:1

He counsels, "He that believeth on me, believeth not on me, but on him that sent me."[540] Therefore who is rejected when refusing to hear counsel on the Word's Sabbath Memorial but His Spirit also, for it written, "The Spirit of the LORD caused him to rest."[541]

17. "He that saith, I know him, and keepeth not his commandments, is a liar, and the truth is not in him";[542] "he is an'tichrist, that denieth the Father and the Son."[543] For this cause His doctrine says, "All men should honour the Son, even as they honour the Father. He that honoureth not the Son honoureth not the Father which hath sent him."[544] How then may one dishonor the Son? He says, "He that hath my commandments, and keepeth them, he it is that loveth me."[545]

18. It is by refusing His immutable word that we dishonor His Son's office, for, as it was the Word who, in the beginning, created all things and then blessed the work of His hands with a Memorial for man's perpetual regeneration, by refusing His "rest," the believer will never come to know the fullness that is in His name for their conversation's character, leaving it that they will not receive the blessing attached to His Spirit, which blessing is *life* for the organs of their faith's mind, and for the flesh of their faith's confidence.

19. Heaven's Faith is not only rejected when refusing to receive conviction on the proper manners of worship and service, it is also the living God's Holy Spirit, which Spirit is the only agent whereby the heart is subdued and the conversation reformed. Yet hear the counsel of His man, "He that rejected me, and receiveth not my words, hath one that judgeth him,"[546] even as it is written, "Ye put it from you, and judge yourselves unworthy."[547]

---

540 John 12:44
541 Isaiah 63:14
542 1 John 2:4
543 1 John 2:22
544 John 5:23
545 John 14:21
546 John 12:48
547 Acts 13:46

20. They who would not have the Creator's will and science govern their understanding prove to be of that class "which glory in appearance, and not in heart."[548] Seeing as how there only rests blessing on the Sabbath appointed of God, to observe another *day* would only be a testament to the righteousness built up in self; for as the word of God is righteousness, and through humble obedience by faith the believer is joined into His righteousness, the word of man is dead and lame, and its glory is only in self. When heaven's throne religion, and the Counsel of that religion, is rejected, another spirit will take the form of *religion*, mingling itself with the emotions, perceptions, and assumptions of the individual, sealing in them "that spirit of an'tichrist,"[549] saying, "Who is the LORD?"[550]

21. It is this spirit that is of the willingly negligent conversation, and "now already is it in the world."[551] This is that spirit of error needing the sacrifice of the Creator to quench it, for "the Father sent the Son to be the Saviour of the world."[552] And we do know that "whatsoever is born of God overcometh the world,"[553] therefore at the end of His creation, the LORD gave birth to the only institution that concealed His refreshing for man to overcome self and the coarse nature of the religious world.

22. "The whole world lieth in wickedness,"[554] including the established precepts ordained by the religious world and for the spirit of the religious world, therefore if there is a profession of the knowledge of the Spirit's law, then there is an acceptance of this wisdom as the only Savior in existence. In that profession there is the spirit of victory, and if there is, in His name, a spirit of victory, then within His mediation there is a spirit of truth, and if a spirit of truth, then we know "the truth is in Jesus,"[555] and if we know and believe the truth is in Jesus,

---

548 2 Corinthians 5:12
549 1 John 4:3
550 Proverbs 30:9
551 1 John 4:3
552 1 John 4:14
553 1 John 5:4
554 1 John 5:19
555 Ephesians 4:21

then we know how it is written, "Thy law is the truth,"[556] and, "All thy commandments are truth,"[557] and, "Sanctify them through thy truth: thy word is truth."[558]

23. That which was mandated by the Spirit for every man, which He too did even join in to; as it says, "He rested on the seventh day";[559] is that which will impute the continual wisdom of victory into the spirit of the mind. None may know that the Creator is that same Word of the living God's Spirit until they allow their hearts to enter into His "rest."

24. One may hear that this is so, one may read that this is so, but there is no thing that will reveal the fact to the heart, and so impress it upon the conscience, like as when His words work within our person when we are "comparing spiritual things with spiritual."[560] "He that keepeth his commandments dwelleth in him, and he in him,"[561] and once "we have known and believed the love that God hath to us,"[562] our comprehension on heavenly things will grow up "unto a perfect man, unto the measure of the statute of the fullness of Christ,"[563] for "this is the victory that overcometh the world, even our faith."[564]

25. His word is everlasting, and that which existed before any dispensation of man in this world, before any empire and institution of man on this earth, is that counsel pointing the believer to His words as their "wisdom, and righteousness, and sanctification, and redemption."[565] The purpose of the Sabbath is revealed in His man's doctrine; in that doctrine is that instruction for the continuation of the law of his LORD's Sabbath. The same God who spoke in the beginning is the same Word who is "an high priest over the house of God,"[566] for the

---

556 Psalm 119:142
557 Psalm 119:151
558 John 17:17
559 Genesis 2:2
560 1 Corinthians 2:13
561 1 John 3:24
562 1 John 4:16
563 Ephesians 4:13
564 1 John 5:4
565 1 Corinthians 1:30
566 Hebrews 10:21

Father has "given all things into his hands"[567] "that he might bring us to God."[568]

26. Through faith in the virtue of the blood of His man, every believer should know His LORD and Father, for in knowing the Father they will know the power of His word and the tone of His voice. Such as learn and do as right students "are sanctified by God the Father, and preserved in Jesus Christ,"[569] to know His name, even as He says, "My people shall know my name,"[570] and, "To him that ordereth his conversation aright will I shew the salvation of God."[571]

27. Let none who profess creation's name reject the learning of its new covenant mediation. "Let all that suffer according to the will of God commit the keeping of their souls to him in well doing, as unto a faithful Creator."[572]

28. It is a terrible thing for the spirit to allow the heart to have control over the members of the mind and body, for if "the soul be without knowledge, it is not good."[573] Every believer should progress in the Spirit's wisdom from eating and digesting that wisdom only, for "out of his mouth cometh knowledge and understanding."[574] The living God would have all who call on His name's commandment to maintain a personal relationship with His words apart from their womb, for even of Abraham He says, "I called him alone."[575]

29. By faith on the instruction of our atonement to the Word's Spirit by the *blood* of His man, it is that the soul of every professor should enter into the "rest" of creation's wisdom. Yet, it is said, "To whom sware he that they should not enter into his rest, but to them that believed not? So we see that they could not enter in because of unbelief."[576]

---

567 John 13:3
568 1 Peter 3:18
569 Jude 1:1
570 Isaiah 52:6
571 Psalm 50:23
572 1 Peter 4:19
573 Proverbs 19:2
574 Proverbs 2:6
575 Isaiah 51:2
576 Hebrews 3:18,19

30. The living God has spoken the word; the believer need but humble their heart that it may feel and receive it. "Through the deceitfulness of sin"[577] the heart will magnify self; as it is said, "When he was strong, his heart was lifted up to his destruction";[578] yet the one born of heaven's will and commandment knows, "We also joy in God through our Lord,"[579] for which cause it is said, "Whosoever believeth that Jesus is the Christ is born of God."[580]

31. None should lack an ever-growing experience in the knowledge of creation's present will and law, and none who profess the name of His throne should lack His judgment's seventh day refreshing. "Our fellowship is with the Father, and with his Son,"[581] and the religion of the heavenly Sanctuary decrees that every one of its members come by the fear of its counsel to reverence every one of its commandments. To greatly enhance our awareness of His abiding presence, the living God has blessed us not only with His doctrine, but also with a Sabbath to sanctify that counsel revealing the "seal of the righteousness of the faith."[582]

---

577 Hebrews 3:13
578 2 Chronicles 26:16
579 Romans 5:11
580 1 John 5:1
581 1 John 1:3
582 Romans 4:11

6

The Israel of God

1. It is written, "He shall save his people from their sins."[583]

2. Notice that a people belong to the living God's man, and to this people belongs deliverance from their own personal and devotional "sins," but who are these people?

3. It is written, "Out of thee shall come a Governor, that shall rule my people Israel."[584]

4. The ones that belong to this man's Faith are those individuals characterized as "Israel," for they are as it is said, "The Israel of God."[585] The His counsel's *Israel* will be recovered from their spiritual negligence against his God's throne, to the end they may better care for self, and for the words of that throne. The LORD's Word will redeem

---

583   Matthew 1:21
584   Matthew 2:6
585   Galatians 6:16

His personal heritage; not an earthy or fleshy tribe or denomination, but that inheritance known only of the living God "accepted in the beloved"[586] through that "Spirit of adoption."[587] The commandment of His voice will remove them very far from their religious error, and we have this confidence because it is said of the Spirit's man, "Whom God hath raised up, having loosed the pains of death: because it was not possible that he should be holden of it."[588]

5. Who is the Israel of God but the brethren or seed of His man's conversation, so then who are His brethren? It is written, "He took on him the seed of Abraham,"[589] and, "Was made of the seed of David according to the flesh."[590]

6. The *Israel* of God bears the spiritual nature and culture of the LORD's man; the conversation of this people is born of the mind of David and Abraham. In spirit and in practice they are of the faith of Abraham, and in the flesh of their faith they, like David, recognize themselves as "sinners" in need of healing.

7. "I acknowledge my transgressions,"[591] they say. "Against thee, thee only, have I sinned, and done this evil in thy sight."[592] "Hide thy face from my sins, and blot out all mine iniquities,"[593] they pray. Yet these will not fall to depression over their condition, for while remembering "the steps of that faith of our father Abraham,"[594] they will diligently consider to "believe on him that raised up Jesus our Lord from the dead,"[595] for "David also describeth the blessedness of the man, unto whom God imputeth righteousness without works."[596]

---

586 Ephesians 1:6
587 Romans 8:15
588 Acts 2:24
589 Hebrews 2:16
590 Romans 1:3
591 Psalm 51:3
592 Psalm 51:4
593 Psalm 51:9
594 Romans 4:12
595 Romans 4:24
596 Romans 4:6

8. David, after his heart condemned him, did not simply cry, "Every man at his best state is altogether vanity,"[597] but he also said, "I am ready to halt,"[598] "I will be sorry for my sin,"[599] and, "Purge me,"[600] "wash me,"[601] "create in me,"[602] "and renew a right spirit within me."[603] What is this that David is saying? What is David admitting by advancing from terrible penitence to a hope of recovery; which recovery seems to be far from his own doing; while his wrong is ever his to claim? He says, "My sin is ever before me,"[604] and, "My sorrow is continually before me,"[605] yet with great boldness he says to the living God, "Restore"[606] "and uphold me";[607] what is David confessing?

9. David is attributing not only the office of forgiveness to the LORD's Spirit, but also the vocation of restorer. David is confessing the name and doctrine of the LORD's Word, and for maintaining the mind of the faith of Abraham in His name, David could say, "Blessed are they whose iniquities are forgiven, and whose sins are covered."[608]

10. David's confidence rests in Abraham's understanding, and in His man's doctrine is David and Abraham's wisdom. For, throughout his life, His man "groaned in the spirit, and was troubled,"[609] nevertheless "in the days of his flesh, when he had offered up prayers and supplications with strong crying and tears unto him that was able to save him from death,"[610] he "was heard in that he feared,"[611] to where

---

597 Psalms 39:5
598 Psalm 38:17
599 Psalm 38:18
600 Psalm 51:7
601 Psalm 51:7
602 Psalm 51:10
603 Psalm 51:10
604 Psalm 51:3
605 Psalm 38:17
606 Psalm 51:12
607 Psalm 51:12
608 Romans 4:7
609 John 11:33
610 Hebrews 5:7
611 Hebrews 5:7

he could say, "The Father hath not left me alone; for I do always those things that please him."[612]

11. How did David know that he was blessed to have his sins forgiven? How could David have had confidence in that which hadn't yet been made official, but was in existence from the beginning of time? How could David trust that a work he set himself to believe on was made certain?

12. It is known that all who "believeth on him that justifieth the ungodly, his faith is counted for righteousness."[613] Faith on the Spirit's will and commandment cannot occur until the mind has its ungodliness revealed to it, for then the person experiments with faith for alleviation at the cost of its *life*, "bearing about in the body the dying of the Lord Jesus, that the life also of Jesus might be made manifest in our body."[614]

13. "I may behold wondrous things out of thy law,"[615] said David, for of old it was said, "If there be laid on him a sum of money, then he shall give for the ransom of his life whatsoever is laid upon him."[616] What does that man of David's line say? He says, "The Son of man came...to give his life a ransom for many."[617] The blessed hope of David!

14. David knew of the Spirit's dispensation through creation's heavenly mediation, for it is David that wrote, concerning the one bound to redemption's science, "His delight is in the law of the LORD; and in his law doth he meditate."[618] The hope of deliverance from the natural disease within the conversation's flesh and from the plague within the heart, would end by creation's new covenant messenger, for David counted the living God's hand most faithful with his heart, seeing as how he says, "Create in me a clean heart."[619]

---

612 John 8:29
613 Romans 4:5
614 2 Corinthians 4:10
615 Psalms 119:18
616 Exodus 21:30
617 Mark 10:45
618 Psalm 1:2
619 Psalms 51:10

15. There is only one who can create, and it is the LORD God's counsel, for it says, "He commanded, and they were created,"[620] and, "The LORD God made the earth and the heavens."[621] David is attributing an exclusive and special office to the LORD's Spirit that is not within himself or any man, and it is the wisdom of ordaining, creating, and sustaining.

16. "Who can bring a clean thing out of an unclean? not one,"[622] yet we know that it was the living God "who created all things by Jesus Christ,"[623] and David counted the Word as that Creator, and as the Creator is that Spirit, it is that David counted on the law of this Spirit's man as some good *thing* by taking knowledge of Abraham's faith, and as this man's speech bore the wisdom of David and Abraham's confidence, it serves that creation's *Israel* should know heaven's Spirit and Faith as that Creator and Judge over His inheritance, to the end they may pray, "There is forgiveness with thee, that thou mayest be feared."[624]

17. Only the Creator could take His own *life* and then retain it; "I lay down my life, that I might take it again,"[625] says the Spirit's Word. David counted the Creator faithful in providing him a new heart and mind; as did Abraham; and for believing on that which spoke of His power, these two men were blessed with His righteousness. This lesson is for "them that suffer according to the will of God,"[626] to "commit the keeping of their souls to him in well doing, as unto a faithful Creator."[627]

18. This is *Israel* of creation's new covenant science. Because "God is a Spirit,"[628] and because "the Spirit of life"[629] is the Word of life,"[630] the Israel of God are the Israel of the Word, and are that creation of

---

620 Psalms 148:5
621 Genesis 2:4
622 Job 14:4
623 Ephesians 3:9
624 Psalms 130:4
625 John 10:17
626 1 Peter 4:19
627 1 Peter 4:19
628 John 4:24
629 Revelation 11:11
630 1 John 1:1

the words within the LORD's heavenly Sanctuary. They are not a race of people; they are not a denomination known to the *world*; they are not seen and heard of on the face of the *earth*; they are "a Jew, which is one inwardly,"[631] "whose praise is not of men, but of God."[632]

19. Now, if these are Jews in the spirit of their mind to the Word's science, this means that if they are of the faith of Abraham then they bear the spiritual heritage of Abraham, for the Jews are of this man's spiritual foundation, and we know how it is said, "Abram the Hebrew."[633] If then the Spirit's Israel possesses the faith of Abraham, it is that they too are Hebrews in spirit of like faith, and being a *Hebrew*, it is that these are "of Sem,"[634] like Abraham, "which was the son of No'e, which was the son of La'mech, which was the son of Mathu'sala, which was the son of E'noch, which was the son of Ja'red, which was the son of Male'leel, which was the son of Cai'nan, which was the son of E'nos, which was the son of Seth, which was the son of Adam, which was the son of God."[635]

20. This is part of the record of "the book of the generation of Jesus Christ, the son of David, the son of Abraham."[636] If then the Israel of God in His man's Faith do trace their roots back to Adam's confidence in Eden's Faith; as the Scriptures plainly declare they should; "there remaineth therefore a rest to the people of God."[637] And this "rest" is as it is said, "He spake in a certain place of the seventh day on this wise, And God did rest the seventh day."[638]

21. Who is a liar but the one professing the name of the LORD's man without His wisdom of restoration? Who is a liar, but the one professing this man's Faith; which is the Faith of the Creator, and of both Abraham and David; and rejecting that Sabbath instituted by His own hand for one of men, or for one of self?

---

631   Romans 2:29
632   Romans 2:29
633   Genesis 14:13
634   Luke 3:36
635   Luke 3:36-38
636   Matthew 1:1
637   Hebrews 4:9
638   Hebrews 4:4

22. The Israel of God will not stumble over the living God's Sabbath. The same one who Created is the same one who suffered for the broken laws and judgments of Eden, which commandments were given to the man Moses and written on stone, which precepts are now to be "written not with ink, but with the Spirit of the living God; not in tables of stone, but in fleshy tables of the heart."[639] It is because none care to remove their faith's intellect from their "vain conversation received by tradition"[640] that there remains a "vail untaken away in the reading of the old testament; which vail is done away in Christ."[641] What is religious error done away in? It is done away in "the knowledge of the Son of God,"[642] that is, in "the doctrine of God our Saviour."[643]

23. Thus, we arrive at where we began, at "Christ" our Savior, for it says, "He shall save his people from their sins."[644] This allows us to understand that since "the Lord Jesus Christ our Saviour"[645] is that aid to cleanse from all "sin," that "sin" is inward, and if inward, then "Jesus Christ," as Paul uses the phrase, is no reference to a man, but to "the commandment of God our Saviour,"[646] which "commandment" is "the doctrine of God our Saviour."[647] Every one examining and doing this commandment and "law of the Spirit"[648] will experience a resurrection from "sin" to never know it within their conversation. This is why His wisdom says, "They shall never perish, neither shall any man pluck them out of my hand. My Father, which gave them me, is greater than all; and no man is able to pluck them out of my Father's hand."[649]

24. The *Israel* of God is wound up in *life* with two; the Father and the knowledge of His commandment for creation; therefore it is said,

---

639   2 Corinthians 3:3
640   1 Peter 1:18
641   2 Corinthians 3:14
642   Ephesians 4:13
643   Titus 2:10
644   Matthew 1:21
645   Titus 1:4
646   Titus 1:3
647   Titus 2:10
648   Romans 8:2
649   John 10:28,29

"Our fellowship is with the Father, and with his Son."[650] His man tells us, "God is a Spirit,"[651] therefore to be joined to the Father is to partake in "fellowship of the Spirit,"[652] that is, in "the communion of the Holy Ghost."[653] "The Spirit of truth, which proceedeth from the Father,"[654] this "Spirit is life because of righteousness,"[655] and we do know how it is said, "All thy commandments are righteousness."[656] The aim of the Spirit's righteousness is therefore our sincere love in the knowledge of His doctrine's intercession for edification, "and this is love, that we walk after his commandments."[657]

25. The fellowship of the Father is of an education administered by "the Spirit of grace,"[658] bringing the doer into personal contact with the living God's religious character, which character is outlined by His Ten Commandments. But the religion of His man is not simply of the Spirit's heart, for the Father has purposed His son and daughter "to be conformed to the image of his Son."[659] His man embraced His Spirit's image within an erroneous conversation, and by the offering of that flesh on the tree, he reconciled all who would learn of and do his name to the Spirit of his conversation. By the counsel of his saying, the laws of the living God's throne will be engraved into the heart, perfecting every conscience by faith "in the doctrine of Christ"[660] to respectably keep His Word's Faith and Ten Commandments.

26. The professed believer is to confess "Christ" as did David and Abraham, and also as did that first messenger of salvation's science, and that confession "through the righteousness of faith."[661] This man's

---

650 1 John 1:3
651 John 4:24
652 Philippians 2:1
653 2 Corinthians 13:14
654 John 15:29
655 Romans 8:10
656 Psalms 119:172
657 2 John 1:6
658 Hebrews 10:29
659 Romans 8:29
660 2 John 1:9
661 Romans 4:13

wisdom is honored because "all the fullness of the Godhead bodily"[662] is given to his mediation of "the Majesty on high."[663] This is why it is written of Christ, "He will magnify the law, and make it honourable."[664] He came to magnify and glorify, to promote and honor, the religious character of His LORD and Father, so that the conversation may stop trying to work *righteousness* to allow righteousness to flow in and from them by an experimental faith on the virtue of His accepted sacrifice.

27. The atonement of the conversation's spirit to the living God's mind of devotion is complete in the course of His man's commandment, therefore it is counseled, "We pray you in Christ's stead, be ye reconciled to God."[665] For even this man taught, "Have faith in God";[666] why? Because "if the Spirit of him that raised up Jesus from the dead dwell in you, he that raised up Christ from the dead shall also quicken your mortal bodies by his Spirit";[667] this is the kingdom and righteousness of the Spirit.

28. It is by faith in creation's present doctrine that every conversation believing on and executing the fact of their conversation's redemption will be made righteous in and before the living God. As Abraham and David believed by faith, the example is for us to live out our personal religion through the law of creation's Spirit, "for as many as are led by the Spirit of God, they are the sons of God."[668]

29. Herein we are able to recognize the Israel of God, even those whose conversation is soberly led by salvation's science. The Spirit is life and health because it delivers not only conviction to the heart, but also a thorough education on the character and promises of the living God, placing the Spirit as the only Agent whereby His name is sealed within the soul, and the intercession of His wisdom as the only channel to commune with that knowledge for "the washing of water by the

---

662 Colossians 2:9
663 Hebrews 8:1
664 Isaiah 42:21
665 2 Corinthians 5:20
666 Mark 11:22
667 Romans 8:11
668 Romans 8:14

word."⁶⁶⁹ But there is more to this Spirit, for it is written, "The Spirit of the LORD caused him to rest."⁶⁷⁰

30. Do we believe on His man's doctrine? Do we believe that his wisdom has creative power to purge our mind from inherited character defects, and to provide us with strength when new and unknown disorders appear to our conscience? "We which have believed do enter into rest";⁶⁷¹ who is a liar but he or she "having a form of godliness, but denying the power thereof"?⁶⁷² "These also resist the truth"⁶⁷³ and are "reprobate concerning the faith,"⁶⁷⁴ but why? The Spirit answers: "These be they who separate themselves, sensual, having not the Spirit."⁶⁷⁵

31. Without the will and commandment of creation's Spirit, we are yet alive to "the body of the sins of the flesh,"⁶⁷⁶ and this is how it becomes easy to miss the necessary stirring and improvement of the heart. There is "rest" and resurrection within the Spirit of heaven's Faith, for the refreshing of creation's law is the blessing of the hope of newness for the recovery of the heart and mind, and this "rest" magnified and blessed by that glorious and sanctified appointment ordained of the Word in the beginning for the seventh day of each week.

32. To ignore the Spirit's Sabbath is to show faithlessness in the doctrine of His wisdom's intercession for sanctification, for the two; the Spirit's Sabbath and the Spirit's intercession; are inseparable. In the Sabbath is creation's benevolence and in heaven's benevolence is creation's Sabbath, which is why this wisdom says, "The Son of man is Lord even of the Sabbath day."⁶⁷⁷

---

669   Ephesians 5:26
670   Isaiah 63:14
671   Hebrews 4:3
672   2 Timothy 3:5
673   2 Timothy 3:8
674   2 Timothy 3:8
675   Jude 1:19
676   Colossians 2:11
677   Matthew 12:8

33. Now, the same Son of man over the Sabbath is the same one that said, "The Son of man hath power on earth to forgive sins."[678] Is it then seen how there is an inconsistency to believe that this man, the minister of the Word's student-patient, can forgive and pardon all things, but the same man has lost the way of his own ministry's Sabbath? Why can he forgive and pardon? It is because his voice is consecrated to be the living God's "merciful and faithful high priest in things pertaining to God, to make reconciliation for the sins of the people."[679] Therefore, with the pardoning of sin before the LORD associated with *his* heavenly ministry, it is that the religion of that ministry is also bound to that same LORD and Spirit, making every law and judgment of that LORD the confidence of his office, including that law stating, "God blessed the seventh day."[680]

34. Remember how He says, "I am the LORD, I change not,"[681] and, "My words shall not pass away"?[682] "The Sabbath was made for man,"[683] says His man, and to those who would refuse counsel on the Word's "rest," while yet believing that they themselves are born of man and *blessed* of *God*; that is, born of Adam; it is that these are born of self, who are also "subverted, and sinneth,"[684] professing "that they know God; but in works they deny him"[685] by remaining faithful to "the perfect manner of the law of the fathers."[686] Refreshing is exactly what the Word's tiding's have ordained for the penitent soul, for their inwards are to be filled with "the fullness of the blessing of the gospel of Christ,"[687] yet where does heaven's Faith draw its eloquence from? It is therefore well to know what it says of the Lord and Governor of the Sabbath, that "on the seventh day he rested, and was refreshed."[688]

---

678   Matthew 9:6
679   Hebrews 2:17
680   Genesis 2:3
681   Malachi 3:6
682   Mark 13:31
683   Mark 2:27
684   Titus 3:11
685   Titus 1:16
686   Acts 22:3
687   Romans 15:29
688   Exodus 31:17

35. Rest and salvation belongs to the *Israel* of creation's commandment, "for salvation is of the Jews,"[689] "which is one inwardly and circumcision is that of the heart, in the spirit."[690] Herein is the reason why David prayed, "Restore unto me the joy of thy salvation,"[691] and, "Renew a right spirit within me."[692] What is it that David was hopeful for? The Spirit saw the religious world bound to spiritual negligence and said, "None saith, Restore,"[693] but here was one on *earth* saying, "Restore," and it was the joy of His salvation that this one longed after. And what was that joy? What was that salvation? It is that hope fulfilling the saying, "That which is born of the Spirit is spirit."[694]

36. It is written, "He shall redeem their soul from deceit and violence,"[695] therefore David knew, "God will redeem my soul from the power of the grave."[696] And wherein did David's heart rest to receive this regeneration by faith? Of him it is written, "The soul of my lord shall be bound in the bundle of life with the LORD thy God."[697] But wherein lay the Word's "life"? It is written, "The Spirit is life,"[698] therefore we know that "he that hath the Son hath life,"[699] and that "if any man have not the Spirit of Christ, he is none of his."[700]

37. Again, to the Israel of God is given rest, learning, refreshing, salvation, and recovery of thought and feeling to "serve in newness of spirit."[701] These are the *people* who are His assembly that He will "save," "ransom," and "redeem" from out of the *earth*, even as they themselves say, "Thou hast redeemed us to God by thy blood out of

---

689   John 4:22
690   Romans 2:29
691   Psalms 51:12
692   Psalm 51:10
693   Isaiah 42:22
694   John 3:6
695   Psalms 72:14
696   Psalms 49:15
697   1 Samuel 25:29
698   Romans 8:10
699   1 John 5:12
700   Romans 8:9
701   Romans 7:6

every kindred, and tongue, and people, and nation."[702] By an experimental faith on his name's confidence, these are them that accept their lot to "be made the righteousness of God in him,"[703] "being redeemed from among men."[704]

38. The *Israel* of creation's understanding will not be void of the name of creation's science, for through this doctrine they will know the name of its Father, even as it says, "No man cometh unto the Father, but by me."[705] The righteousness of God will not house within the heart of one who does not care to learn reform, of one who does not care to aggravate the Word's will to secure knowledge of His wisdom to their conversation's conscience. The full life, death, and heavenly ministry of His man will lead the student to advance in creation's standard by faith, which is why His man also says, "Every man therefore that hath heard, and hath learned of the Father, cometh unto me."[706]

39. Creation's Faith is to lead our conversation to honest repentance towards our personally violating the living God's commandments, for from the anguish of such an experience the heart will confess in greater and yet greater tones, "There is none other name under heaven given among men, whereby we must be saved."[707] It is ordained that "the name of our Lord Jesus Christ may be glorified in you, and ye in him, according to the grace of our God and the Lord Jesus Christ,"[708] "therefore leaving the principles of the doctrine of Christ, let us go on unto perfection,"[709] as it says, "Perfect, as pertaining to the conscience."[710]

40. The work of redemption for the soul begins upon honest acceptance and execution of the Spirit's doctrine, and that work is of the Spirit given to man by heaven's learning to have His name bring health into the conversation's inwards. The individual must now study after

---

702 Revelation 5:9
703 2 Corinthians 5:21
704 Revelation 14:4
705 John 14:6
706 John 6:45
707 Acts 4:12
708 2 Thessalonians 1:12
709 Hebrews 6:1
710 Hebrews 9:9

the Word's voice and exist in that voice by faith, eradicating from their soul temple that "old" label, "Them that walk after the flesh in the lust of uncleanness, and despise government."[711]

41. The knowledge of the Spirit's man is Governor over the members of our faith's "body," therefore, if we are in this understanding, "our old man is crucified with him, that the body of sin might be destroyed, that henceforth we should not serve sin."[712] Blessed hope! The believer is no longer held to "sin," for His man, "in the likeness of sinful flesh, and for sin, condemned sin in the flesh"[713] "in his own body on the tree, that we, being dead to sins, should live unto righteousness."[714] The purpose for his mission was to establish his Father's name in the *earth* without "sin," and because "the strength of sin is the law,"[715] we may keep a right conversation to the Spirit's Faith without the philosophy of the religious law to know the Spirit's benevolence, even as it says, "That he might bring us to God,"[716] and, "Bringing many sons unto glory."[717]

42. The *Israel* of God is rescued from their "sins" and is not rescued in their religious error, for which reason it is said, "Let every one that nameth the name of Christ depart from iniquity."[718] *Israel* is recovered away from their spiritual negligence; they are given a new mind to live out their conversation when once committing to trust in that counsel pronouncing, "Behold the Lamb of God, which taketh away."[719] His man took away that wall of separation between the mind and the Word of Eden, and today the saying is fulfilled, "He shall stand and feed in the strength of the LORD, in the majesty of the name of the LORD his God; and they shall abide."[720]

---

711 2 Peter 2:10
712 Romans 6:6
713 Romans 8:3
714 1 Peter 2:24
715 1 Corinthians 15:56
716 1 Peter 3:18
717 Hebrews 2:10
718 2 Timothy 2:19
719 John 1:29
720 Micah 5:4

43. Concerning "the enmity, even the law of commandments contained in ordinances,"[721] this man, by his passing on the tree, "took it out of the way, nailing it to his cross,"[722] condemning, in every generation thereafter, the pen of priests and elders that our conscience may be "renewed in knowledge."[723] Today is the year and "time of reformation."[724] It is now time to take the Spirit's instruction and personally examine it, whether it is that Faith born to "persuade men, or God,"[725] for "to whom sware he that they should not enter into his rest, but to them that believed not?"[726]

44. It is time to soberly trust the living God, because "whosoever believeth that Jesus is the Christ is born of God,"[727] "and he that hath not the Son of God hath not life."[728] The Israel of God is no denominated race of people; they are alike "having the same spirit of faith"[729] by "that one and the selfsame Spirit,"[730] knowing their "conversation is in heaven"[731] "unto the city of the living God, the heavenly Jerusalem,"[732] "where Christ sitteth on the right hand of God."[733]

45. The Christian must willingly allow their conversation to "be offered upon the sacrifice and service"[734] "for the work of Christ,"[735] and such a mind is born of great "patience and comfort of the scriptures."[736] "The work of righteousness shall be peace; and the effect of righteousness quietness and assurance for ever":[737] "for thus saith the

---

721 Ephesians 2:15
722 Colossians 2:14
723 Colossians 3:10
724 Hebrews 9:10
725 Galatians 1:10
726 Hebrews 3:18
727 1 John 5:1
728 1 John 5:12
729 2 Corinthians 4:13
730 1 Corinthians 12:11
731 Philippians 3:20
732 Hebrews 12:22
733 Colossians 3:1
734 Philippians 2:17
735 Philippians 2:30
736 Romans 15:4
737 Isaiah 32:17

Lord GOD, the Holy One of Israel; In returning and rest shall ye be saved; in quietness and in confidence shall be your strength: and ye would not."[738]

46. It is time to observe the saying, "Thou art he that took me out of the womb,"[739] for there is "rest" and redemption on the side of faith. "It pleased God, who separated me from my mother's womb, and called me by his grace,"[740] says the apostle, and that separation caused by "the gospel of the grace of God,"[741] for it is "the grace of God that bringeth salvation."[742]

47. His man's saying for creation is sown in power to the offspring of Adam that he or she may not remain in Adam's spiritual estate, but rather serve the Spirit's Word in the spirit through the name and spiritual confidence of the second Adam. "Let us therefore fear, lest, a promise being left us of entering into his rest, any of you should seem to come short of it."[743]

48. They that fear the living God and worship Him that made all things, by whom all things consist, by the spirit of their conversation's conscience, these are that *Israel* "which keep the commandments of God, and have the testimony of Jesus Christ."[744] Thus, because they have held to the principle written within them by the Spirit's finger, only this Israel will hear, "Well done, good and faithful servant; thou hast been faithful over a few things, I will make thee ruler over many things: enter thou into the joy of thy lord."[745]

---

738 Isaiah 30:15
739 Psalms 22:9
740 Galatians 1:15
741 Acts 20:24
742 Titus 2:11
743 Hebrews 4:1
744 Revelation 12:17
745 Matthew 25:23

7

He That Sanctifies

1. Let the one professing the confidence of His man observe the saying, "He that sanctifieth and they who are sanctified are all of one."[746]

2. This man prays, "That they all may be one; as thou, Father, art in me, and I in thee, that they also may be one in us,"[747] that is, "I in them, and thou in me, that they may be made perfect in one,"[748] because he says, "I am in my Father, and ye in me, and I in you."[749]

3. The living God's doctrine has power to sanctify the spiritual understanding. There is only *one* that has authority to sanctify, and it says, "The very God of peace sanctify you wholly."[750] It is the Word that

---

746 Hebrews 2:11
747 John 17:21
748 John 17:23
749 John 14:20
750 1 Thessalonians 5:23

does sanctify its steward, which is why its baptism is "with the washing of water by the word."[751] It is this Word that blesses and has all wisdom to hallow and make clean, wherefore it is well to remember that this Spirit is understood as, "He that sanctifieth."[752]

4. "He is not a man, as I am";[753] that is, a "man, whose breath is in his nostrils";[754] for He says, "I am the LORD thy God, the Holy One of Israel, thy Saviour,"[755] and, "Be still, and know that I am God."[756] Who is that Holy One? Said one of a contrary mind, "What have we to do with thee, thou Jesus of Nazareth?"[757] "I know thee who thou art, the Holy One of God."[758] It is this same "Jesus Christ" who, of old, is that *Holy One* and *Savior* of his people *Israel*, for what was written of him? It says, "They shall smite the judge of Israel,"[759] "yet out of thee shall he come forth unto me that is to be ruler in Israel; whose goings forth have been from of old, from everlasting."[760] "It is he which was ordained of God to be the Judge of quick and dead,"[761] and of this wisdom, which wisdom is the God and Ruler of *Israel*, it is known, "The word of our God shall stand forever."[762]

5. Is it true that "Christ" sanctifies? Seeing as how "the Lord Jesus Christ our Saviour"[763] is, in reality, "the commandment of God our Saviour,"[764] it is well to know that "the commandment of the LORD is pure, enlightening the eyes."[765]

---

751 Ephesians 5:26
752 Hebrews 2:11
753 Job 9:32
754 Isaiah 2:22
755 Isaiah 43:3
756 Psalms 46:10
757 Mark 1:24
758 Mark 1:24
759 Micah 5:1
760 Micah 5:2
761 Acts 10:42
762 Isaiah 40:8
763 Titus 1:4
764 Titus 1:3
765 Psalm 19:8

6. "Jesus Christ" is a term denoting the commandment and "doctrine of God our Saviour,"[766] and when once this commandment is brought in to the spirit of the conversation's mind; for we are counseled, "Be renewed in the spirit of your mind";[767] "the eyes of your understanding being enlightened"[768] will confess, "Thy law is the truth."[769] Thus, "by one offering he hath perfected for ever them that are sanctified"[770] by "the law of the Spirit of life,"[771] and "perfect, as pertaining to the conscience."[772] The conversation's conscience is that body to be dressed and sanctified of the Spirit's law and counsel, which is why it is said, "He that sanctifieth."[773]

7. Now, He that sanctifies is "the author of eternal salvation,"[774] "having obtained eternal redemption for us"[775] "through the eternal Spirit."[776] By faith in the merits of his man's virtue, the Christian is called to "receive the promise of eternal inheritance,"[777] for after He was "of God exalted, and having received of the Father the promise of the Holy Ghost, he hath shed forth this"[778] on us that we may be "sanctified by the Holy Ghost,"[779] that is, "by the power of the Spirit of God."[780] Concerning the goodness within the Spirit for the inward parts, it is said, "With great power,"[781] and, "Great grace,"[782] for it is "the grace of God that bringeth salvation."[783] "Through sanctification

---

766 Titus 2:10
767 Ephesians 4:23
768 Ephesians 1:18
769 Psalm 119:142
770 Hebrews 10:14
771 Romans 8:2
772 Hebrews 9:9
773 Hebrews 2:11
774 Hebrews 5:9
775 Hebrews 9:12
776 Hebrews 9:14
777 Hebrews 9:15
778 Acts 2:33
779 Romans 15:16
780 Romans 15:19
781 Acts 4:33
782 Acts 4:33
783 Titus 2:11

of the Spirit,"[784] the one sick in "sin"; that is, in religious error; is to "receive abundance of grace"[785] that they may confess, "I delight in the law of God,"[786] yet only when once confessing, "I live by the faith of the Son of God,"[787] and, "I serve with my spirit in the gospel of his Son."[788]

8. The professed believer should remember that at the root and foundation of redemption's science is the knowledge of His man's name, which name is the *Savior* of His *Israel*, "whose goings forth have been from of old, from everlasting."[789] If this Faith is that same God of Israel, then it is that this Spirit was the God of Abraham, and if Abraham's God, it was the God of Noah, and He being the God of Noah was the God and Creator of man; of Adam; of whom we all derive our natural spiritual estate, even as did the Spirit's man. For this man "took not on him the nature of angels; but he took on him the seed of Abraham."[790]

9. The "nature" and the "seed," these two are the same reference, for in another place it is said, "Jesus Christ of the seed of David,"[791] and again, "Christ cometh of the seed of David, and of the town of Beth'lehem, where David was."[792] The seed is the nature, and the nature is of the town, and the town is "of the house and lineage of David."[793]

10. Now David was the son of Jesse, and Jesse was the son of O'bed, and O'bed of Bo'az, and Bo'az of Sal'mon. Sal'mon was the son of Nah'shon and Nah'shon was the son of Ammin'adab; "Ram begat Ammina'dab,"[794] "and Hez'ron begat Ram";[795] "Pha'rez begat Hez'ron"[796] and Pha'rez "was the son of Juda, which was the son of

---

784 1 Peter 1:2
785 Romans 5:17
786 Romans 7:22
787 Galatians 2:20
788 Romans 1:9
789 Micah 5:2
790 Hebrews 2:16
791 2 Timothy 2:8
792 John 7:42
793 Luke 2:4
794 Ruth 4:19
795 Ruth 4:19
796 Ruth 4:18

Jacob, which was the son of Isaac, which was the son of Abraham."[797] If, then, His man is of the seed of Abraham and of the lineage of David, it is then that he also derives his form from Adam, and "as in Adam all die,"[798] "as the children are partakers of flesh and blood, he also himself likewise took part of the same."[799]

11. It should now be known that He who was since time everlasting; "who is before all things"[800] and by whom "all things were created";[801] "being found in fashion as a man, he humbled himself, and became obedient unto death."[802] With his own *blood* he purchased "wisdom, and righteousness, and sanctification, and redemption"[803] for all who would believe on and live out their conversation by the fact. "For the joy that was set before him he endured the cross, despising the shame,"[804] to the end "he might be a merciful and faithful high priest in things pertaining to God, to make reconciliation for the sins of the people."[805]

12. As soon as the conversation's reconciliation to the Spirit's throne is accepted as a fact, the reformer's conversation will be given into the hands of His Word for sanctification. Herein the believer says, "We also joy in God through our Lord Jesus Christ, by whom we have now received the atonement."[806]

13. Reconciliation to the Spirit is the beginning of creation's new covenant work so that we "might serve him without fear, in holiness and righteousness before him, all the days of our life."[807] Therefore the work of sanctification is not the work of one day or of one year, it is a work of bringing the inwards of the conversation under the instruction of creation's will and law for the revival and reform of our faith's

---

797 Luke 3:33,34
798 1 Corinthians 15:22
799 Hebrews 2:14
800 Colossians 1:17
801 Colossians 1:16
802 Philippians 2:8
803 1 Corinthians 1:30
804 Hebrews 12:2
805 Hebrews 2:17
806 Romans 5:11
807 Luke 1:74,75

conscience, for it is the Spirit's intention to "purge your conscience from dead works to serve the living God."[808]

14. Now "we know that the Son of God is come, and hath given us an understanding, that we may know him that is true,"[809] and this is why it says, "If ye keep my commandments, ye shall abide in my love; even as I have kept my Father's commandments, and abide in his love."[810] As he lived in his Father's name and existed in His righteousness; for "learned he obedience"[811] in this manner; so too should the one given to his doctrine remain faithful to his words, existing in his course of learning by an experimental faith on his name for learning the name of his Father, for we are counseled, "Live through him,"[812] and again, "Live according to God in the spirit."[813]

15. Now, if his saying is that *Savior* of *Israel*, and in being Savior of *Israel* is become the God of *Israel*; for "unto the Son he saith, Thy throne, O God";[814] it is that the Spirit's *Israel* should know the precepts of their God, and the most blatant commandment pronouncing, "He that sanctifieth,"[815] is that commandment established from everlasting, saying, "God blessed the seventh day, and sanctified it."[816]

16. There is sanctification within heaven's Faith for the doer of creation's science to receive "the seal of circumcision, a seal of the righteousness of the faith."[817] The purpose of the Spirit's gift in giving us His man's name was that he might "deliver us, and purge away our sins,"[818] as it is written, "Who gave himself for our sins, that he might deliver us."[819] Notice that it was this man who gave his conversation in

---

808   Hebrews 9:14
809   1 John 5:20
810   John 15:10
811   IIebrews 5.8
812   1 John 4:9
813   1 Peter 4:6
814   Hebrews 1:8
815   Hebrews 2:11
816   Genesis 2:3
817   Romans 4:11
818   Psalms 79:9
819   Galatians 1:4

exchange for ours "while we were yet sinners"[820] and "alienated and enemies"[821] in our "mind by wicked works."[822]

17. The inwards of our faith's *body* needed to be properly ransomed from the religious world's chain; there was no *thing* worthy of man to God as a perfect substitute for their violation of His voice than the *body* of His man's faith. It is for this reason that this fact is eternally true: "It is he that hath made us, and not we ourselves."[823]

18. Man being subject to the spirit of man means that man has no escape of any *thing* within or without himself. It is God "that giveth breath"[824] "and spirit,"[825] therefore concerning the redemption of ministers and stewards, it is only the Spirit that can sanctify the mind of the conversation, and as the God that suffered and regenerated from the tree is the Word of Creation, it is that His commandments do not fail. This is why He says, "The word is gone out of my mouth in righteousness, and shall not return,"[826] for it is that He that sanctifies the spirit yet upholds a day to more thoroughly sanctify both soul and spirit.

19. Is not the ordained redemption a second creation? Here is the current work of heaven for the believer: "To be conformed to the image of his Son."[827]

20. Man failed his only opportunity to perfectly exist in the living God's religious character, "but when the fullness of the time was come, God sent forth his Son, made of a woman, made under the law, to redeem them that were under the law,"[828] "that he might be just, and the justifier of him which believeth in Jesus."[829] Henceforth the penitent should exist in his man's higher learning "for the remission of sins that are past."[830]

---

820 Romans 5:8
821 Colossians 1:21
822 Colossians 1:21
823 Psalms 100:3
824 Isaiah 42:5
825 Isaiah 42:5
826 Isaiah 45:23
827 Romans 8:29
828 Galatians 4:4
829 Romans 3:26
830 Romans 3:25

21. The entire plan of redemption, so that the reformer may again come into harmony with the name and commandments of the living God, is the creation of the inward man into the image of his man's conversation through mental or doctrinal sanctification. Thus, it is said of our conversation's blessing through His doctrine's mediation, that God has gathered it together "in the body of his flesh through death"[831] unto His throne, but why? It says, "To present you holy and unblameable and unreprovable in his sight,"[832] to the end "we should be holy and without blame before him in love."[833] He that sanctifies the soul is the same who ordained a "rest" for the conversation on the Sabbath of His name, for He is who says, "I the LORD do sanctify Israel."[834]

22. It is for this reason that He counsels His household, "The children of Israel shall keep the Sabbath, to observe the Sabbath throughout their generations, for a perpetual covenant."[835] And what is the living God's counsel concerning any covenant drawn out of His mouth? He says, "My covenant will I not break, nor alter the thing that is gone out of my lips."[836] Therefore who would be so bold as to claim service to His man's name, and while remaining unfaithful to His covenant, but a liar? Isn't it written, "Hereby we do know that we know him, if we keep his commandments"?[837]

23. Now the Jewish covenant was registered to *God*, yet now it is "Jesus the mediator of the new covenant."[838] Thus far the Christian is bound to know and keep two modern covenants when professing the knowledge of His chief apostle: that one of the Sabbath existing with the Word in the beginning; which this same Word blessed and ordained; and that covenant known as the "remembrance of his mercy"[839] "to Abraham,

---

831 Colossians 1:21,22
832 Colossians 1:22
833 Ephesians 1:4
834 Ezekiel 37:28
835 Exodus 31:16
836 Psalms 89:34
837 1 John 2:3
838 Hebrews 12:24
839 Luke 1:54

and to his seed forever."[840] That "old" or former covenant was, "Obey my voice indeed, and keep my covenant";[841] and that obedience through "the handwriting of ordinances";[842] but the Spirit "hath in these last days spoken unto us by his Son,"[843] therefore He said, "Hear ye him,"[844] and His man says, "Hear the voice of the Son of God,"[845] and, "If any man hear my voice, and open."[846] Only the Word can undo that which He has ordained, wherefore when "he saith, A new covenant, he hath made the first old."[847]

24. The Sabbath commandment has nothing to do with the Jewish or Christian economy, but rather everything to do with the living God's core manner of worship and service.

25. The Sabbath existed with man as a covenant between man's spirit and God's Spirit, and the LORD God has not revoked this law of His Faith. The mother of His man once said, "His mercy is on them that fear him from generation to generation,"[848] and then she says, "He hath holpen his servant Israel, in remembrance of his mercy."[849] Why does Mary rehearse the generational blessing of the LORD God's mercy? And in reference to this, why does she then pick up the subject of the covenant established in Abraham's name and course of learning? Where did Mary receive her doctrine? It is written, "And shewing mercy unto thousands of them that love me, and keep my commandments."[850]

26. At the center of the Spirit's commandments is the same reference made by the mother of His man, for she kept and blessed the Creator's ten precepts. And further, she uses a specific word relating to the promised covenant, saying, "Remembrance,"[851] in that the Spirit

---

840 Luke 1:55
841 Exodus 19:5
842 Colossians 2:14
843 Hebrews 1:2
844 Matthew 17:5
845 John 5:25
846 Revelation 3:20
847 Hebrews 8:13
848 Luke 1:50
849 Luke 1:54
850 Exodus 20:6
851 Luke 1:54

said, "Remember the Sabbath,"[852] because His *Israel* confesses, "The desire of our soul is to thy name, and to the remembrance of thee."[853] Herein we may understand that Mary kept the Sabbath of the living God, which Sabbath He instituted at creation.

27. It was His man that "taketh away the first, that he may establish the second,"[854] and that second is in reality the first that was ever decreed, in that the true covenant "was confirmed before of God in Christ."[855]

28. "Now to Abraham and his seed were the promises made. He saith not, And to seeds, as of many; but as of one, And to thy seed, which is Christ."[856]

29. The literal nation of Israel was to be a depositary of the living God's name and doctrine to the religious world; they were to bear within their conversation's character the same religious character of the living God, but truly His man "said unto them, Full well ye reject the commandment of God, that ye may keep your own tradition."[857] What commandment did the priests and elders put off doing? Surely that commandment which compelled him to say, "If ye were Abraham's children, ye would do the works of Abraham,"[858] which works are "through the righteousness of faith,"[859] because it is written, "God imputeth righteousness without works."[860] Now there was no Moses in the time of Abraham, for Abraham obeyed the precepts of the garden while they that issued from him "forsook the LORD God of their fathers,"[861] changing "the truth of God into a lie, and worshipped and served the creature more than the Creator."[862]

---

852 Exodus 20:8
853 Isaiah 26:8
854 Hebrews 10:9
855 Galatians 3:17
856 Galatians 3:16
857 Mark 7:8
858 John 8:39
859 Romans 4:13
860 Romans 4:6
861 Judges 2:12
862 Romans 1:25

30. It was that old covenant, and that former standard of Moses, that was to perish for use to those who should be "risen with him through the faith of the operation of God."[863] "That which was made glorious had no glory in this respect, by reason of the glory that excelleth. For if that which is done away was glorious, much more that which remaineth is glorious."[864] And what is it that now remains for us? "The ministration of the spirit"[865] and "the ministration of righteousness"[866] centered within heavenly Sanctuary under the wings of that "which entereth into that within the veil; whither the forerunner is for us entered, even Jesus, made an high priest for ever";[867] is ours to claim.

31. He that sanctifies would have all to know that the Ten Commandments of His throne are joined to His new covenant Faith, and joined to His doctrine is that name of His Spirit known and recognized within His seventh day's Sabbath. The same work of creation is the same work of redemption regarding the conversation's inwards, and to the conversation wrestling with His Spirit's voice to gain an understanding of a right and sufficient diet, to that spirit is given a "rest" known only to that *Israel* joined to "the afflictions of the gospel."[868] "Let us labour therefore to enter into that rest"[869] "of the blessing of the gospel of Christ,"[870] to the end we may know "he spake in a certain place of the seventh day on this wise, And God did rest the seventh day from all his works."[871]

32. "There remaineth therefore a rest to the people of God,"[872] "for we which have believed do enter into rest."[873] If there is one professing hope of sanctification in creation's new covenant science, then it is that they should know of the original and everlasting regeneration to endure

---

863 Colossians 2:12
864 2 Corinthians 3:10,11
865 2 Corinthians 3:8
866 2 Corinthians 3:9
867 Hebrews 6:20
868 2 Timothy 1:8
869 Hebrews 4:11
870 Romans 15:29
871 Hebrews 4:4
872 Hebrews 4:9
873 Hebrews 4:3

a joy in the purification of that course. Creation's present baptism is not without the sanctification of the living God's seventh-day Sabbath, for every word of Scripture belongs to His Word, and whosoever should say, "I know him, and keepeth not his commandments, is a liar, and the truth is not in him."[874]

33. The Spirit that said, "I sanctify myself,"[875] is no different from Him of whom it says, "On the seventh day he rested, and was refreshed."[876] Can that which the Godhead joined in to be of a nature to fit the description, "That was against us, which was contrary to us"?[877] How is it that the hard heart of the human being yet refuses to observe His own voice saying, "The Son of man is Lord also of the Sabbath,"[878] and, "The Sabbath was made for man"?[879] Yet the word of condemnation from the *One* they profess is gone out against them, saying, "Ye therefore hear them not, because ye are not of God,"[880] and, "Ye will not believe";[881] "ye have not his word abiding in you,"[882] and, "I know you, that ye have not the love of God in you."[883]

34. The Spirit's doctrine gives to the reformer the seal of the righteousness of their faith in that doctrine, which seal is understood by one's entrance in to the refreshing of His seventh day. Whosoever will claim His man's name without those precepts ordained for man at the beginning of creation serves another *Christ*, and in serving another *Christ*, they will, "because they received not the love of the truth,"[884] be given another hope. This Spirit's words do not change and are not diminished unless by His own Person, and to claim Him that sanctifies without the Sabbath of that sanctification is to "stumble at noonday as

---

874   1 John 2:4
875   John 17:19
876   Exodus 31:17
877   Colossians 2:14
878   Luke 6:5
879   Mark 2:27
880   John 8:47
881   Luke 22:67
882   John 5:38
883   John 5:42
884   1 Thessalonians 2:10

in the night."⁸⁸⁵ Truly we are then become them that fulfill the saying, "They crucify to themselves the Son of God afresh, and put him to an open shame."⁸⁸⁶

35. Today, our counsel is, "I have set before thee an open door, and no man can shut it,"⁸⁸⁷ yet how is it still reported, "Who is there among you that would shut the doors for nought?"⁸⁸⁸ "He that rejecteth me, and receiveth not my words, hath one that judgeth him,"⁸⁸⁹ says His man, for of a truth, "he that is such is subverted, and sinneth, being condemned of himself."⁸⁹⁰

36. "The LORD hath a controversy with the nations,"⁸⁹¹ and, "Hear the word of the LORD, ye children of Israel: for the LORD hath a controversy with the inhabitants of the land":⁸⁹² "Whether is easier, to say, Thy sins be forgiven thee; or to say, Rise up and walk?"⁸⁹³ For "without controversy great is the mystery of godliness: God was manifest in the flesh";⁸⁹⁴ therefore "sanctify the Lord God in your hearts"⁸⁹⁵ you that are "far off, and to him that is near, saith the LORD; and I will heal him."⁸⁹⁶

37. "Sanctify the LORD of hosts himself; and let him be your fear, and let him be your dread."⁸⁹⁷ "They that sanctify themselves, and purify themselves in the gardens behind one tree in the midst, eating swine's flesh, and the abomination, and the mouse, shall be consumed together, saith the LORD. For I know their works and their thoughts:

---

885 Isaiah 59:10
886 Hebrews 6:6
887 Revelation 3:8
888 Malachi 1:10
889 John 12:48
890 Titus 3:11
891 Jeremiah 25:31
892 Hosea 4:1
893 Luke 5:23
894 1 Timothy 3:16
895 1 Peter 3:15
896 Isaiah 57:19
897 Isaiah 8:13

it shall come, that I will gather all nations and tongues; and they shall come, and see my glory."[898]

38. "Seeing then that all these things shall be dissolved, what manner of persons ought ye to be in all holy conversation and godliness"?[899] "Account that the longsuffering of our Lord is salvation";[900] "this is good and acceptable in the sight of God our Saviour; who will have all men to be saved, and to come unto the knowledge of the truth."[901] Therefore hear creation's present decree: "Thou wilt perform the truth to Jacob, and the mercy to Abraham, which thou hast sworn unto our fathers from the days of old."[902]

---

898   Isaiah 66:17,18
899   2 peter 3:11
900   2 Peter 3:15
901   1 Timothy 2:3,4
902   Micah 7:20

8

The Inward Voice Of The Gospel

1. "As much as in me is, I am not ashamed of the gospel of Christ: for it is the power of God unto salvation to every one that believeth."[903] "Therein is the righteousness of God revealed from faith to faith: as it is written, The just shall live by faith."[904]

2. What is the gospel of Christ? Says the apostle, "It is the power of God."[905] What is the power of God? It is written, "Thy power and thy glory."[906] The power of God is the glory of God, and wherein do we find the glory of God but in the gospel of Christ. Wherein does the glory of Christ originate, which glory is contained in His doctrine? It is said,

---

903 Romans 1:16
904 Romans 1:17
905 Romans 1:16
906 Psalms 63:2

"We beheld his glory, the glory as of the only begotten of the Father."[907] That which is of the gospel of Christ is the glory of the LORD His Father. Thus, if the glory of God is the power of God, then that within the voice of Christ should be "the righteousness of God revealed."[908]

3. The gospel of Christ is the living God's benevolence ordained for soul redemption by faith to every one who would believe on this promise: "To give his life a ransom for many"[909] "to save them to the uttermost that come unto God by him."[910]

4. God's Priest desires to bring the believer where? It is said, "Christ also hath once suffered for sins...that he might bring us to God."[911] The believer is to be gathered in by His man's doctrine for spiritual perfection to be delivered unto God, as it says, "Having predestinated us unto the adoption of children by Jesus Christ to himself, according to the good pleasure of his will."[912] It is by the living God's wisdom that we are to be brought, by our faith on that counsel, to His Spirit's will, and should the heart consent to "the word of the Lord Jesus,"[913] which is "the word of reconciliation,"[914] it is that we "might be made the righteousness of God in him."[915]

5. But how is it that we are to be redeemed? The believer is inwardly recovered through faith, but faith in what? It is recorded, "Save me, O God, by thy name."[916] It is by faith on the virtue of His man's name that the believer will be made "holy and unblameable and unreprovable in his sight."[917]

6. Creation's new covenant wisdom longs "to present you faultless before the presence of his glory with exceeding joy,"[918] for it is

---

907 John 1:14
908 Romans 1:17
909 Mark 10:45
910 Hebrews 7.25
911 1 Peter 3:18
912 Ephesians 1:5
913 Acts 19:10
914 2 Corinthians 5:19
915 2 Corinthians 5:21
916 Psalms 54:1
917 Colossians 1:22
918 Jude 1:24

Him whom "God hath set forth to be a propitiation through faith in his blood, to declare his righteousness for the remission of sins."[919] Before one may encounter the living God's revealed glory, to hallow and admire and rest in that goodness, it is that the believer must take hold of the light within His man's name, which "name" is the praise and blessing of His will and intention.

7. Why does the believer need His man's spiritual understanding? It is written, "Wherein he hath made us accepted in the beloved"[920] "for the remission of sins."[921] Without accepting His man's course of learning, one exudes "a zeal of God, but not according to knowledge."[922] "There is none other name under heaven given among men, whereby we must be saved,"[923] for only through the edification of His man's voice may it be said, "Leaving the principles of the doctrine of Christ, let us go on unto perfection."[924] Where is one to find themselves when once belief is secured in this doctrine's mediation? To excellence or to perfection; for this reason it says, "His name alone is excellent,"[925] and for this cause it says of this wisdom, "Bringing many sons unto glory."[926]

8. The gospel is the revealed glory of God to place that glory of God within the one in whom that glory is revealed. The law of his man's doctrine is the road to acceptably keep the commandments of God, and this keeping "through the faith of Christ, the righteousness which is of God by faith."[927]

9. This is the gospel, for it is "the light of the knowledge of the glory of God in the face of Jesus Christ."[928] It is the light of what in Christ? The knowledge of his God's glory, for it says, "The earth shall

---

919 Romans 3:24
920 Ephesians 1:6
921 Romans 3:25
922 Romans 10:2
923 Acts 4:12
924 Hebrews 6:1
925 Psalms 148:13
926 Hebrews 2:10
927 Philippians 3:9
928 2 Corinthians 4:6

be filled with the knowledge of the glory of the LORD."[929] This is why the Father says of His chief apostle, "I have put my spirit upon him"[930] "and the isles shall wait for his law."[931] For whose law should the Gentile denominations wait for? For the law of His Son, which is why the Father then says, "A law shall proceed from me,"[932] and His man confirms, "I proceeded forth and came from God."[933]

10. We know that "whatsoever is born of God overcometh the world,"[934] and we know of "the city of the living God,"[935] and of the Son who has confessed that only He "is in the bosom of the Father,"[936] and that "the LORD came from Si'nai...with ten thousands of saints: from his right hand went a fiery law."[937]

11. The city of God with all that is therein, the ten laws of God, and the doctrine of God, are all given us personally from the living God. The religious world was to wait on the His man's spiritual law of life because only through this Faith could anyone come to the Spirit of his God; that is, come to perfectly love and do the acceptable will of His God's Spirit.

12. "According to his good pleasure which he"; He God the Father; "hath purposed in himself";[938] it is that by obeying the voice of his man's commandment that we may know the living God to further our recovery from mental and spiritual sin against Him. "The law of Christ"[939] is that which points the believer "unto the city of the living God, the heavenly Jerusalem...and to Jesus the mediator of the new covenant,"[940] allowing the believer to personally know "God the Judge of all."[941]

---

929 Habakkuk 2:14
930 Isaiah 42:1
931 Isaiah 42:4
932 Isaiah 51:4
933 John 8:42
934 1 John 5:4
935 Hebrews 12:22
936 John 1:18
937 Deuteronomy 33:2
938 Ephesians 1:9
939 Galatians 6:2
940 Hebrews 12:22-24
941 Hebrews 12:23

13. The righteousness of God; the praise of God as found in the law of His Spirit's wisdom; is revealed in the his man's tidings for the believer to know and keep, for such "righteousness of God which is by faith of Jesus Christ"[942] is the end of the gospel that we may "be conformed to the image of his Son."[943] Therefore, by "the excellency of the knowledge of Christ Jesus,"[944] the Christian will declare, "I may know him."[945] And if it is that God would have us conformed or reconciled to His religious character, this is doubtless a work of a second creation, which is why it is said, "The new man, which after God is created."[946]

14. Creation's science, "who is before all things, and by whom all things consist";[947] for in the beginning it was "God, who created all things by Jesus Christ";[948] plainly desires to purify the soul temple that its character may rest within it, and that its works may come forth from it. "The new man, which is renewed in knowledge after the image of him that created him,"[949] is the second creation of a being within the first, therefore to the second man there must also be a "rest" for his conversation, even as there was to the first, wherefore it is confirmed, "We which have believed do enter into rest."[950]

15. He who said, "Come unto me...and I will give you rest,"[951] in the beginning said, "Six days shall work be done: but the seventh day is the Sabbath of rest, an holy convocation."[952] Now, "God blessed the seventh day,"[953] and "I know that, whatsoever God doeth, it shall be for ever: nothing can be put to it, nor any thing taken from it: and God

---

942 Romans 3:22
943 Romans 8:29
944 Philippians 3:8
945 Philippians 3:9
946 Ephesians 4:24
947 Colossians 1:9
948 Ephesians 3:9
949 Colossians 3:10
950 Hebrews 4:3
951 Matthew 11:28
952 Leviticus 23:3
953 Genesis 2:3

doeth it, that men should fear before him."⁹⁵⁴ This is why it says, "Thou blessest, O LORD, and it shall be blessed for ever."⁹⁵⁵ Our entrance into the living God's "rest" on His seventh day is a sign witnessing to our devotion to His law of creation, wherefore if His man's commandment, who is over this creation, blesses our conversation, then the science of righteousness is a labor that will not be shunned or put off, which is why we are counseled, "Awake to righteousness."⁹⁵⁶

16. "Do we provoke the Lord to jealousy? are we stronger than he?"⁹⁵⁷ One of old confessed, "God is not a man, that he should lie; neither the son of man, that he should repent: hath he said, and shall he not do it? or hath he spoken, and shall he not make it good? Behold, I have received commandment to bless: and he hath blessed; and I cannot reverse it."⁹⁵⁸

17. The living God has commanded His name's Memorial; can that commandment be reversed? Never can it be reversed, not by any one other than Him, and His faithful understand this fact, saying within themselves, "He hath blessed; and I cannot reverse it."⁹⁵⁹

18. God blessed the seventh day, but what does that mean? He sanctified this day and set it apart from every other day with His own seal and blessing, for which cause, when creation's new dispensation began, His man confirmed his ministry's allegiance to His LORD's Sabbath by saying, "The Son of man is Lord even of the Sabbath day."⁹⁶⁰

19. But to who does the "rest" of the Sabbath belong? Notice that if His man spoke of those *sabbaths* of the Jews, He would have said *sabbaths*, plural, but He plainly says, Sabbath, singular. The Spirit says, "The children of Israel shall keep the Sabbath,"⁹⁶¹ for the Sabbath is for the *Israel* of God; but who are they? It is written of His host,

---

954 Ecclesiastes 3:14
955 1 Chronicles 17:27
956 1 Corinthians 15:34
957 1 Corinthians 10:22
958 Numbers 23:19,20
959 Numbers 23:20
960 Matthew 12:8
961 Exodus 31:16

"The people shall dwell alone, and shall not be reckoned among the nations."[962]

20. "They are not all Israel, which are of Israel,"[963] counsels the apostle; for there is a difference in keeping the seventh day and partaking of the seventh day's Sabbath "rest," in that one bears the character of Israel while the other is nominally after the form. The *Israel* of God are not reckoned among any earthy group, nor are they denominated, for these are of God and created by His wisdom and are known of Him while they are on *earth*, therefore being the creation of God they know the rest of their LORD and Father, for their experience matches the father of their heritage, as it says, "As a prince hast thou power with God and with men, and hast prevailed."[964] "Every one that is called by my name," says the Spirit, "I have created him for my glory, I have formed him; yea, I have made him,"[965] which is why only these can say, "I cannot go beyond the commandment of the LORD, to do either good or bad of mine own mind."[966]

21. One cannot have the creative power of the gospel to conquer "sin," and applied by the same God of creation, without the character of that God present in the experience. How the Spirit of God turns the spirit of the mind against self for the recuperation of self is "the mystery of godliness."[967] Thus, "As thou knowest not what is the way of the spirit, nor how the bones do grow in the womb of her that is with child: even so thou knowest not the works of God who maketh all,"[968] it is written.

22. We do not know His methods, but it means nothing to the one who is of faith, for the work is supernatural and extremely incredible, and "if thou canst believe, all things are possible to him that believeth."[969] What thing is possible for the one who would believe on His

---

962   Numbers 23:9
963   Romans 9:6
964   Genesis 32:28
965   Isaiah 43:7
966   Numbers 24:13
967   1 Timothy 3:16
968   Ecclesiastes 11:5
969   Mark 9:23

man's name and saying? It is that "we might be made the righteousness of God in him,"[970] and, that "the righteousness of the law might be fulfilled in us,"[971] and, that "the body of sin might be destroyed, that henceforth we should not serve sin,"[972] and, that "by the obedience of one shall many be made righteous"[973] through "abundance of grace and of the gift of righteousness,"[974] and, that "we might receive the promise of the Spirit."[975] Therefore "thanks be to God, which giveth us the victory through our Lord Jesus Christ."[976]

23. All of these things, and more, are done by faith in His man's name that we may know the living God to fall in awe of His religious character, and to have restored in us the image of disinterested love wrapped within the comfort of His Sabbath's "rest" and refreshing. All things are for the believer, "and if ye be Christ's,"[977] "Christ is God's,"[978] for "then are ye Abraham's seed,"[979] "or rather are known of God."[980] Being known of God, it is that we "joy in God through our Lord";[981] our "fellowship in the gospel"[982] awakens us to the "fellowship of the Spirit";[983] for the entire purpose of the Spirit's Faith is to cause every believing soul to remain "alive unto God through Jesus Christ."[984]

24. Who do believers become alive to? The believer is risen by His man's name "through the faith of the operation of God"[985] to know the benefit of His commandment's intercession, therefore it is said,

---

970	2 Corinthians 5:21
971	Romans 8:4
972	Romans 6:6
973	Romans 5:19
974	Romans 5:17
975	Galatians 3:14
976	1 Corinthians 15:57
977	Galatians 3:29
978	1 Corinthians 3:23
979	Galatians 3:29
980	Galatians 4:9
981	Romans 5:11
982	Philippians 1:5
983	Philippians 2:1
984	Romans 6:11
985	Colossians 2:12

"Our fellowship is with the Father, and with his Son Jesus Christ,"[986] or rather, is of "fellowship of the Spirit"[987] "to speak the mystery of Christ."[988] It is "that God sent his only begotten Son into the world, that we might live through him,"[989] therefore "being reconciled we shall be saved by his life."[990] "We were reconciled to God by the death of his Son,"[991] and our reconciliation does not remove the precepts of his God from us, but greatly magnifies them for our conversation, for we by faith rest in that "glory that excelleth."[992]

25. This is the living God's Faith, and to the believer belongs "the fulness of the blessing of the gospel of Christ"[993] to advance in it. It is this gospel that is the announcement and pronunciation of the Spirit's righteousness and the duty of the Christian, for the religion of heaven's throne is the revelation of the Spirit's law conquering the mind of an erroneous religious conversation, even as "God was in Christ."[994] This is the mystery that the believer is to speak, and it is all by faith in the blessed merits of His man's voice, for "without faith it is impossible to please him."[995]

26. It is by faith that the same creative power that called all things to be; which power still upholds all that was spoken into existence; will enter into the spirit of the conversation's conscience, delivering health to the soul when once it does "receive with meekness the engrafted word."[996] Creation's present doctrine is the Spirit's glory leading to conversational deliverance from inherited and cultivated religious negligence, and the redemption of His *Israel* is "through sanctification of the Spirit and belief of the truth"[997] to the end that these may

---

986 1 John 1:3
987 Philippians 2:1
988 Colossians 4:3
989 1 John 4:9
990 Romans 5:10
991 Romans 5:10
992 2 Corinthians 3:10
993 Romans 15:29
994 2 Corinthians 5:19
995 Hebrews 11:6
996 James 1:21
997 2 Thessalonians 2:14

receive "the sign of circumcision, a seal of the righteousness of the faith."⁹⁹⁸ "For he spake in a certain place of the seventh day on this wise,"⁹⁹⁹ seeing as how "there remaineth therefore a rest to the people of God."¹⁰⁰⁰

27. The saying of His man is creation's power unto the conversation's salvation, and it is an ever-living fact that by this law, all who would mentally and spiritually believe on it would find harmony with the image of the One who spoke it. This image is revealed by the fourth commandment of His seventh day, and our compliance with that Faith, transforming our mind into the likeness of our Creator, will lead us to care for the Memorial of that Faith's song, moving us to say, "The desire of our soul is to thy name, and to the remembrance of thee."¹⁰⁰¹ This Faith, because it is the living God's Product; as His man says, "The words that I speak unto you I speak not of myself,"¹⁰⁰² and, "I have not spoken of myself; but the Father which sent me, he gave me a commandment, what I should say, and what I should speak";¹⁰⁰³ it is the means whereby we love Him, "and this is love, that we walk after his commandments."¹⁰⁰⁴

28. Again, who is the Author of this doctrine? Hear the witness of it: "He whom God hath sent speaketh the words of God."¹⁰⁰⁵ Yet on whom should the faith of the believer rest? It is said, "The Father loveth the Son, and hath given all things into his hand,"¹⁰⁰⁶ and again, "Looking unto Jesus the author and finisher of our faith."¹⁰⁰⁷

29. By faith, the believer is to look to the wisdom of God's man for the end that his Father purposed through his doctrine, that is, "like as Christ was raised up from the dead by the glory of the Father, even so

---

998   Romans 4:11
999   Hebrews 4:4
1000 Hebrews 4:9
1001 Isaiah 26:8
1002 John 14:10
1003 John 12:49
1004 2 John 1:6
1005 John 3:34
1006 John 3:35
1007 Hebrews 12:2

we also should walk in newness of life."[1008] Like symbolizes like, and like as "death hath no more dominion over him,"[1009] "he that raised up Christ from the dead shall also quicken your mortal bodies by his Spirit"[1010] to fulfill the saying, "I will put my spirit within you, and cause you to walk in my statutes, and ye shall keep my judgments, and do them."[1011]

30. The wisdom and new covenant charge of the living God is that which is to repair our inward parts so that we may sincerely confess, "I delight in the law of God after the inward man."[1012] The work of redemption is the labor of His voice in bringing man back to full allegiance with His religious character through the means wrought by His man's name, yet the believer must know, "It is given in the behalf of Christ, not only to believe on him, but also to suffer for his sake."[1013] For this cause, the spirit of the mind is to confess, "For peace I had great bitterness,"[1014] to the end it may hear, "Come unto me, all ye that labour and are heavy laden, and I will give you rest."[1015]

31. The work of righteousness is a vocation most grievous against the inward impaired nature of the person, therefore to the *Israel* of God a season of refreshing is allotted for their toil with self. To the believer of salvation's science belongs the seventh day's perpetual covenant, which covenant was given at none other time than creation. His gospel is of washing, of rest, and of regeneration, and so too is the seventh day's Sabbath ordained by the same Spirit of the same doctrine. That spoken of by the Father, unless retracted or redacted by Him personally, "it is that which shall be."[1016]

1008   Romans 6:4
1009   Romans 6:9
1010   Romans 8:11
1011   Ezekiel 36:27
1012   Romans 7:22
1013   Philippians 1:29
1014   Isaiah 38:17
1015   Matthew 11:28
1016   Ecclesiastes 1:9

9

The Gospel Of The Sabbath

1. "Now there is at Jerusalem by the sheep market a pool, which is called in the Hebrew tongue Bethes'da, having five porches. In these lay a great multitude of impotent folk, of blind, halt, withered, waiting for the moving of the water."[1017]

2. "And a certain man was there, which had an infirmity thirty and eight years. When Jesus saw him lie, and knew that he had been now a long time in that case, he saith unto him, Wilt thou be made whole? The impotent man answered him, Sir, I have no man, when the water is troubled, to put me into the pool: but while I am coming, another steppeth down before me. Jesus saith unto him, Rise, take up thy bed, and walk. And immediately the man was made whole, and took up his bed, and walked: and on the same day was the Sabbath."[1018]

1017 John 5:1-3
1018 John 5:5-9

3. It is clearly discerned how that the Spirit's doctrine and the Spirit's Sabbath are without separation, for His man confessed, "My Father worketh hitherto, and I work."[1019] The work of salvation's science draws its foundation from the work of the Sabbath, for, the law and substance of wholeness is "in the fullness of the blessing of the gospel of Christ,"[1020] and "we which have believed"[1021] in that counsel to be made whole "do enter into rest."[1022]

4. Heaven's Faith sends the mind to creation; after the Word had spoken all things into existence, He rested on the seventh day from His endeavor; and as His man said to the man, "Rise," it was that by believing on and exercising faith on the counsel of his voice, the same creative power that, of old, constructed invisible elements to visible permanence presently made the error within his members right. It is known that it was the Word "who created all things by Jesus Christ,"[1023] therefore on this day, a certain man became an example of the Spirit's will by His man's creating doctrine.

5. In that man, by the same power of creation, and by the voice of the living God's doctrine, wholeness occurred to free his mind from "sin"; both personal and devotional; by faith in the judgment of creation's new covenant charge.

Therefore "as the Father hath life in himself; so hath he given to the Son to have life in himself,"[1024] and for this cause the apostle writes, "He that hath the Son hath life."[1025]

6. It is that "the Spirit is life,"[1026] and it is "life" because the Spirit adds to our faith's intellect "the grace of life."[1027] As the seventh day's Sabbath is the declaration of the living God's authority as God, so on the Sabbath His man preached the law of recovery.

1019 John 5:17
1020 Romans 15:29
1021 Hebrews 4:3
1022 Hebrews 4:3
1023 Ephesians 3:9
1024 John 5:26
1025 1 John 5:12
1026 Romans 8:10
1027 1 Peter 3:7

7. He who spoke in the beginning is the same that spoke on *earth* within the *body* of His man's faith, who consented to suffer the lot and penalty of negligent ministers, later ascending up to the throne of the Father to claim the office of High Priest and Intercessor for every mind dawning a lame *body* of faith. The Sabbath is the Memorial of the Spirit's creative power, and so too in the gospel is that same power to be fulfilled within man's inwards by faith on the voice of its authority to create the conversation perfect, and "perfect, as pertaining to the conscience."[1028] The spirit of the mind is to be renewed on "the knowledge of his will in all wisdom and spiritual understanding"[1029] to fit heaven's religious character, and this new work of creation, which is a work of regeneration, is done by doing "the words of his holiness"[1030] for "the washing of regeneration, and reviewing of the Holy Ghost."[1031]

8. This is why creation's Faith says, "That which is born of the Spirit is spirit,"[1032] for, "the spirit of truth"[1033] is of "even the Spirit of truth,"[1034] and as it says, "Be filled with the Spirit,"[1035] truly it is counseled, "Be filled with all the fullness of God."[1036] Herein we have before us the substance that allowed it to be known, "Immediately the man was made whole, and took up his bed, and walked,"[1037] even the substance of wisdom for newness of spiritual thought and feeling, which is why it is said, "Thou desirest truth in the inward parts: and in the hidden part thou shalt make me to know wisdom,"[1038] and, "Be ye transformed by the renewing of your mind."[1039]

1028 Hebrews 9:9
1029 Colossians 1:9
1030 Jeremiah 23:9
1031 Titus 3:5
1032 John 3:6
1033 1 John 4:6
1034 John 15:26
1035 Ephesians 5:18
1036 Ephesians 3:19
1037 John 5:9
1038 Psalm 51:6
1039 Romans 12:2

9. This man heard heaven's "wholesome words, even the words of our Lord Jesus Christ,"[1040] which words are that "doctrine which is according to godliness."[1041] Creation's law said, "Wilt thou be made whole?"[1042] and as the man obeyed the hope contained in these words, he "became heir of the righteousness which is by faith"[1043] when acting on what he had heard. On the day that these things were done, "on the same day was the Sabbath"[1044] to express that, for the confidence of the heavenly Sanctuary, both the Father and the spiritual understanding of that Building are working for the health of man, and that also, concerning that benevolence, "there remaineth a rest to the people of God."[1045]

10. Now, concerning the Word and Father of this kindness, "the world was made by him, and the world knew him not,"[1046] yet it was "that he should be made manifest to Israel."[1047] "He came unto his own,"[1048] but was neither received nor regarded by them that should have known His doctrine's face, but His thinking and feeling creation will know the Faith and Creator of their faith's person, for it says, "The children of Israel shall keep the Sabbath...for a perpetual covenant."[1049]

11. To claim His man's speech without the Sabbath is to possess his name without its redeeming power; it is to excel in a conversation "having a form of godliness, but denying the power thereof."[1050] To claim the living God's law of creation without His religious character is to receive another doctrine for another salvation from another *God*.

1040 1 Timothy 6:3
1041 1 Timothy 6:3
1042 John 5:6
1043 Hebrews 11:7
1044 John 5:9
1045 Hebrews 4:9
1046 John 1:10
1047 John 1:31
1048 John 1:11
1049 Exodus 31:16
1050 2 Timothy 3:5

12. The Jews believed that His man "had broken the Sabbath"[1051] by edifying on the Sabbath, but if they had known his saying, they would have known that what he did in their presence, and what that same Word did before man's existence, was of the same work. If they had known the living God's voice, they would have rejoiced in that done by His man on the seventh day. His man knew of the vile and unnecessary burden that the pretenders of the Faith had laid on his God's Sabbath, therefore to His *Israel*, he would educate them through things unseen that they may cherish the example of the things discerned to their conscience.

13. This man was sick for thirty-eight years, and around him rested "a great multitude of impotent folk, of blind, halt, withered,"[1052] and looking at such as these are, it is easy to conclude that they were in a condition "without form and void,"[1053] for at the beginning, "darkness was upon the face of the deep."[1054] Now, the deep are the waters, and "the waters...are peoples, and multitudes, and nations, and tongues,"[1055] therefore concerning this "deep" and these "waters," it is written, "Jesus went unto them, walking on the sea."[1056]

14. It would be this man's understanding that would banish religious darkness and bring life and spiritual rightness to light, for this sick man fulfilled the saying, "Without Christ,"[1057] and, "Without God in the world";[1058] that is, "having the understanding darkened, being alienated from the life of God."[1059] Such a people, concerning their faith's "body," "from the sole of the foot even unto the head there is no soundness in it; but wounds, and bruises, and putrifying sores."[1060] But as He that "commanded, and it stood fast"[1061] in the beginning, said,

---

1051 John 5:18
1052 John 5:3
1053 Genesis 1:2
1054 Genesis 1:2
1055 Revelation 17:15
1056 Matthew 14:25
1057 Ephesians 2:12
1058 Ephesians 2:12
1059 Ephesians 4:18
1060 Isaiah 1:6
1061 Psalms 33:9

"Rise,"[1062] his voice's creative power met the faith of that man to create and regenerate his limbs to complete newness.

15. Creation is not only the exhibit of the Spirit's power and wisdom, but also of how that knowledge flourishes within the thing wherein it is sent. Thus, "through faith we understand that the worlds were framed by the word of God, so that things which are seen were not made of things which do appear."[1063] "He spake, and it was done";[1064] in the beginning "he commanded, and they were created";[1065] and how was it that what He had said came to pass exactly as it was thought? It was by an exercised faith on His voice that every substance of life came together to perform what was intended. The root of creation's law is in the foundation of the living God's righteousness or kindness, and that ground watered and nurtured by "showers of blessing"[1066] from His thoughts, even "with all spiritual blessings"[1067] "to the praise of the glory of his grace"[1068] through that "revelation in the knowledge of him."[1069]

16. As the man heard His man's doctrine, from believing on and acting out that counsel, he was accounted righteous to receive the full measure of the blessing from doing redemption's law, even "grace according to the measure of the gift of Christ"[1070] for creation. This is why it says, "Where sin abounded, grace did much more abound."[1071]

17. Without creation's present grace, no mind will be able to conquer the infirmity that has for years confused and depressed it. Without taking personal knowledge on the fact that the Spirit's voice will conquer the defects of the conversation's character to elevate the

---

1062 John 5:8
1063 Hebrews 11:3
1064 Psalms 33:9
1065 Psalms 148:5
1066 Ezekiel 34:26
1067 Ephesians 1:3
1068 Ephesians 1:6
1069 Ephesians 1:17
1070 Ephesians 4:7
1071 Romans 5:20

thoughts of the heart, there will be a continual withering and pining away in the filth of self, and of the religious world, because of fear. This is why the record of creation was written for our observation, and this is why the record of the Spirit's Sabbath is given for our examination and participation.

18. The law of the Sabbath and the law of righteousness by faith cannot be separated from creation's present course of learning, for, after His work, He rested and blessed the seventh day, and for the new spirit created by the knowledge of His man's name, there yet rests the same Sabbath by the same Creator of the same creative power. If there is one professing His man's full doctrine, that one will not be void of the refreshing guaranteed by the law and judgment of his voice, and from that education they will know that for them belongs a day to cease the toil of their soul, even as the living God and His active Commandment ceased their toil of the earth and the heavens to better comprehend that good venture of Their heart.

19. His man preached the Spirit's will and law on the Sabbath day not to emphasize heaven's kindness above the Sabbath, for both the Faith and Sabbath of the living God are of the same Father and Spirit, and the creation being an example representing the experience man should know. His man performed this good work on the seventh day to confirm that his doctrine is indeed that Lord of the Father's seventh-day Sabbath, and that this Sabbath celebrates the glory of that Lord and Faith of the living God, which commandment is ordained for the conversation's conscience "to be conformed to the image of his Son."[1072]

20. The man by the supposed troubled water, he represents them that would rely on religious and traditional superstitious commandments to provoke thought for *health*. He knew this man, and he knew the mental, physical, emotional, and spiritual place where he was at, yet "Jesus saith unto him, Rise, take up thy bed, and walk,"[1073] for only that done in faith of the charge of God will procure the medicine to conquer self.

1072 Romans 8:29
1073 John 5:8

21. "Now it was not written for his sake alone, that it was imputed to him; but for us also, to whom it shall be imputed, if we believe on him that raised up Jesus our Lord from the dead."[1074] And this is why the apostle writes, "We which have believed do enter into rest,"[1075] "for he spake in a certain place of the seventh day."[1076]

22. The same God of Creation, with the same creative power, is yet "the author and finisher of our faith."[1077] It is most certainly written, "The gospel of Christ...is the power of God unto salvation,"[1078] for in this Faith the same creative material found in the creation is present, therefore the same "rest" of that same One is ever alive to the one strengthened by that material, for at the heart of the Spirit's *Hebrew* is the Sabbath of His own hand.

23. The Jews made His Sabbath a burden; as they also did to His name; and to the Gentile world, the living God's seventh day was looked at as one of vain weariness. His man exposed the fact of the Sabbath, that not only is this day a celebration of the fame of creation within the Spirit's doctrine, but that the seventh day is also a season of mental and spiritual edification for the soul, *body*, and spirit, of our faith.

24. After pure faith is achieved in the counsel of reconciliation, from faith the experience will flow into creation's school where its virtue will be studied and the spirit will be aggravated to advance from virtue to knowledge, and from knowledge to temperance, and from temperance to patience, and from patience to godliness, and from godliness to self-sacrificing love for kin of like faith, and then for all others. This is the work of creation that is accomplished through the Word's benevolence by faith in the wisdom of His Spirit to provide the necessary education on His will. Such a daily work needs an appointed day of "rest," which is why the Spirit has said, "In returning and rest shall ye be saved."[1079]

1074 Romans 4:23,24
1075 Hebrews 4:3
1076 Hebrews 4:4
1077 Hebrews 12:2
1078 Romans 1:16
1079 Isaiah 30:15

25. There is a twofold work: to turn the conversation's conscience to the living God's science and to accept that "rest" of His science; then will the mind receive knowledge to remain in "the kindness and love of God our Saviour toward man."[1080] This "turn" is not complete unless the refreshing of this course is observed and studied after, which is why it says, "We which have believed do enter into rest."[1081]

26. Salvation's assembly is known not only by how they "turned to God from idols to serve the living and true God,"[1082] but how that they maintain the heart and spirit of their faith to continually keep warring with self by the refreshing received through His Sabbath blessing. By faith in creation's new covenant counsel, this man was healed on the living God's Sabbath, therefore if His man should heal on this day, and suffer the attitude of the willingly ignorant, then how much health must be contained within it for us?

27. This was not the first time he saw these people or even observed this man, for the superstition of this pool of water was known. He could have chosen any other day to join his doctrine to, but no other day would have sufficed as did that Sabbath his Word personally spoke in to existence.

28. How then may one claim this Spirit's man without this Spirit's Sabbath? How may one claim that they serve the Creator without creation's Sabbath? And to the one professing this God's name and Sabbath, it should be heard and examined, "Grow in grace, and in the knowledge of our Lord and Saviour,"[1083] for if one lacks creation's grace then they are yet unchanged in heart and in mind, being alive to "sin" against creation's interceding commandment.

29. Faith in this commandment will deliver to the mind that medicine to combat "sin"; both personal and spiritual; and a thoughtful examination of self by that instruction, will keep the conversation in the presence of the living God's religious character, keeping the mind continually fed. The law of the creation of the new inward being is the

---

1080   Titus 3:4
1081   Hebrews 4:3
1082   1 Thessalonians 1:9
1083   2 Peter 3:18

joy of the believing conversation to not only keep, but to also apply to, because in so doing, they will receive a heart to honor every one of His commandments, seeing as how "this is the love of God, that we keep his commandments."[1084]

1084 1 John 5:3

10

The Heritage Of The People Of God

1. Why did the LORD prescribe a weekly Sabbath for man on the seventh day? Why was it necessary for His Spirit to bless and sanctify a day for "rest"? What should His kind of *man* even need to "rest" from? What's the point?

2. To them that would stubbornly hold that the blessing confined to the seventh day is "against us"[1085] and "contrary to us,"[1086] it must be explained why God Himself would subject Himself to a curse in which He Himself found beneficial, to then have taken "it out of the way, nailing it to his cross."[1087]

1085 Colossians 2:14
1086 Colossians 2:14
1087 Colossians 2:14

3. Scripture says, "He rested on the seventh day from all his work which he had made,"[1088] and after subjecting Himself to something supposedly contrary to Himself, He then "blessed the seventh day, and sanctified it."[1089] Such strange activity compels one to ask, "Who is the Creator?"

4. It says, "In the beginning God created."[1090] As God created in the beginning, the beginning is then the subject, or rather the author, of creation. Who then is it through whom God created? Scripture says, "His dear Son"[1091] "who is the beginning, the firstborn from the dead."[1092] "All things were created by him,"[1093] for it was "God, who created all things by Jesus Christ,"[1094] making God, or the living God's Spirit, the means whereby all things are born and do continue.

5. The LORD God created the heavens and the earth by His Spirit, and this same Spirit says, "The Sabbath was made for man."[1095] This Spirit was there before any religious world of man was thought of, and He was there to hear and participate in the ordination of the Sabbath. He who could have finished creation in one day, in one hour, in one second by His voice, took six full days to perfect the vision of His LORD, for it says, "The Word was with God, and the Word was God. The same was in the beginning with God."[1096]

6. He who could have finished creating by one word spent time on six different days to perfect what was first conceived in thought. Indeed "he spake, and it was done; he commanded, and it stood fast,"[1097] yet He exercised discretion to make certain the function and order of His product. The living God took six days for what could have been done in one, for not even God Himself would rush Himself because of the

---

1088 Genesis 2:2
1089 Genesis 2:3
1090 Genesis 1:1
1091 Colossians 1:13
1092 Colossians 1:18
1093 Colossians 1:16
1094 Ephesians 3:9
1095 Mark 2:27
1096 John 1:1,2
1097 Psalms 33:9

excitement within Himself, but His revealed temperance is a revelation of love, and is fit to be linked to that one who "humbled himself, and became obedient unto death."[1098]

7. These two characters are herein synonymous; the Creator and that Word found within the *body* of His man's faith; therefore He confirms, "The Son of man is Lord also of the Sabbath."[1099]

8. Scripture tells, "The everlasting God, the LORD, the Creator of the ends of the earth, fainteth not, neither is weary,"[1100] yet it is written, "In six days the LORD made heaven and earth, and on the seventh day he rested, and was refreshed."[1101]

9. The Word, at creation, did not experience that weariness His man experienced within his person, as it says, "Jesus therefore, being wearied with his journey, sat."[1102] "As the children are partakers of flesh and blood, he also himself likewise took part of the same";[1103] that is, formed "in the likeness of sinful flesh"[1104] and "made of a woman."[1105]

10. That which the Word experienced at the end of creation was not human or mortal weariness, nor may it ever be so vainly thought of. Creation's endeavor moved the Creator, and so after He stilled His hands, and with also His voice and spirit, He was refreshed in mind and revived by joy from taking knowledge of His labor, learning that such a "rest" was so wonderful that even His thinking and feeling creation should be partakers of it with Him. Something came out from the living God's Spirit at the end of creation, and after thinking on what had come out from Him, "knowing in himself that virtue had gone out of him,"[1106] "God blessed the seventh day, and sanctified it."[1107]

1098 Philippians 2:8
1099 Mark 2:28
1100 Isaiah 40:28
1101 Exodus 31:17
1102 John 4:6
1103 Hebrews 2:14
1104 Romans 8:3
1105 Galatians 4:4
1106 Mark 5:30
1107 Genesis 2:3

11. The Sabbath was made for man, and even in his sinless state the seventh day was blessed and ordained for them, bearing testimony that this "rest" for man is most crucial to his service to creation's wisdom, and to his fellows. The Sabbath being that institution which has ever been, it is that the "rest" observed by the Spirit and fixed for man should follow the same pattern from which it was born. For this cause His man says, "I have given you an example, that ye should do as I have done,"[1108] for which cause the apostle writes, "The Son of God is come, and hath given us an understanding, that we may know him."[1109] Again it is written, "Christ also suffered for us, leaving us an example,"[1110] and these things of him "are written for our admonition,"[1111] "written for our learning, that we through patience and comfort of the scriptures might have hope"[1112] in His every word.

12. The entire creation is an example of the work to be done within the erroneous conversation by faith on the Spirit's law of creation, and on the virtue of the merits and knowledge of that sacrificed doctrine. The heart of the believer is to be "created in righteousness and true holiness,"[1113] "renewed in knowledge after the image of him that created him."[1114] In the beginning "God created man in his own image,"[1115] and now man is "to be conformed to the image of his Son."[1116]

13. All things in Scripture explain the law of His wisdom's heavenly mediation. All things in Scripture relay the Spirit's wisdom concerning the doctrine of His man's Faith "that thou mayest fear this glorious and fearful name, THE LORD THY GOD."[1117]

14. Adam and Eve were not created to be lazy, but to continue creation's essence from investigating the portal from which that essence

---

1108 John 13:15
1109 1 John 5:20
1110 1 Peter 2:21
1111 1 Corinthians 10:11
1112 Romans 15:4
1113 Ephesians 4:24
1114 Colossians 3:10
1115 Genesis 1:27
1116 Romans 8:29
1117 Deuteronomy 28:58

was conceived. Creation may have ceased, the living God may have saw and called all things to be *good* and full of health, yet man was never expected to stop advancing in *life* and sober *love*; in knowledge and in benevolent godliness; but they were to exercise the faculties of their mind that they may obtain creation's precepts for a right moral and intellectual culture to regulate their conversation. Even at that time they were told, "To him that overcometh will I give to eat of the hidden man'na,"[1118] for "his understanding is infinite,"[1119] and with that power which worked within the tree of life, man was to continue creation within self by faith on the Word's voice by "the tree of life, and eat, and live for ever."[1120]

15. Adam was not free from committing error in his sinless religious state; proof is seen in that he willfully erred within and against his conscience after his wife had been deceived and then deceived him. The couple in Eden had much to overcome, much that their newly born and innocent conversations were unaware of and unaccustomed to, for the living God could not forcefully make them subject to His voice; they would need a personal and willing experience with that voice to acquire unadulterated love for that voice.

16. After religious error occured, it became much more difficult for them to overcome self to know their Creator. The LORD then devised a plan, "I will put enmity between thee and the woman,"[1121] He said, and to define this "enmity," "unto Adam also and to his wife did the LORD God make coats of skins, and clothed them."[1122] Herein the Spirit explained the second creation that He would do "through the redemption that is in Christ,"[1123] for by "faith in his blood,"[1124] every willing mind receives "his righteousness for the remission of sins,"[1125]

1118 Revelation 2:17
1119 Psalms 147:5
1120 Genesis 3:22
1121 Genesis 3:15
1122 Genesis 3:21
1123 Romans 3:24
1124 Romans 3:25
1125 Romans 3:25

for which cause it is said, "Put ye on the Lord Jesus Christ, and make not provision for the flesh."[1126]

17. Our faith's first parents fell away from the Spirit's understanding by giving way to base passions that magnified intemperance and spiritual rebellion. This is that spirit resting in them that they knew nothing about, and from handling their environment, from communing with creation's law and message, they were to advance in heart and in mind, having untold precepts written within their mind from examining what was formed before them.

18. This labor is most arduous, involving much mental anguish to subdue the mind to allow creation's voice into the soul's temple. Even in their sinless state this work was most naturally unattractive, and we have proof of this by the fact that Eve saw the cursed "tree to be desired to make one wise."[1127]

19. Eve did not care to tax herself to know her God, convincing herself that what had been forbidden should have excelled her knowledge in heavenly things. A sinless spiritual state does not mean that there is not an atmosphere of sin against the living God's name, nor that one has no sin within their conversation's heart and *body*, and the living God, knowing this, took into consideration the labor of man to separate a day of "rest" for him to temporarily quit the charge, "Afflict your souls."[1128]

20. Besides having to obtain a living education from God to overcome foreign dispositions within themselves that *blessed* mental and spiritual disobedience, the garden was not free from strange energy, as it says, "The serpent was more subtil."[1129] God knew that creatures contrary to His religious character existed. *God* constructed this strange creature, and He knew that such creatures could baffle man to provoke a certain stumbling from Him, yet man should not be left without a Memorial of His voice to keep them in remembrance of His person.

1126 Romans 13:14
1127 Genesis 3:6
1128 Leviticus 23:27
1129 Genesis 3:1

This is why it is said, "Put ye on the Lord Jesus Christ, and make not provision for the flesh."[1130]

21. By a living faith in His man's name, the believing conversation will be given his righteousness to receive the precious gifts and promises of his Spirit for overcoming the mind of their faith's *flesh*. The pair in Eden had it no easier than us, yet "God having provided some better thing for us"[1131] ordained "that the promise by faith of Jesus Christ might be given to them that believe."[1132] The "promise of the life that now is,"[1133] it is by faith purposed to lead us in to a personal religion with the religion of Eden, and such a religion needs a "rest" for the spirit of the conversation, which "rest" is to revive the conversation's conscience for continuing to pick up the work of self-development in heaven's light.

22. As the Word, in the beginning, worked and then rested and was refreshed, so too He charges man, "Break up your fallow ground"[1134] "and ye shall find rest unto your souls."[1135]

23. The faithful are to hear the counsel, "Break off thy sins,"[1136] and as they cooperate with His Spirit's will and charge, they are to know that the work of reform and refreshing will not happen in a week, or in a month, or in a year, or in eight years. Therefore remember the Sabbath of the living God, that His mentality may refresh your spirit and revive your faith's senses. "Remember the Sabbath day, to keep it holy,"[1137] "for in six days the LORD made heaven and earth, the sea, and all that in them is, and rested the seventh day: wherefore the LORD blessed the Sabbath day, and hallowed it."[1138]

24. The seventh day is that Memorial for the power of the Spirit's voice, for the labor of *Israel* is not after the inherited culture of the

---

1130 Romans 13:14
1131 Hebrews 11:40
1132 Galatians 3:22
1133 1 Timothy 4:8
1134 Jeremiah 4:3
1135 Matthew 11:29
1136 Daniel 4:27
1137 Exodus 20:8
1138 Exodus 20:11

natural religious tradition, but is of worship within the spirit by faith on that voice of creation's new covenant, for the knowledge within that doctrine is to create, inwardly, a new creature.

25. Man is to be formed by "the Spirit of the living God"[1139] "in fleshy tables of the heart,"[1140] and that done in the beginning is an example of that work to be finished within the conversation's conscience.

26. All things are to be done through faith in creation's wisdom, for "through faith we understand that the worlds were framed by the word of God."[1141] The believing conversation is privileged to enjoy the process of purification when once handling simple faith with confidence in the word of spiritual ransom and redemption, and as the individual faithfully handles creation's instruction; even as Christ Himself also handled the word of His Father, saying, "I know him, and keep his saying";[1142] so too the believer will be given the holy "rest" of creation's law to let be what was done during the week, and to regenerate their conversation by His words to endure what should come after. Truly, then, "there remaineth therefore a rest to the people of God."[1143]

27. Is love yet seen in the Sabbath? Must the heart refuse the special celebration that the living God confided to the seventh day of the week? Can the reader discern the relevance of this day's hours? What is the end of the Sabbath but a cessation of weary labor to rest under the shadow of the living God for beneficial knowledge of His name?

28. Of old it is written, "The LORD God took the man, and put him into the garden of Eden to dress it and to keep it,"[1144] and now He has charged, "Sow to yourselves in righteousness, reap in mercy; break up your fallow ground."[1145]

29. Man at the present is not fit to dress and keep the ground of his heart by his self, therefore we have *One* who has "fled for refuge to lay

---

1139 2 Corinthians 3:3
1140 2 Corinthians 3:3
1141 Hebrews 11:3
1142 John 8:55
1143 Hebrews 4:9
1144 Genesis 2:15
1145 Hosea 10:12

hold upon the hope set before us,"[1146] "even Jesus, made an high priest for ever after the order of Melchis'edec."[1147]

30. As the reformer cooperates with the doctrine of this High Priest, they will know their High Priest to receive life to continue their conversation with His name, for "the Spirit is life."[1148] This is why the apostle writes, "He that hath the Son hath life,"[1149] for out of the Spirit comes "the grace of life"[1150] that all who should suffer self to famish should "reign in life by one, Jesus Christ."[1151]

31. The gospel cannot be separated from the seventh day's Sabbath, for the same doctrine is Lord over both, and in both; in His Faith and His Sabbath; His love is supremely magnified.

32. Even though we have such a great High Priest who, "when he had by himself purged our sins, sat down on the right hand of the Majesty on high,"[1152] the work to apply for membership to his High Priestly Ministration is personal. The Godhead has done Their part; recovery of the mind of the conversation's conscience is available "by the washing of regeneration, and renewing of the Holy Ghost";[1153] yet that work of righteousness cannot take place until creation's Faith is made into an active personal Savior.

33. The benefits of reconciliation will not take place until the heart will accept the condition spoken of by the living God's Spirit, and He says, "A covenant with me by sacrifice."[1154] When the heart may say, "I made a covenant with mine eyes,"[1155] then will the Spirit teach that spirit "the excellency of the knowledge of Christ,"[1156] for it is written, "We which have believed do enter into rest":[1157] "for he spake in a

---

1146 Hebrews 6:18
1147 Hebrews 6:20
1148 Romans 8:10
1149 1 John 5:12
1150 1 Peter 3:7
1151 Romans 5:17
1152 Hebrews 1:3
1153 Titus 3:5
1154 Psalms 50:5
1155 Job 31:1
1156 Philippians 3:8
1157 Hebrews 4:3

certain place of the seventh day on this wise, And God did rest the seventh day from all his works."[1158]

34. When once the heart surrenders to the doctrine of the living God's man, the soul will know the "rest" appointed for it. His Faith is of justification; justification is another word for sanctification; by faith on the knowledge of his doctrine's operation to recover the lost spiritual faculties of man's conversation. There is therefore, for them that are creations of this counsel's intercession, only one Sabbath, and that Sabbath rests on the seventh day. To bring man closer to His throne, to allow man the opportunity to know the place of His strength and sufficiency when warring against self, to allow man the opportunity to remember the hope for him, the Sabbath was given that man may rejoice in the sustaining wisdom of the Spirit's grace. Herein is a blessed institution of the living God for His *Israel* born of His second Adam's spiritual understanding, for the He knows the deficiencies in man and what He did not naturally place within him, that as man would, through His counsel, faithfully work in self that which is contrary to self's religious nature, they may "rest" and find place for soul rejuvenation.

1158 Hebrews 4:4

11

The Power And Order Of His Blessing

1. Says Scripture, "God blessed the seventh day, and sanctified it,"[1159] therefore we know that no change can happen to this ordained season of worship, for Scripture plainly confesses, "Thou blessest, O LORD, and it shall be blessed for ever."[1160]

2. The seventh day's "rest" is the blessed appointment of heaven's wisdom. That which the voice of God does bless is blessed for ever, and for this reason it is written, "The Strength of Israel will not lie nor repent: for he is not a man, that he should repent."[1161]

3. All who profess His man's name should not only know his doctrine's living Sabbath of regeneration, but also the power of that

---

1159   Genesis 2:3
1160   1 Chronicles 17:27
1161   1 Samuel 15:29

refreshing, yet there is no advancing knowledge on the living God's Sabbath because "we sought him not after the due order."[1162]

4. The order ordained for the believer is found in the counsel, "Be ye mindful always of his covenant; the word which he commanded,"[1163] "even the covenant which he made with Abraham"[1164] "and hath confirmed the same to Jacob for a law, and to Israel for an everlasting covenant."[1165]

5. Notice that the order to know His wisdom is contained within a covenant, and this covenant is understood to be a word, and this "word" is called a law. There is a law to be observed that is to deliver the penitent soul certain precepts of personal religious order to honestly maintain their conversation, and this word of law is found in the saying, "A law shall proceed from me."[1166] "My righteousness,"[1167] "my salvation is gone forth,"[1168] says the living God, "and the isles shall wait for his law."[1169]

6. This law is "the law of Christ"[1170] expressed "through the blood of the everlasting covenant,"[1171] even "the doctrine of Christ"[1172] "confirmed before of God in Christ, the law."[1173] The order of this covenant is "through the righteousness of faith,"[1174] which is "the righteousness of the law"[1175] as taught by "the faith of Abraham,"[1176] for "the word of righteousness"[1177] is after "the righteousness which is by faith."[1178]

1162 1 Chronicles 15:13
1163 1 Chronicles 16:15
1164 1 Chronicles 16:16
1165 1 Chronicles 16:17
1166 Isaiah 51:4
1167 Isaiah 51:5
1168 Isaiah 51:5
1169 Isaiah 42:4
1170 Galatians 6:2
1171 Hebrews 13:20
1172 2 John 1:9
1173 Galatians 3:17
1174 Romans 4:13
1175 Romans 2:26
1176 Romans 4:16
1177 Hcbrews 5:13
1178 Hebrews 11:7

7. The Spirit's law and doctrine speaks to this point, as it says, "We might be justified by faith,"[1179] therefore being justified, or rather sanctified by an experimental faith, it should be heard, "We which have believed do enter into rest."[1180] "For he spake in a certain place of the seventh day on this wise, And God did rest the seventh day from all his works."[1181] Therefore because the law of His man's Faith is chained to His wisdom's seventh-day Sabbath, "as the Holy Ghost saith, To day if ye will hear his voice, harden not your hearts."[1182]

8. No conversation should lack the precepts of the living God's Faith, or the law of His Sabbath, if it considers its understanding to be faithful to His and His chief apostle's name. The precepts of His Faith lead in to His "rest," for "to whom sware he that they should not enter into his rest, but to them that believed not?"[1183] It is because of secret unbelief that there exists an error "untaken away in the reading of the old testament; which vail is done away in Christ,"[1184] that is, which spiritual negligence is corrected by exercising faith on creation's present spiritual understanding.

9. The wisdom of heaven is not without the Sabbath of heaven's Father, and the law of His man's speech is not without the ten immutable laws of his Father. His man, with his own mouth, says, "Blessed are they that hear the word of God, and keep it,"[1185] and if they that hear are blessed, and His wisdom's blessing is for ever, then there is no doubt concerning the certainty of the counsel: "The word of our God shall stand for ever."[1186]

10. What then is the word or counsel concerning His seventh day's appointment? It says, "God blessed the seventh day, and sanctified it."[1187]

1179 Galatians 2:16
1180 Hebrews 4:3
1181 Hebrews 4:4
1182 Hebrews 3:7
1183 Hebrews 3:18
1184 2 Corinthians 3:14
1185 Luke 11:28
1186 Isaiah 40:8
1187 Genesis 2:3

11. "Thou blessest, O LORD, and it shall be blessed for ever."[1188] "What his soul desireth, even that he doeth,"[1189] and "whatsoever God doeth, it shall be for ever: nothing can be put to it, nor anything taken from it."[1190] Amen.

12. Blessed is the living God's seventh day's Sabbath, and blessed are them "that do his commandments, hearkening unto the voice of his word."[1191]

13. "Arise therefore, and be doing, and the LORD be with thee."[1192] "Know thou the God of thy father, and serve him with a perfect heart and with a willing mind,"[1193] for creation's law, who is our Mediator for health, says, "I ascend to my Father, and your Father; and to my God, and your God."[1194]

1188 1 Chronicles 17:27
1189 Job 23:13
1190 Ecclesiastes 3:14
1191 Psalms 103:20
1192 1 Chronicles 22:16
1193 1 Chronicles 28:9
1194 John 20:17

12

Which Abideth For Ever

1. Says Scripture, "The word of God, which liveth and abideth for ever."[1195]

2. The word of God is not just living; it has been alive as long as the One who originally spoke it. "God is not a man, that he should lie; neither the son of man, that he should repent: hath he said, and shall he not do it? or hath he spoken, and shall he not make it good?"[1196]

3. The living and breathing word of God does not change. The hand of man can alter it just as much as the Author of that word can think to be vandalized; there is in fact no thing that man can do to extinguish His voice. The most man can do is transform "the truth of God into a lie."[1197] Nevertheless, "what if some did not believe? shall their unbelief make the faith of God without effect?"[1198]

1195   1 Peter 1:23
1196   Numbers 23:19
1197   Romans 1:25
1198   Romans 3:3

4. Where does this living counsel come from? Why is it that when the word spoken by this wisdom meets the material of the air, and when the conscience of the invisible environment vibrates with the intention of His heart, that that word is received by nature to be a living force as soon as He speaks it?

5. Upon his conversion, the king of Babylon said, "I praised and honoured him that liveth for ever, whose dominion is an everlasting dominion, and his kingdom is from generation to generation."[1199] That great voice of life proceeds from Him that has ever existed, from Him that has been since all things were, for this is "him that sat on the throne, who liveth for ever and ever,"[1200] who the apostle saw in vision as the center of *heaven's* entire universe. The Word's counsel lives and abides for ever because it is born from One who lives and abides for ever, and for His faithful sons and daughters, the counsel is, "He that doeth the will of God abideth for ever."[1201]

6. The entire purpose for His man's offering was for the conversation's inwards to ever advance in "understanding what the will of the Lord is."[1202] What does the living God say on every thing contained in that will and purpose of His name? "I know the thoughts that I think toward you, saith the LORD, thoughts of peace, and not of evil, to give you an expected end."[1203]

7. Every word of God is filled with exactly this, even "on earth peace, good will toward men."[1204] Now, that "peace" and "good" is in reality "abundance of peace"[1205] in the form of "abundance of grace."[1206] That good purpose of His will towards man came after the blood of His man appeased His wrath towards *man's* inwards. Because this gift is now received in the form of His own mind of devotion, through the name

---

1199   Daniel 4:34
1200   Revelation 4:9
1201   1 John 2:17
1202   Ephesians 5:17
1203   Jeremiah 29:11
1204   Luke 2:14
1205   Psalms 72:7
1206   Romans 5:17

and wisdom of His man, "we might receive the promise of the Spirit through faith."[1207]

8. By "the Spirit of grace,"[1208] every believer is "to be conformed to the image of his Son";[1209] "changed into the same image from glory to glory, even as by the Spirit of the Lord."[1210] Because this Spirit is given the office of transforming the corrupt and foul religious conversation in to the image of His man's conversation, and because "the Spirit of truth"[1211] "proceedeth from the Father,"[1212] this Spirit's every word is binding to every professed believer of His science. The creation of His Faith's new creature is but a revelation born for sending the mind back to the beginning of all things, and as the mind finds itself confronted with the living God in every thing concerning creation, they are then brought to hear one of the living laws of that Word of creation, that "God blessed the seventh day, and sanctified it."[1213]

9. Remember, "The word of God is ever lasting,"[1214] and, "Whoso hears and does the will of God, their conversation will also live as long, and grow in the same strength of, that word."[1215]

10. Before any religious denomination created its self, before man separated from Eden's Spirit and Counsel, even before man had the chance to entertain separation from His name, the living word of God said, "God blessed and hallowed His seventh day, and sanctified it."[1216] Herein is the word of God. It ever lives and cannot fail or be removed, and it has not been removed, and it will ever remain the same "not only in this world, but also in that which is to come."[1217]

11. The LORD's mouth sanctioned the seventh day above all other days, and in that endorsement He also declares His will, saying, "Six

---

1207 Galatians 3:14
1208 Hebrews 10:29
1209 Romans 8:29
1210 2 Corinthians 3:18
1211 John 15:26
1212 John 15:26
1213 Genesis 2:3
1214 Isaiah 40:8
1215 1 John 2:17
1216 Genesis 2:3
1217 Ephesians 1:21

days shall work be done: but the seventh day is the Sabbath of rest, an holy convocation; ye shall do no work therein: it is the Sabbath of the LORD."[1218] "It is a sign between me and the children of Israel for ever...for a perpetual covenant."[1219]

12. God once said, concerning one of His tribes, "Out of thee shall come a Governor, that shall rule my people Israel."[1220] Now, when it says, "The veil of the temple was rent in twain from the top to the bottom,"[1221] the saying was fulfilled, "Where is the bill of your mother's divorcement, whom I have put away?"[1222] The temple ripping in two, exposing what no eye ever saw, except the seed of a particular tribe, occurred to strengthen the notion that the LORD of the Hebrews had removed His Faith from *earth*, and from men of the religious world, in to His heavenly Sanctuary. The saying was fulfilled, "Neither shall the priests the Levites want a man before me,"[1223] for the Spirit's religion, and the Spirit's assembly, were to no longer find themselves under a literal theocracy, but rather under a spiritual course headed by the living God's spiritual understanding, who is appointed as that High Priest over creation's new covenant science.

13. Thus, "the Israel of God"[1224] is no longer a literal people under a literal earthy denomination subscribing to some doctrinal tradition by some *Moses*, but are rather them who bear the likeness of their God and High Priest, being "filled with the knowledge of his will in all wisdom and spiritual understanding."[1225]

14. Every thing of God is now firstly of a mental and spiritual nature. This is why the commandment is, "Worship God in the spirit,"[1226] and, "Live according to God in the spirit."[1227] For this cause, never forget to

---

1218 Leviticus 23:3
1219 Exodus 31:16,17
1220 Matthew 2:6
1221 Mark 15:38
1222 Isaiah 50:1
1223 Jeremiah 33:18
1224 Galatians 6:16
1225 Colossians 1:9
1226 Philippians 3:3
1227 1 Peter 4:6

soberly "rejoice in Christ Jesus,"[1228] for "we also joy in God through our Lord Jesus Christ, by whom we have now received the atonement."[1229] To rejoice therefore in "Christ" is, in reality, to magnify "the doctrine of Christ,"[1230] and to magnify the law of "Christ" is to hear and do the counsel, "Be filled with all the fulness of God,"[1231] that is, "Be filled with the Spirit."[1232]

15. Because "it pleased the Father that in him should all fulness dwell,"[1233] whosoever has His man's understanding has the fullness of his mind of devotion, and that fullness drawn from "the law of the Spirit of life."[1234] Because the LORD's Spirit proceeds from Him, the mind of that Spirit is ordained to bring the believer of the God of that Spirit to the wisdom of that Spirit. Thus, the foundation of the high priestly office of His doctrine is, "He might bring us to God."[1235] And is this a lie? Hear the Word's man speaking on the ministration of creation's law: "He is able also to save them to the uttermost that come unto God by him, seeing he ever liveth to make intercession for them."[1236]

16. Because "God is a Spirit,"[1237] to be brought to "God" is to have the conversation's conscience brought into the domain and classroom of the living God's new covenant wisdom. The entire purpose of His man's doctrine is to place man, by an experimental faith on His present charge, into the hand of the living God for a right education and revival, that the human being may learn how to properly reform and strengthen its mental and moral faculties. Such an experience is reserved for them who, with all of their heart and mind and soul, directly confess to heaven's will and law, "I will not let thee go, except thou bless me."[1238]

1228 Philippians 3:3
1229 Romans 5:11
1230 2 John 1:9
1231 Ephesians 3:19
1232 Ephesians 5:18
1233 Colossians 1:19
1234 Romans 8:2
1235 1 Peter 3:18
1236 Hebrews 7:25
1237 John 4:24
1238 Genesis 32:26

17. Who is this that dare say such a thing? Says the Spirit, "Thy name shall be called no more Jacob, but Israel."[1239] Thus, for the one who is so bold to hear and do the charge, "Handle me, and see,"[1240] that "one shall say, I am the LORD'S."[1241]

18. Herein we have proved that no thing of the living God literally belongs to any one tribe or religious denomination, but is rather left for the individual soul that is fervently desirous to personally know His name and operation. Therefore, for the author of this book and chapter, and for his reader, no matter who they may be, "through him we both have access by one Spirit unto the Father."[1242]

19. All may possess the religious character that fulfills the name and conversation of *Israel*, but how? Says the Spirit, "If ye be willing and obedient."[1243] And if we are afraid to be willing, and are also afraid to be obedient to His present law of creation, what does the Spirit say on this subject? He says, "Call unto me, and I will answer thee, and shew thee great and mighty things, which thou knowest not."[1244]

20. Tradition, whether inherited or self-cultivated, can honestly do nothing for the soul of any one in the sight of the Godhead. Vain religious thoughts and imaginations, superstitions and policies that aggravate that true work of creation, "philosophy and vain deceit, after the tradition of men,"[1245] can do no thing. Creation's spiritual assembly maintains "spiritual sacrifices"[1246] that procure "spiritual blessings,"[1247] which blessings, given upon our active faith on what ultimately proceeds out of the living God's mouth, will help the heart of the conversation's mind understand "that the law is spiritual."[1248]

1239 Genesis 32:28
1240 Luke 24:39
1241 Isaiah 44:5
1242 Ephesians 2:18
1243 Isaiah 1:19
1244 Jeremiah 33:3
1245 Colossians 2:8
1246 1 Peter 2:5
1247 Ephesians 1:3
1248 Romans 7:14

21. The living God's commandments are for the mind as well as for the flesh of our faith. "By the washing of regeneration, and renewing of the Holy Ghost,"[1249] the individual is to have the saying fulfilled in them, "I will put my law in their inward parts, and write it in their hearts."[1250] The spirit of the conversation is to become that new ark containing the Godhead's will and testament. Every one of the Spirit's ten laws is to be engraved within the heart when once atonement to His wisdom is accepted. And since the Spirit is that Agent for inward renewal and regeneration, that same Spirit of God will not let the reformer's faith exist without telling them, "In returning and rest shall ye be saved."[1251]

22. For this cause He says, "The sons of the stranger, that join themselves to the LORD, to serve him, and to love the name of the LORD, to be his servants, every one that keepeth the Sabbath from polluting it, and taketh hold of my covenant; even them will I bring to my holy mountain, and make them joyful in my house of prayer."[1252]

23. We, who are not of literal Hebrew descent, yet profess a faith and confidence in that Spirit of the ancient Hebrews, are in fact the strangers spoken of by Him. The living God did not will for any one to be negligent towards that day of edification He ordained after creation. Before there was ever a distinction between bloodline and stranger, man was right before God, and He never designed for there to be a separation from His manner of worship and service. What should tie the human race together, what should place humanity in remembrance of its weakness to better exist with one another, and what should engrave within the mind of the human being his or her duty to one another, came in the form of a Memorial to be celebrated once every week, and on the last day of the week, to re-establish their devotion and thanksgiving to the Giver of their being's prosperity. This is why it says, "Remember the Sabbath day."[1253]

1249 Titus 3:5
1250 Jeremiah 31:33
1251 Isaiah 30:15
1252 Isaiah 56:6,7
1253 Exodus 29:8

24. Although His word is ever a living and established fact, the living God knew that the spiritual ignorance within mankind would drive them from Him. Nevertheless, "the times of this ignorance God winked at; but now commandeth all men every where to repent."[1254]

25. This side of "sin," we need not be as faithless as them that came before us. The Spirit's voice lives and abides for ever; "it shall be for ever: nothing can be put to it, nor any thing taken from it: and God doeth it, that men should fear before him."[1255] So then if we believe whatever we believe concerning His man, must it be ignored that God Himself will create our conversation's character to fit into His chief son's mold? And if in fact this process of redemption by His wisdom is a second creation, if this same God said of old, "The seventh year shall be a sabbath of rest unto the land,"[1256] how much more valuable is a soul to the land?

26. To every one who would know the Spirit of creation, and to all who are known of His Spirit, His Sabbath is a perpetual covenant that cannot be broken, and that God Himself has not cast off. This word from the beginning, concerning the seventh day, is ever living, simply because of the One who first spoke it.

1254 Acts 17:30
1255 Ecclesiastes 3:14
1256 Leviticus 25:4

13

The Banner Of His Faith

1. Who loves the living God's spiritual understanding? Who cares for this Spirit's law and commandment? Who finds the law of heaven's Faith beyond amiable? Who is even so bold as to observe this course of learning, and to trust on this wisdom, that it can also create their conversation in similar likeness to His chief messenger's? If there is sincere love for both the Father and His ministering wisdom, and if there is unadulterated trust in that Spirit, should not such affection find open confession?

2. If the chambers of the heart are filled with this Spirit's voice, and if the soul temple has consented to have its Faith as its primary Minister, how may we know that our devotion is elevated above the *flesh's* perception? Scripture says, "Thou hast given a banner to them that fear thee, that it may be displayed because of the truth."[1257]

1257 Psalms 60:4

3. The flag of the Spirit's nationality bears witness to the purity of our conversation, for it is implanted within the ground of our faith, and is ever present before the door of the house of our religious character. "Upon the posts of thy house, and on thy gates,"[1258] should rest the ensign of the county from which our confidence is.

4. Every citizen loves their country, and every lawful foreigner taking on a new country, even though they have the memory of their original land, will, for the liberty of that new place, pick up the manners and service of that new country. The Spirit's faithful, devoutly attached to their new country, will therefore say, "I am a stranger with thee, and a sojourner."[1259]

5. "They that say such things declare plainly that they seek a country."[1260] "They desire a better country, that is, an heavenly: wherefore God is not ashamed to be called their God: for he hath prepared for them a city."[1261]

6. It is the banner of the City of the living God that pronounces entire affiliation with Him, and it is given that His name and virtue may be on full display to justify what the resources of that new land accomplishes in its citizen, and what it will do for every one willing to know it. If there is a love for this Spirit, then there also needs to be a love for the country of this Spirit. Should the counsel have been given in vain, "Ye are no more strangers and foreigners, but fellowcitizens with the saints, and of the household of God"?[1262] Every one who would be a friend of the Godhead is a stranger and a pilgrim to *earth*, other nationalities and persuasions amounting to no weight in *His* sight.

7. Is it false to say such things? It is said, "All nations";[1263] in reality, all religious denominations; "before him are as nothing; and they are counted to him less than nothing, and vanity."[1264] This is why it is says, "Ye were not redeemed with corruptible things, as silver and gold, from

---

1258 Deuteronomy 6:9
1259 Psalms 39:12
1260 Hebrews 11:14
1261 Hebrews 11:16
1262 Ephesians 2:19
1263 Isaiah 40:17
1264 Isaiah 40:17

your vain conversation received by tradition from your fathers."[1265] Instead, "sanctify the Lord God in your hearts,"[1266] for it is written, "Their righteousness is of me, saith the LORD."[1267]

8. Applying to the Spirit's law and learning will procure health "multiplied unto you through the knowledge of God, and of Jesus our Lord."[1268] It is this obtained knowledge that shines forth from our person upon the sphere of our existence.

9. Because our "fellowship in the gospel"[1269] is joined to the "fellowship of the Spirit,"[1270] the Spirit's Faith is but "the fellowship of the mystery"[1271] encouraging the faithful reformer to "speak the mystery of Christ."[1272] The banner that is given to them that fear this mystery is that ensign conveying the message of a successful campaign of heaven's wisdom within the heart, for it is "the sign of circumcision, a seal of the righteousness of the faith."[1273] Thus, every citizen of the living God's City, wherein rests that Church maintained by His Spirit's wisdom of creation, is a banner for proof of the Spirit's creative power, and of the authenticity of His name's fame, which name is given in the form of a the seal upon the conversation reiterating His fame, which name is sealed by His seventh day's Sabbath.

10. The time will come when the word will again be fulfilled, "I will send those that escape of them unto the nations"[1274] "that have not heard my fame."[1275] What is the LORD's fame? He says, "That have not heard my fame, neither have seen my glory."[1276]

11. His fame is His glory, so what then is the living God's glory? Says the psalmist, "Blessed be his glorious name for ever: and let the

---

1265 1 Peter 1:18
1266 1 Peter 3:15
1267 Isaiah 54:17
1268 2 Peter 1:2
1269 Philippians 1:5
1270 Philippians 2:1
1271 Ephesians 3:9
1272 Colossians 4:3
1273 Romans 4:11
1274 Isaiah 66:19
1275 Isaiah 66:19
1276 Isaiah 66:19

whole earth be filled with his glory";[1277] in reality this means, "The earth shall be filled with the knowledge of the glory of the LORD."[1278]

12. The fame and the glory of God is in fact the knowledge of His name. What is this knowledge? It is "the light of the knowledge of the glory of God in the face of Jesus Christ."[1279] This wisdom preaches, "God was manifest in the flesh, justified in the Spirit,"[1280] for creation's science is after that which is called, "The mystery of godliness."[1281]

13. The living God's spiritual understanding is that Spirit and Creator, and *He* does not say in vain, "I make all things new."[1282] From a strange void of nothingness, the Spirit formed the earth into a habitable place, and this example is for us who are alive this side of "sin" and creation.

14. The endeavor of making the physical world is finished. All things currently exist as they did in the beginning, for when He stopped creating, what was then created was sufficient to continue as long as His Spirit decreed that it should. The power of His voice, and the living stream of His thoughts, constructed the frame of our realm from what was once a base and barren *earth*, and, that it should no longer be unfruitful, the same creative power of the Word of creation is ordained to enter into the *dead* heart of the personal religion, moving the conversation to be "fruitful in every good work, and increasing in the knowledge of God."[1283]

15. Just as darkness clung to the earth, and just as error against His fame naturally fills the members of the human conversation, so now it is possible to "put on the new man, which after God is created in righteousness and true holiness."[1284] Thus, as the saying goes, "In God we trust," so what is read on the Spirit's banner is, "Which after God is created."[1285]

1277   Psalms 72:19
1278   Habakkuk 2:14
1279   2 Corinthians 4:6
1280   1 Timothy 3:16
1281   1 Timothy 3:16
1282   Revelation 21:5
1283   Colossians 1:10
1284   Ephesians 4:24
1285   Ephesians 4:24

16. Because "God is a Spirit,"[1286] "God" in the *flesh* is the Spirit of God within the spiritually erroneous *body* of faith, and this is the will of creation's mystery. The Spirit has officially ordained a second creation to commence within the soul holding dear to the knowledge and illustration of His sacrifice on the tree. Therefore, the one who accepts the revelation of His man will say, "The Spirit of God hath made me, and the breath of the Almighty hath given me life."[1287]

17. The fame and glory of God puts the saying to rest, "Who can bring a clean thing out of an unclean?"[1288] for the Spirit's name is seen in how He "is able to keep you from falling, and to present you faultless before the presence of his glory."[1289] Because it is the Word's purpose to form a new creature in the midst of an already existing erroneous conversation, the counsel should be heard, "In his temple doth every one speak of his glory."[1290]

18. In the living God's heavenly Temple, every *thing* within that Building, every instrument and article within the Spirit's *Places*, exemplifies the virtue of His name and purpose. This is why He counsels, "Look unto me, and be ye saved."[1291]

19. His man is not on a tree. His man is not in the *earth* or under the earth. The Spirit Himself is telling His active host to look to His name, to look at His person, to search after His spiritual understanding, and this means that He has a Place where His throne dwells, and that He expects His host to be there with Him where He is. Where then are we to look? "Look upon Zion, the city of our solemnities,"[1292] we are counseled. And this is why Paul counsels, "Ye are come unto mount Si'on, and unto the city of the living God."[1293]

20. This is the living God's Country of, and that means whereby every citizen knows, and is continually advancing in knowledge of this

---

1286 John 4:24
1287 Job 33:4
1288 Job 14:4
1289 Jude 1:24
1290 Psalms 29:9
1291 Isaiah 45:22
1292 Isaiah 33:20
1293 Hebrews 12:22

Land's counsels. Because this is the Spirit's country, the name of the LORD of this country is found in every place of this country, and on every thing within it. Should the heart allow the eye to operate through faith, should the believer of heaven's Faith so boldly enter this City through its course of learning, to then obtain a free pass into the Spirit's Temple to join the congregation of His spiritual confidence, every *thing* seen will reveal the fact that God Himself does not want the newcomer to leave. As the ear soberly hears of creation's sacrifice, and follows that offering into the living God's Places, the vision of His salvation's science will encourage the soul to continue its good fight of faith in the commandment that overcame all religious things for the sake of their conversation's newness.

21. His man once healed a man. After he had done a series of things with him to test his faith, these things being finished, "he went his way therefore, and washed, and came seeing."[1294] But being sent away and healed away from him, people, curious of this man that he spoke of, said "unto him, Where is he? He said, I know not."[1295] He had only accepted a doctrine by faith, and this in fact healed him, but he never once saw the man.

22. This blind man loved the *God* taught to him by his parents. Every thing he heard of God on the Sabbath or at home, every thing he heard of the Christ of God by John and his disciples, it caused him to make sure that "the law of his God is in his heart."[1296] Thus, when approached by His man, His man had already known him, and this man had already been anticipating the one who perfectly pronounced to him the righteousness of his LORD, and when he finally saw his face, he never, until the day that he died, turned from it.

23. This man saw the glory of the Spirit's name in the face of His Son, or rather, he now knew the Word's will from what obedience to that voice of commandment had previously bestowed on him. It is not enough to believe on *God*, because not even God Himself would have us satisfied on unproven belief, theory, or superstition. Belief is not

---

1294 John 9:7
1295 John 9:12
1296 Psalms 37:31

emotional, belief is not formed by any public opinion, and any thing related to God cannot be self-sustained without containing some contaminating force. Right belief is rather obtained from experience, from perceiving and actively taking knowledge of the LORD God's operation, and this knowledge does "not stand in the wisdom of men, but in the power of God."[1297]

24. When this man saw His chief apostle, it was then that he could honesty say, "I worship thy name."[1298] And when those around him had heard his testimony, they could say with him, "We believe, not because of thy saying: for we have heard him ourselves, and know."[1299] This is the required experience necessary to obtain citizenship for the heavenly country. It is that while in this Place, and while under the reign of that meditation joined to the LORD God's throne, every precept of that throne will be written and engraved within the soul's temple by His Spirit's chief counsel, even as it says, "Written not with ink, but with the Spirit of the living God."[1300]

25. This ministration points to "the righteousness of God without the law."[1301] This "law" is that instruction of *perfection*, for "perfection were by the Levit'ical priesthood."[1302] The glory of God is now without "the blood of bulls and of goats, and the ashes of an heifer sprinkling the unclean";[1303] it is today without "meats and drinks, and divers washings, and carnal ordinances";[1304] it is without "both gifts and sacrifices, that could not make him that did the service perfect, as pertaining to the conscience."[1305] The fame of God is seen in that His thoughts care to inhabit the soul temple so that His name can personally cleanse the conversation's conscience from the taint of a carnal religious nature, only to fill it with the nature of His own religious character. This is why

---

1297 1 Corinthians 2:5
1298 John 9:38
1299 John 4:42
1300 2 Corinthians 3:3
1301 Romans 3:21
1302 Hebrews 7:11
1303 Hebrews 9:13
1304 Hebrews 9:10
1305 Hebrews 9:9

the apostle preaches that the Spirit has "given unto us exceeding great and precious promises: that by these ye might be partakers of the divine nature."[1306]

26. Every bit of our faith in creation's present law, and of our faithful application to its praise, seals to our spirit the power to overcome self, to retain His knowledge, and to cultivate and properly express the benevolent spirit attached to such an endeavor. This work of righteousness, this work of familiarizing self with the atmosphere of *heaven*, fulfills the counsel, "Put on the new man, which is renewed in knowledge after the image of him that created him."[1307]

27. When once the reformer confesses creation's law as their faith's personal Savior and Governor, it is then expected that the believer come to intimately know their Savior's ministry, and the Wisdom or Word conducting it. They are to see both the Father and His Son with their own eyes of understanding,[1308] and with their own hands. This is that work allotted for the six days of every week after the Sabbath of the seventh, and what a strenuous and most exhausting work it is. Self-development in the Godhead's presence calls for abstaining from strange and injurious mental and spiritual indulgences, and such an education that is filled with tremendous agitation needs a time of "rest."

28. Man was not created to exist without anything to do. God made Adam, and fixed him in the place that He put him, so that he could study the operation of his environment to further obtain the mind of His God. God gave Adam not just the ability to obtain knowledge, but to engineer creations in reference to the perceived weight of justice that his creation derived its essence from. Man, should he have never had in him a desire to entertain religious error, would have existed without an itching for spiritual falsehood, and with a more powerfully inclined mind towards sound reason and right religion, that he may spend his days searching after creation's conversation, to do it, that he may express the terrible majesty, and the admirable character, of his Creator, to his fellow thinking and feeling creatures.

1306 2 Peter 1:4
1307 Colossians 3:10
1308 Ephesians 1:18

29. The new mind that God hopes to install within the believer is in fact a new creation within an old creation that already has habits, tendencies, likes, dislikes, prejudices, and certain favorite pleasures, and this is what makes heaven-appointed conversion so painful. It therefore does not make sense why the God of creation should keep the sanctified day of His "rest" from the soul and spirit that He is repairing and sanctifying.

30. Due to such a process of purification, because the work of the religion of *heaven's* Faith is mentally and spiritually taxing, and because the days of this purification are hard, and at times overwhelming, the Spirit's wisdom comforts its host by saying, "The Son of man is Lord also of the Sabbath."[1309] It was this wisdom's Word who originally ordained the Sabbath for Adam, and because "the last Adam";[1310] this wisdom's chief man; "was made a quickening spirit,"[1311] the Sabbath of Adam stands for the spirit whom the Spirit would quicken. Humanity now stands under the second Adam's operation, and the work of reformation yet rests under the same banner of that operation's Spirit.

31. It is a blessing to know that what God sanctions does ever continue. "Whatsoever God doeth, it shall be for ever: nothing can be put to it, nor any thing taken from it: and God doeth it, that men should fear before him."[1312]

32. Only them that fear and respect His name will receive that banner bearing witness to the work of His intention. The living God is known by the fact that He is "God, who quickeneth the dead, and calleth those things which be not as though they were."[1313]

33. God has ordained, through faith on the law and doctrine of "the word of reconciliation,"[1314] that we, being *dead* through "the body of the sins of the flesh"[1315] "might live through him."[1316] It is counseled, "If ye through the Spirit do mortify the deeds of the body, ye shall

---

1309 Luke 6:5
1310 1 Corinthians 15:45
1311 1 Corinthians 15:45
1312 Ecclesiastes 3:14
1313 Romans 4:17
1314 2 Corinthians 5:19
1315 Colossians 2:11
1316 1 John 4:9

live,"¹³¹⁷ for such an individual born of the religion of this Spirit is a walking epistle of the power and wisdom of *heaven's* throne. It is that sign of His Sabbath, and all that it embodies as relating to the authority of His wisdom's voice to make new what was once old and lacking, that is given to the faithful as a seal of their faith in His spiritual baptism, and as a token of proof concerning the Place of their residence for health and for recovery.

1317 Romans 8:13

14

Into My Rest

1. The Sabbath is often spoken against due to something Paul once charged the church of the Corinthians. Paul writes, "Concerning the collection for the saints, as I have given order to the churches of Gala'tia, even so do ye. Upon the first day of the week let every one of you lay by him in store, as God hath prospered him, that there be no gatherings when I come."[1318]

2. A collection is in relation to a total sum of some *thing* concerning some charitable purpose. Paul charged not just the Corinthian churches, but also the churches of Gala'tia with the same charge of letting the collections rest on the first day of the week, to the end that, on the first day of the week, there should be no gathering for this sum of collection to be taken by the elders of the churches.

1318 1 Corinthians 16:2

3. Again, "Let every one of you lay by him in store, as God hath prospered him,"[1319] he writes. We know that this collection is for worship service based on how it is written, "Why hast thou not required of the Levites to bring in out of Judah and out of Jerusalem the collection"?[1320]

4. "They that are of the sons of Levi, who receive the office of the priesthood,"[1321] are those types of figures who receive the offerings of the people. Because he is writing to churches, the only collection that he can be speaking of is that collection circulating throughout the body of the church when assembled. We therefore read to confirm this thought: "We should bring the firstfruits of our dough, and our offerings, and the fruit of all manner of trees, of wine and of oil, unto the priests, to the chambers of the house of our God; and the tithes of our ground unto the Levites, that the same Levites might have the tithes in all the cities of our tillage."[1322]

5. Paul is counseling the chief ministers and elders of churches to lay up what they have, avoiding doing any thing on the first day of the week. But what, in fact, does it mean to "lay up in store"? We read: "Is not this laid up in store with me, and sealed up among my treasures?"[1323]

6. To lay up in store means to seal up your actions, to remain still, to cease movement, to stop action, and this is why it may be misconstrued for a command to uphold the first day as a sacred appointment. This misunderstanding is not even close to enumerating the fact of the request that Paul makes concerning the first day of the week.

7. Because Paul only ministered to Gentile churches; for he once wrote, "I should be the minister of Jesus Christ to the Gentiles,"[1324] and also, when he met John and Peter for the first time, he writes of the commission given him and his companions by them, "That we should go unto the heathen";[1325] their fashion for honoring the sun was formerly celebrated on the first day of the week. Being turned, from

---

1319 1 Corinthians 16:2
1320 2 Chronicles 24:6
1321 Hebrews 7:5
1322 Nehemiah 10:37
1323 Deuteronomy 32:34
1324 Romans 15:15
1325 Galatians 2:9

their former pagan religion, to the apostles' doctrine, sun worship need not be advocated, even though Paul is writing to churches under Roman jurisdiction.

8. As Roman citizens, the religion of the State was synonymous with the civil laws of the State. The Roman state was, in itself, a god, and her emperor perceived as a man born from their god, thus any *thing* out of the mouth of the emperor is as if a god had said it, and any law of Rome perceived to be upheld by the weight of *divine* credibility.

9. When Paul wrote his epistles, he wrote them in the midst of controversy. He counseled converted pagan ministers of the Jewish religion at a time when going against the ancestral religious heritage of Rome meant death. To reject the Roman laws concerning its State religion was to become an enemy of the State, which is why most professing the living God's doctrine were at this time called atheists, for they rejected the gods of their heritage, and as a result suffered persecution in many forms.

10. Also at this time when Paul is writing to the Corinthians, many professing creation's present law were still worshipping their ancestral sun god, who, in Scripture, is called, Ba'al,[1326] or Tam'muz,[1327] or Mo'loch.[1328] Because of this, Paul had to write to the elders, "Have no fellowship with the unfruitful works of darkness, but rather reprove them,"[1329] and, "It is a shame even to speak of those things which are done of them in secret."[1330]

11. It was not only Paul who was seeing falsehood occur in the Christian church, but the living God also. He reported His observation: "Thou hast tried them which say they are apostles, and are not, and hast found them liars."[1331]

12. Because these churches were upholding the same ceremonial rites as their pagan counterparts, because they were honoring the same

---

1326 Jeremiah 11:13
1327 Ezekiel 8:14
1328 Amos 5:26
1329 Ephesians 5:11
1330 Ephesians 5:12
1331 Revelation 2:2

"days, and months, and times, and years"[1332] of the pagan priesthoods and congregations of Rome, Paul wrote to them, "I am afraid of you, lest I have bestowed upon you labour in vain."[1333] This is why he counseled the Corinthians, "Keep in memory what I preached unto you, unless ye have believed in vain."[1334]

13. The Gentile converts to Judaism were finding it hard to observe just exactly what the apostles were teaching because "the word preached did not profit them, not being mixed with faith in them that heard it."[1335] There is more to hearing than receiving, and that is actually doing what you have heard because you believe it to be certain.

14. Many of the churches failed to do for themselves because they did not, in reality, believe what they had heard. Belief does not come by hearing a discourse or from reading a book. Belief comes from experiencing what the mind has taken from what it has discovered, to then prove its benefit by physically exercising the limbs of the heart to move the body to retain the fact of what the mind perceives to be right. This is why "the kingdom of God is not in word, but in power,"[1336] and why Paul counseled the Roman churches, "Be ye transformed by the renewing of your mind, that ye may prove what is that good, and acceptable, and perfect, will of God."[1337]

15. Bearing in mind that Paul was given the task of mentoring, as far as he could without damaging their faith, formerly pagan ministers who were converted to the Jewish religion, it should be held in consideration that his position was very difficult. He knew that if any one church of the Gentile Jews should be caught honoring Sunday as any *day*, further confusion to the precepts laid by the living God would be drawn, and greater animosity towards the Spirit of those commandments. This in fact did occur because of their disobedience: the people who sought after the Bible's God were spoken against by pagan philosophers,

---

1332 Galatians 4:10
1333 Galatians 4:11
1334 1 Corinthians 15:2
1335 Hebrews 4:2
1336 1 Corinthians 4:20
1337 Romans 12:2

magistrates, priests, emperors and citizens, as being fraudulent and hypocritical, for they saw their same images used for worship by Christians in their worship, and they saw these Christians honoring the same universal day of the sun to a foreign *God* of their knowledge.

16. The living God's cause is always after fulfilling the saying in a people, "Ye shall be a peculiar treasure unto me above all people."[1338] A distinct peculiarity of His people from all other people is their reverence for the seventh day that He specifically set apart from the other days of the week. Paul knew this, but because Gentile Jewish ministers "did not like to retain God in their knowledge,"[1339] they did not know, neither did they understand this.

17. At times, for their stubbornness and lethargic hearts, Paul even had to raise his voice at them, only to later say, "Though I made you sorry with a letter, I do not repent, though I did repent: for I perceive that the same epistle hath made you sorry, though it were but for a season."[1340] And again, "I wrote this same unto you, lest, when I came, I should have sorrow from them of whom I ought to rejoice; having confidence in you all, that my joy is the joy of you all."[1341]

18. But they did not want to share Paul's joy. For he writes of how they mocked him, saying, "His letters, say they, are weighty and powerful; but his bodily presence is weak, and his speech contemptible."[1342]

19. The Gentile churches didn't believe that Paul was actually a man appointed specifically by the living God. This is why he wrote, "Mine answer to them that do examine me is this...Am I not an apostle? am I not free? have I not seen Jesus Christ our Lord? are not ye my work in the Lord? If I be not an apostle unto others, yet doubtless I am to you: for the seal of mine apostleship are ye in the Lord."[1343]

20. Nevertheless, because he dealt with countless bickering against his doctrine, at last he sarcastically said, "If he that cometh preacheth

---

1338 Exodus 19:5
1339 Romans 1:28
1340 2 Corinthians 7:8
1341 2 Corinthians 2:3
1342 2 Corinthians 10:10
1343 1 Corinthians 9:1-3

another Jesus, whom we have not preached, or if ye receive another spirit, which ye have not received, or another gospel, which ye have not accepted, ye might well bear with him. For I suppose I was not a whit behind the very chiefest apostles."[1344]

21. Now that a bit of the spirit of this ancient period is before our mind, and now that we have heard the thoughts and feelings of Paul concerning the ones he sought to educate, and their demeanor towards him, we can now see that Paul was requesting that every soul seal up themselves in their own houses on the first day of the week, keeping from any assembling together that might work for the hurt of the foundation of the living God's doctrine.

22. That word "let" means rest or quit. Paul was counseling ministers to quit all activities regarding worship service, wherein the collection of money should be put together, on the first day of the week. Whenever Paul should get to the Corinthians, just as he told them of Gala'tia, "Above all things, do not do any thing on the first evening and morning concerning the gifts you have for me (Paul), or for your service together in the living God's presence." "For he spake in a certain place of the seventh day on this wise,"[1345] writes Paul, "And God did rest the seventh day from all his works. And in this place again (on the seventh evening and morning), If they shall enter into my rest."[1346]

1344 2 Corinthians 11:4,5
1345 Hebrews 4:4
1346 Hebrews 4:4,5

15

The Day Of The Sun

1. Christian ministers express the fact of Sunday sacredness due to the premise that the greatest work of *Christ*, the resurrection, commenced on the first day of the week. It is quite interesting to note that when the Bible talks about *Christ* rising from the grave, the majority of the sources in Scripture do not say that *Christ* rose on the first day of the week, but rather on the third day.

2. The only one reference pointing to a first day resurrection states, "When Jesus was risen early the first day of the week, he appeared first to Mary Magdale'ne."[1347] There are no other sure references connecting the first day to *Christ*, but rather the man himself said, "The Son of man must suffer many things, and be rejected of the elders and chief priests and scribes, and be slain, and be raised the third day."[1348]

1347 Mark 16:9
1348 Luke 9:22

Even years after the resurrection, Paul still taught, "Christ died for our sins according to the scriptures; and that he was buried, and that he rose again the third day according to the scriptures."[1349]

3. Although I do not intend to list every "third day" reference, I have given two, and "at the mouth of two witnesses, or at the mouth of three witnesses, shall the matter be established."[1350] Therefore, based upon the testimony of various scriptures, along with the voice of the living God's man, plus the counsel of Paul above twenty years after the fact, *Christ* did not resurrect from the grave on the first day of the week, but rather on the third day.

4. The living God's man never utters the words "first day" when speaking about himself. "The Son of man shall be betrayed into the hands of men,"[1351] he says, "and they shall kill him, and the third day he shall be raised again."[1352]

5. There is a reason why this man avoided mentioning "the first day," and it was because Israel had long since begun to serve the god of the sun. When it says, in reference to the people that professed His name, "Ye have borne the tabernacle of your Mo'loch and Chi'un your images, the star of your god, which ye made to yourselves,"[1353] and, "There sat women weeping for Tam'muz,"[1354] the Bible is mentioning the name of the same sun god reverence by the different people of various pagan nations. To one nation he was called Mo'loch, to another Apollo, to another Hercules, to another Ba'al, to another Mithra, to another Tam'muz.

6. *Jesus* grew up in Israel. This man heard the various conversations of the gods in his own land and by his own people. This is why Scripture reports, "The world knew him not,"[1355] and, "His own received him not."[1356]

1349 1 Corinthians 15:3,4
1350 Deuteronomy 19:15
1351 Matthew 17:22
1352 Matthew 17:23
1353 Amos 5:26
1354 Ezekiel 8:14
1355 John 1:10
1356 John 1:11

7. How is it that the people of God could have ever missed His face? And when he was born, why should it have been written of the king of Jerusalem, that "he was troubled, and all Jerusalem with him"?[1357]

8. They looked for, and desired, "another Jesus."[1358] Throughout his entire life, the living God's man saw the temples to foreign gods in the land professedly dedicated to *the living God*. He saw the priests of the temple of *God* sacrificing to the sun god of the Gentiles, and before he was even born, the living God said to them that ordered the temple, "According to the number of thy cities were thy gods, O Judah; and according to the number of the streets of Jerusalem have ye set up altars to that shameful thing, even altars to burn incense unto Ba'al."[1359]

9. *Jesus* was very familiar with the first day church service of the pagan priesthoods within and outside of Israel. When he came into the Jewish world, institutionalized paganism was at its height in glory. Many of the priests of the temple of *God* set up foundations to pagan gods in the east and west, being educated in Egyptian religious arts and sciences. These priests then took what they obtained from ministers who had no knowledge of the living God and mingled it with the sayings of Moses, creating strange religious laws and precepts for service toward *God* that, in reality, had no weight.

10. This is why the living God's man said of the Jewish philosophical sects of his day, "Hypocrites! for ye are as graves which appear not, and the men that walk over them are not aware of them."[1360] And to show that this practice was not new, it is even anciently recorded of Israel, "The children of Israel did secretly those things that were not right against the LORD their God."[1361] "They burnt incense in all the high places, as did the heathen whom the LORD carried away before them."[1362] "They left all the commandments of the LORD their God,

---

1357 Matthew 2:3
1358 2 Corinthians 10:4
1359 Jeremiah 11:31
1360 Luke 11:44
1361 2 Kings 17:9
1362 2 Kings 17:11

and made them molten images, even two calves, and made a grove, and worshipped all the host of heaven, and served Ba'al."[1363]

11. Sun, and sun-day worship, is no new thing, but is rather an old religious plague. The living God's man knew about the Roman sun worship that existed in Israel and in Judah, which is why, never from his mouth, would he ever mention his rising on the first day of the week, for he already knew the perverted intention of "false apostles, deceitful workers, transforming themselves into the apostles of Christ."[1364]

12. Therefore because not even this man entertained the saying of any *thing* connected to the first day of the week, should we? In reality, Sunday sacredness should, of a truth, be third day sacredness, but why is not any one honoring *Christ* on the third day?

13. The preference for a "third day" does not fit into the pagan practice. The answer is that "Satan himself is transformed into an angel of light"[1365] by the fathers of a spurious first day holiday. Because the sun god is in reality Satan himself, Ba'al worship is Satan worship, and first day worship belongs to the father of its heritage. This is why the institution prominent for disguising a false worship to *God* under a Christian garb devoted to the sun god is called "the abomination that maketh desolate,"[1366] and why the man of that institution is called "the son of perdition."[1367]

14. What is perdition? Paul writes: "We are not of them who draw back unto perdition."[1368]

15. Perdition is drawing back into a religious habit after there is open revelation made to the conscience of the falsehood within that habit. Perdition is the height of mental and spiritual loss wherein one is drawn back into one's damaging religious ways. What then is the perdition that one in Paul's day may have committed? Because the only people that comprised the early churches were Jews and pagan converts

---

1363 2 Kings 17:16
1364 2 Corinthians 11:13
1365 2 Corinthians 11:14
1366 Daniel 11:31
1367 2 Thessalonians 2:3
1368 Hebrews 10:39

to Judaism, perdition would be gravitating back into the practice of honoring justification before *God* through various days and feasts and gifts and sacrifices that ritualistic culture cherishes.

16. When Paul began to see many ministers turning away from the true fact of service to creation's present commandment, he wrote, "If I build again the things which I destroyed, I make myself a transgressor."[1369] Paul began to see a new *faith* administered by "false brethren unawares brought in,"[1370] who sought only to "pervert the gospel of Christ,"[1371] and it was built upon the foundation of transgressing the new covenant's will and wisdom.

17. It did not take long before the supposed Gentile Jewish converts began to turn back to their old pagan Roman heritages. Just as Israel anciently did secretly those things that were not right, even now Paul had to write, "Have no fellowship with the unfruitful works of darkness, but rather reprove them. For it is a shame even to speak of those things which are done of them in secret."[1372]

18. The new covenant's apostles were seeing the professed converts of that covenant promise fall back into their ancestral religious heritage, and at the same time develop a religion separate from the religion of that apostolic church at Jerusalem. This is what prompted Paul to write, "I fear, lest by any means, as the serpent beguiled Eve though his subtilty, so your minds should be corrupted from the simplicity that is in Christ."[1373]

19. The spirit of the Christian church was changing. She had enacted rites of communion similar to her pagan counterparts, ecclesiastical laws according to *their* faith, and at this time, officially maintained the same pagan sun-day festival of the Roman religious world, only now the god of the sun was translated to be *Jesus*, their "Sun of righteousness."[1374]

[1369] Galatians 2:18
[1370] Galatians 2:4
[1371] Galatians 1:7
[1372] Ephesians 5:11,12
[1373] 2 Corinthians 2:11
[1374] Malachi 4:2

20. Since pagans attributed the sun god as being that "great light," Christians attributed their deluded worship on the day of the sun to *Christ* due to him being referenced as "the Sun of righteousness,"[1375] and by him saying of himself, "I am the light of the world."[1376] The reality is that the "Christian" institution that began this practice was, and still is, a pagan cult, and the god that they honor is not that living God, but rather an angel of *light* familiar to their pagan lineage and contrary to all things concerning creation.

21. If God Himself was anciently upset that individuals claiming to serve Him upheld a false god and a false sun-day to serve that god in their places of worship, would not that same God be drawn to the same fury? "Ye cannot drink the cup of the Lord, and the cup of devils: ye cannot be partakers of the Lord's table, and of the table of devils. Do we provoke the Lord to jealousy? are we stronger than he?"[1377] For this cause this Spirit says, "I am the LORD, I change not."[1378] This is why His man, with his own mouth says, "The Son of man is Lord also of the Sabbath,"[1379] and "he spake in a certain place of the seventh day on this wise."[1380]

22. Who is "Lord" of the living God's Sabbath? It says, "The Son of man." In order for his doctrine to be that Son, or that Minister, Intercessor, or High Priest for the living God's benevolence, his doctrinal commandment would have to have a special position in the presence of God. This is why it says, "He hath by inheritance obtained a more excellent name,"[1381] and, "We have not an high priest which cannot be touched with the feeling of our infirmities."[1382]

23. The word "son" is better understood as one drawn out to the service of God. If His man's speech is the Son of mankind, this means that his word of counsel is the Servant and Benefactor to the

---

1375 Malachi 4:2
1376 John 8:12
1377 1 Corinthians 10:21,22
1378 Malachi 3:6
1379 Luke 6:5
1380 Hebrews 4:4
1381 Hebrews 1:4
1382 Hebrews 4:15

unsavory religious character in ministers, that that counsel may bring the disagreeable mind within that conversation into perfect harmony with the living God's religious character. In bringing the foul conscience of the conversation to this wisdom, it is that it is conditioning the heart and mind to stand in the living God's presence, to look Him in His face that it may again commune with that wisdom separated from them by "sin."

24. Therefore, because "we have an advocate with the Father"[1383] "we draw nigh unto God."[1384] And because we are admitted into intimate fellowship with Him through His Faith, the one drawn out to that commandment will know and love the seventh-day Sabbath of that wisdom, which His man has said nothing about changing or abolishing. But now, under the dispensation of creation's science, that very same Sabbath of creation is established and flourishes.

25. Since creation's commandment is the Minister of the penitent mind, and because this counsel emphasizes the creation of a new heart and mind, and because the Sabbath is for that specific creation of this commandment, His man's speech is most emphatically the face of the seventh day's institution. This is why it is important to personally know the living God's new covenant will and wisdom.

26. "God blessed the seventh day, and sanctified it."[1385] "Whatsoever God doeth, it shall be for ever: nothing can be put to it, nor any thing taken from it: and God doeth it, that men should fear before him."[1386] Because this is an everlasting fact, and the seventh-day Sabbath a perpetual covenant between Him and His faithful, it is therefore written, "Thou blessest, O LORD, and it shall be blessed for ever."[1387]

1383   1 John 2:1
1384   Hebrews 7:19
1385   Genesis 2:3
1386   Ecclesiastes 3:14
1387   1 Chronicles 17:27

16

Wrath's Assignment

1. It is not good that the living God's Sabbath is not rightly known or celebrated, wherefore the Spirit still counsels all; great and small; professing *His* name, "Ye bring more wrath upon Israel by profaning the Sabbath."[1388]

2. The high of rank and the low of rank in *Israel* fail in rightly discerning the name and knowledge of the Spirit's Faith because of a failure to learn of that Faith's Sabbath. There is only one God in existence, and "God is the LORD,"[1389] even "the LORD, the most high God, the possessor of heaven and earth."[1390] From Genesis to the Revelation, the living God is that "blessed and only Potentate, the King of

---

1388 Nehemiah 13:18
1389 Psalm 118:27
1390 Genesis 14:22

kings, and Lord of lords,"[1391] and must we believe that any failure to learn of and do His voice will not be visited?

3. "Wrath" today exists, and "the wrath of God is revealed from heaven against all ungodliness and unrighteousness of men, who hold the truth in unrighteousness."[1392] Concerning the definition of "unrighteousness," we read, "All unrighteousness is sin,"[1393] and concerning that "sin" defining "unrighteousness," we read, "The strength of sin is the law."[1394]

4. The "law" here mentioned is the legal religious law of priests and elders; "the law of commandments contained in ordinances."[1395] The religious law is today "sin" to the living God's Faith, for, "having abolished in his flesh the enmity, even the law of commandments contained in ordinances,"[1396] the LORD's man "took it out of the way, nailing it to his cross."[1397] "Wrath," or trouble within our spiritual understanding, is therefore become our lot by subscribing to what is accursed and nailed to the tree. It is therefore well to know that "Christ hath redeemed us from the curse of the law."[1398]

5. Knowledge of the fact that "Christ hath redeemed us from the curse of the law"[1399] is crucial to our keeping a pure conversation because "whatsoever is not of faith is sin,"[1400] "and the law is not of faith."[1401]

6. Whatsoever halts faith's right exercise and learning is "sin" to the living God's will and wisdom, which is why His man's ministry was blessed "to redeem them that were under the law,"[1402] and is today still blessed to "purge your conscience from dead works to serve the living

---

1391 1 Timothy 6:15
1392 Romans 1:18
1393 1 John 5:17
1394 1 Corinthians 15:56
1395 Ephesians 2:15
1396 Ephesians 2:15
1397 Colossians 2:14
1398 Galatians 3:13
1399 Galatians 3:13
1400 Romans 14:23
1401 Galatians 3:12
1402 Galatians 4:5

God."[1403] Seeing as how "the sting of death is sin; and the strength of sin is the law";[1404] "dead works" are of that manner of worship and service nailed to the tree, which devotion "sanctifieth to the purifying of the flesh"[1405] when, in reality, the conversation is to be "perfect, as pertaining to the conscience."[1406]

7. The religious law is an unsatisfactory route for right blessing because it fails to wash and dress the mind, which baptism only occurs "with the washing of water by the word,"[1407] which is why it says, "Sanctify them through thy truth: thy word is truth,"[1408] and, "Ye are clean through the word which I have spoken."[1409] All righteousness is in transforming the mind by learning of and doing the words of creation's science, but all unrighteousness is "after the commandments and doctrines of men,"[1410] that is, "through philosophy and vain deceit, after the tradition of men."[1411]

8. As the LORD's man lay passed away on the tree, the illustration reveals the passing away of the pen of flesh from the living God's religious character, leaving the inwards crucified to the strength of "sin" for faithfully acquiring knowledge to live by. Now, what is nailed to the tree is accursed of the Spirit's Word for "wrath" to the doer of them, which is why it says, "He that is hanged is accursed of God."[1412]

9. Again, as we observe the LORD's man on the tree, it is not that we are observing a man suspended between heaven and earth, but are, to the Spirit's mind, witnessing a religious ideology, with its conversation, nailed to the tree. Therefore, "having abolished in his flesh the enmity, even the law of commandments contained in ordinances,"[1413] this Spirit's man has for ever established what transgression against the

---

1403 Hebrews 9:14
1404 1 Corinthians 15:56
1405 Hebrews 9:13
1406 Hebrews 9:9
1407 Ephesians 5:26
1408 John 17:17
1409 John 15:3
1410 Colossians 2:22
1411 Colossians 2:8
1412 Deuteronomy 21:23
1413 Ephesians 2:15

living God is, moving the sober observer to say, "If I build again the things which I destroyed, I make myself a transgressor."[1414]

10. With this man on the tree, "the handwriting of ordinances"[1415] is for ever destroyed from the LORD God's doctrine, and "not only in this world, but also in that which is to come."[1416] Therefore to hear any *Christ* today preaching, "Righteousness come by the law,"[1417] it is to hear a false and counterfeit *Christ* speaking against the fact of the LORD's Word for creation, seeing as how His "Christ hath redeemed us from the curse of the law, being made a curse for us: for it is written, Cursed is every one that hangeth on a tree."[1418]

11. If it is that our religious conversation does hang on the speech and routine of this tree, and of what is nailed to it, it is well to know that our religious conversation is accursed. It is accursed for mental and spiritual growth and development, for by doing what is of no weight for the living God's kindness, we own the rebuke, "God shall send them strong delusion, that they should believe a lie: that they all might be damned who believed not the truth, but had pleasure in unrighteousness."[1419]

12. "Wrath" is given when the name and science of the living God is held in "unrighteousness," and "all unrighteousness is sin,"[1420] "and the strength of sin is the law."[1421] When the Word's Faith is forwarded by "the law of commandments contained in ordinances,"[1422] we may understand that what is born from that creed is "sin" against creation's present will. For this reason, we may understand that we are all conceived in "sin" against heaven's new covenant will and doctrine by the fact that the spirit and philosophy of the tree naturally rules our heart. Again, wrath is given when the living God's name is mishandled,

---

1414 Galatians 2:15
1415 Colossians 2:14
1416 Ephesians 1:21
1417 Galatians 2:21
1418 Galatians 3:13
1419 2 Thessalonians 2:11,12
1420 1 John 5:17
1421 1 Corinthians 15:56
1422 Ephesians 2:15

and there is no greater display of religious error against the Spirit's name than desecrating His seventh-day Sabbath.

13. Why is there no greater error? How can the author say such a thing? Plainly we read, "God blessed the seventh day, and sanctified it,"[1423] therefore the only way this Sabbath can be forgotten is through a religious law put forth by a priest or minister.

14. For, have we no knowledge that "whatsoever God doeth, it shall be for ever: nothing can be put to it, nor any thing taken from it"?[1424] Are we ignorant of the fact that "what therefore God hath joined together, let not man put asunder"?[1425] If God blessed the seventh day with His Sabbath, it is evident that God has joined the Sabbath and the seventh day together; again, error against the living God's commandment is due to entertaining "sin," "and the strength of sin is the law."[1426] We may therefore understand that our conversation is "sinful" and "unrighteous" when found subject to "the handwriting of ordinances."[1427]

15. And we remain in spiritual negligence by no accident, for "wrath" is become our lot. This wrath is not physical because the issue is not against any physical thing, but is "against spiritual wickedness in high places."[1428] Wherefore we should think on the "death" that Adam suffered by the tree when understanding what wrath we should experience by clinging to the tree and its accursed philosophy.

16. Adam died no physical death, but by taking the tree to be a law for *righteousness*, their "death" was to their *eyes*, even as it says, "The eyes of your understanding."[1429] A subscription to that mind nailed the tree is a death to spiritual perception and comprehension, fulfilling the saying, "They have not known nor understood: for he hath shut their eyes, that they cannot see; and their hearts, that they cannot

---

1423 Genesis 2:3
1424 Ecclesiastes 3:14
1425 Mark 10:9
1426 1 Corinthians 15:56
1427 Colossians 2:14
1428 Ephesians 6:12
1429 Ephesians 1:18

understand."[1430] Thus, when blatantly hearing, "In the beginning was the Word, and the Word was with God, and the Word was God,"[1431] it is wrath that keeps the mind ignorant to that fact that the LORD's Spirit is that Word who blessed the seventh day to hold His Sabbath refreshing.

17. Because there is no other LORD or Word, there is no other Sabbath, for this is a Sabbath celebrating creation, as it says, "Create in me a clean heart, O God."[1432] Thus, every doer of the Word's Faith says, "The law of the Spirit of life in Christ Jesus hath made me free from the law of sin and death,"[1433] allowing the heart of the conversation's mind to understand that "God blessed the seventh day."[1434]

18. Our conversation, like as our lungs need air, needs His Sabbath "rest"; remove air from the lungs and the brain with the body fails. There is no other period of time blessed of the living God for revealing His name and intention to us than the seventh day's hours. Learning continues from the first day to the sixth, but on the seventh day, all unnecessary labor to learn is halted for the matchless revelation of that labor's aim.

19. Creation is the sum of the living God's Sabbath; the hours of this day are blessed to greatly reveal creation's science to the conversation's conscience. To have no knowledge of this Sabbath's appointment is to uphold a conversation without knowledge of redemption, which ignorance is understood by wasting the heart's energy on *sabbaths* entirely contrary to that of heaven's. We may therefore understand a contrary *sabbath* by the LORD's own actions during the days when His man slept, for it was "God the Father, who raised him from the dead."[1435]

20. If His man brought up his own self on the first day, then we ought to believe that it is a lie to say, "Christ hath redeemed us from the curse of the law,"[1436] for his rising during the LORD's Sabbath

---

1430 Isaiah 44:18
1431 John 1:1
1432 Psalm 51:10
1433 Romans 8:2
1434 Genesis 2:3
1435 Galatians 1:1
1436 Galatians 3:12

plainly cancels out that Sabbath for a *sabbath* of his own devising. But since this did not happen, if the LORD brought up His man on the second day, we ought to think it a lie to believe that this man's flesh was given "to redeem them that were under the law,"[1437] for the LORD would have then violated His own Sabbath, leaving us free to invent a *sabbath* of our own.

21. But since none of these things occurred, but that the LORD's Spirit, "in the end of the Sabbath, as it began to dawn toward the first day of the week,"[1438] brought up His man from the grave, it is evident that this Spirit, by refraining from laboring during His Sabbath, has for ever associated His seventh day to His man's name, wherefore to profane that name would mean to profane His Sabbath. And truly the name of His Son is violated, and that violation understood by priests and ministers inventing and forwarding religious laws and traditions to forward an agenda contrary to salvatioin's science, when it is that His "Christ hath redeemed us from the curse of the law, being made a curse for us: for it is written, Cursed is every one that hangeth on a tree."[1439]

22. That Spirit of creation is the living God's Word or Counsel of creation, wherefore if the Word has accursed that spirit and persuasion nailed to the tree, then it is that what remains without the tree is our assignment, which vocation is understood by how it says, "Fear God, and give glory to him; for the hour of his judgment is come: and worship him that made heaven, and earth, and the sea, and the fountains of waters."[1440]

23. The Spirit's "judgment" is what the Spirit's chief minister preaches, saying, "For judgment I am come into this world."[1441] He or she doing the judgment of his speech will worship Him that creates, understanding why it says, "In six days the LORD made heaven and

---

1437 Galatians 4:5
1438 Matthew 28:1
1439 Galatians 3:12
1440 Revelation 14:7
1441 John 9:39

earth, the sea, and all that in them is, and rested the seventh day: wherefore the LORD blessed the Sabbath day, and hallowed it."[1442]

24. By comprehending the Word of creation, "knowledge of his will in all wisdom and spiritual understanding"[1443] will dawn upon the conscience, moving the person to confess, "Thou blessest, O LORD, and it shall be blessed for ever."[1444] But who can know the perpetuity of His blessing without being blessed by His spiritual understanding? What does it even mean to be blessed by the living God's spiritual understanding? We read, "I will pour my spirit upon thy seed, and my blessing upon thine offspring,"[1445] and, "I will pour out my spirit unto you, I will make known my words unto you."[1446]

25. Because "a spirit hath not flesh and bones,"[1447] blessing cannot appear by any physical or natural means, which is why "that which is born of the Spirit is spirit."[1448] We are blessed by the intercession of creation's new covenant will as our conversation's conscience retains the wisdom and knowledge of His Spirit's voice through it, which is why his man says, "I know him, and keep his saying."[1449]

26. It is our responsibility to keep the Spirit's saying, and that keeping is only by mental taxation and spiritual discernment. The Spirit's righteousness is in creating a new mind of worship and service within the religious character, allowing us to perceive that "the righteousness of God without the law is manifested."[1450]

27. "Christ is the end of the law for righteousness to every one that believeth,"[1451] and we understand that we are unbelievers when subscribing to that philosophy nailed to the tree, which philosophy teaches, "Righteousness come by the law."[1452] It is therefore a fact that

---

1442 Exodus 20:11
1443 Colossians 1:9
1444 1 Chronicles 17:27
1445 Isaiah 44:3
1446 Proverbs 1:23
1447 Luke 24:39
1448 John 3:6
1449 John 8:55
1450 Romans 3:21
1451 Romans 10:4
1452 Galatians 2:21

a third day, or a first day *sabbath,* is "sin" to the living God's Faith, for it is plainly a religious law.

28. If the LORD's "Christ hath redeemed us from the curse of the law,"[1453] and we are yet bound to the religious law, then it is evident that such as subscribe to religious error "crucify to themselves the Son of God afresh, and put him to an open shame."[1454] Such as consent to spiritual wrong and "not only do the same, but have pleasure in them that do them,"[1455] have chosen unrighteousness to be the "God" of their conversation, and have elected spiritual "death" to rule over their heart. Again, "the sting of death is sin; and the strength of sin is the law";[1456] therefore with the "God" of sin subtly destroying our heart, our *eyes* are taken from us, leaving us with no mind to pray, "Lighten mine eyes, lest I sleep the sleep of death."[1457]

29. The LORD's man nailed "death's" religious sleep to the tree, and by that act, also unsealed for us the employment of his heart, saying, "Father, into thy hands I commend my spirit."[1458]

30. With that fleshy conversation passed away into the heavenly Sanctuary, what remains is the resurrection of the spirit of the mind from that dead *body,* to the end we may confidently say, "The law of the Spirit of life in Christ Jesus hath made me free from the law of sin and death."[1459] This benevolence is the reason why "God blessed the seventh day, and sanctified it,"[1460] and to be without the Word's Sabbath is to confess that we have not known or experienced "the kindness and love of God our Saviour toward man."[1461]

31. Our spiritual intelligence is dwarfed by our failure to actually comprehend the institution blessed to the seventh day. The seventh day is not the Sabbath per se; no *day* is the Sabbath; the Sabbath is an

---

1453 Galatians 3:13
1454 Hebrews 6:6
1455 Romans 1:32
1456 1 Corinthians 15:56
1457 Psalm 13:3
1458 Luke 23:46
1459 Romans 8:2
1460 Genesis 2:3
1461 Titus 3:4

appointment of creation blessed by the living God's voice and occurring every seventh day of every week. We can therefore keep the seventh day without ever knowing or experiencing the Sabbath, just as we may keep the handwritten first day to experience the same nothingness.

32. The seventh day holds the conversation's refreshing, and this "refreshing" is understood by how it says, "Precept must be upon precept, precept upon precept; line upon line, line upon line; here a little, and there a little...To whom he said, This is the rest wherewith ye may cause the weary to rest."[1462]

33. The "rest" of the Sabbath day is mental and spiritual alleviation, which refreshing occurs only when "comparing spiritual things with spiritual."[1463] The seventh day is sanctified, or set apart, for increasing our understanding on the living God's name, which is why, when explaining His "rest" and "refreshing," it says, "Whom shall he teach knowledge? and whom shall he make to understand doctrine?"[1464] The "refreshing" of the seventh day is mental and spiritual rejuvenation by the knowledge of creation's doctrine, which is why He likens His refreshing to an outpouring of rain, saying, "My doctrine shall drop as the rain."[1465]

34. The living God's Sabbath is a twenty-four hour period of time filling up the inward parts with "showers of blessing,"[1466] and concerning the definition of this "filling," it says, "I am full of power by the spirit of the LORD, and of judgment, and of might,"[1467] and, "I have filled him with the spirit of God, in wisdom, and in understanding, and in knowledge."[1468]

35. To be "filled" with the "Spirit" is to be consumed with the knowledge of creation's present wisdom, and the Sabbath of the seventh day is blessed to accomplish this filling within every mind thoughtfully examining His words. His Sabbath is meant to further enlighten the

---

1462 Isaiah 28:10-12
1463 1 Corinthians 2:13
1464 Isaiah 28:9
1465 Deuteronomy 32:2
1466 Ezekiel 34:26
1467 Micah 3:8
1468 Exodus 31:3

eyes of our faith and strengthen the organs of our mind on His name and science, and "wisdom strengtheneth."[1469]

36. If it is that we sincerely love the name of His benevolence; which "name" is His thoughtfulness towards our faith's inwards; then we cannot miss His Sabbath, for it is our opportunity to commune with heaven's throne by a channel that cannot be disturbed. The week presents circumstances to kill our heart from this channel, but on the seventh day, it is open without any interference, which is why it is well to remain still or quiet during these hours that, as we examine His voice, we may have a clear entrance into the promised edification.

1469   Ecclesiastes 7:19

17

From The Beginning

1. It is well that, when doubtful or perplexed about any thing concerning the living God's course of learning, we return to the true beginning of that course, for "this is the commandment, That, as ye have heard from the beginning, ye should walk in it."[1470] There is no thing established at creation that is contrary to the living God's present science, and we may say so because, when pressed about the issue of divorce, His man says, "But from the beginning of the creation God made them male and female."[1471]

2. We may investigate every issue concerning spiritual wisdom or religious error by examining the philosophy of creation's wisdom, for "this is the commandment, That, as ye have heard from the beginning,

---

1470   2 John 1:6
1471   Mark 10:6

ye should walk in it."[1472] Instead of justifying the pen of Moses, the Spirit's man took his speech, and them that heard it, to the beginning of the living God's Faith, for the only authority on the living God's commandment is the Spirit that pronounces it. Therefore seeing as how "in the beginning was the Word, and the Word was with God, and the Word was God,"[1473] it is that the only reasonable explanation for any thing in Scripture must come from weighing what perplexes the mind with the Word's original counsel and judgment.

3. If the living God's man returned to creation to explain marriage and divorce, should we not also look to creation for information on charity, faith, sanctification by an experimental faith, personal and individual accountability before His voice, repentance, education, diet, and the Sabbath? If we should not think to return to creation for knowledge of the heavenly Sanctuary's religion, we make it a lie to believe how it says, "Christ also suffered for us, leaving us an example, that ye should follow his steps,"[1474] and, "The Son of God is come, and hath given us an understanding."[1475]

4. In this example of divorce used by the Word's chief apostle, the mind is directed to creation for comprehending a rule of learning, namely, that "this is the commandment, That, as ye have heard from the beginning, ye should walk in it."[1476] Ignoring the hand of Moses, this man would not put any saying above that established counsel of his LORD and Father when He therefore "planted a garden eastward in Eden."[1477]

5. We should not think this "garden" to be a literal colorful field, for one said unto Peter, "Did not I see thee in the garden with him?"[1478] Concerning this "garden," "when they had sung an hymn, they went out into the mount of Olives."[1479]

1472 2 John 1:6
1473 John 1:1
1474 1 Peter 2:21
1475 1 John 5:20
1476 2 John 1:6
1477 Genesis 2:8
1478 John 18:26
1479 Mark 14:26

6. The "garden" is a "mount," and a "mount" is figurative language for a church or a temple, as it says, "The mountain of the house of the LORD,"[1480] and, "Them will I bring to my holy mountain, and make them joyful in my house of prayer,"[1481] and, "Solomon began to build the house of the LORD at Jerusalem in mount Mori'ah."[1482]

7. The garden of Eden was a "house" of Eden, and, again, a "house" is language representing a "church," as it says, "The house of God, which is the church of the living God."[1483] Thus, when returning the mind to Eden, the LORD's man is putting Jewish elders in remembrance that before Moses' hand existed, and before Abraham's circumcision, there was in Eden that founding church of the living God's name and operation, even "the spirit of wisdom and revelation in the knowledge of him."[1484]

8. All issues concerning the LORD God's Faith return to this beginning understanding, for the commandment of Eden is the Spirit's Word, and this is that "Spirit of truth, which proceedeth from the Father,"[1485] of whom it says, "And the Word was God. The same was in the beginning with God. All things were made by him; and without him was not any thing made that was made."[1486] Thus, there should be no confusion on what the LORD God of creation has to say about any thing concerning His Faith, and especially about that Sabbath confessing His Faith.

9. If, for divorce, His man directs the attention to the doctrine of Eden's church, then in this present age that we now live in, when the question is over another pillar of Eden's Faith, which is the seventh-day Sabbath, must we think that the living God's new covenant messenger will not begin his answer with, "From the beginning of the creation God made,"[1487] when asked, "When is the Sabbath?"

1480 Micah 4:1
1481 Isaiah 56:7
1482 2 Chronicles 3:1
1483 1 Timothy 3:15
1484 Ephesians 1:17
1485 John 15:26
1486 John 1:1-3
1487 Mark 10:6

10. The LORD's man is anointed to forward the religion of Eden, and to make honorable that law and judgment returning the mind to Eden's Spirit and Counsel. How can the author say such a thing? When explaining the bill of divorcing, by passing over Moses' hand, His man puts to rest the philosophical persuasion born by flesh to appease flesh by bringing the mind to understand the ultimate authority on the issue, even the One that first uttered the commandment.

11. The living God, at creation, uttered no change in His commandment for marriage, allowing us to understand that He never imagined *divorce* at all. It is for this reason that the LORD's man says, "For the hardness of your heart he wrote you this precept. But from the beginning of the creation God made them male and female. For this cause shall a man leave his father and mother, and cleave to his wife."[1488]

12. Not only does he explain the irrational fever that moved Moses to write such a law, but the Spirit's man also quotes that record of Genesis, establishing the fact that pen and ink is not above the voice of the living God. This fact he further testifies of when "blotting out the handwriting of ordinances"[1489] on the tree. This flesh, when on the tree, illustrates that religious ideology separating the spirit of the mind from creation's Spirit, and seeing as how he was "made under the law,"[1490] it is that this His "Christ hath redeemed us from the curse of the law,"[1491] for it says, "He that is hanged is accursed of God."[1492]

13. What is hanged on the tree is, in reality, not a man, but rather a religious conversation symbolized by the flesh of a man. Therefore "having abolished in his flesh the enmity, even the law of commandments contained in ordinances,"[1493] this man openly defines "sin" to every age thereafter, "and the strength of sin is the law."[1494]

14. This man gave no real attention to what Moses had written concerning divorce because it ultimately entertained "sin" against the

---

1488 Mark 10:5-7
1489 Colossians 2:14
1490 Galatians 4:4
1491 Galatians 3:13
1492 Deuteronomy 21:23
1493 Ephesians 2:15
1494 1 Corinthians 15:56

Word's intention. It is the Word's will to "purge your conscience from dead works to serve the living God,"[1495] and whatsoever halts this sanctification is "sin" encouraging "dead works," which "works" are born to avoid the heart's confrontation with heaven's mind.

15. *Marriage*, as is no thing is life, is not meant to be easy, but should rightly challenge every thought and feeling to develop the person into a more perfect creation, and "perfect, as pertaining to the conscience."[1496] Error occurs where communication fails, and separation from heaven's throne is deemed a viable option when unnecessary silence, impatience, and spiritual intemperance govern the being.

16. *Divorce* is given no attention by the Word at creation because His blessing rests on the sincerely married pair, but if not sincerely married, what do we imagine can help convert our flesh-based heart to love what we, in reality, have no interest in loving? Likewise this living God's blessing rests upon His seventh-day Sabbath, but if not sanctified by His manner of love, must we, whose conversation is not sanctified by His commandment, think to sanctify what only a sanctified spirit can honor?

17. There is no other Sabbath of the living God than that Sabbath founded by His Word at creation. If "the Word was made flesh, and dwelt among us,"[1497] must we believe that this same Word of creation should change His mind on His own doctrine? This Word does not speak of His own mind, but is of the LORD God's heart, even as it says, "The Word was with God, and the Word was God."[1498]

18. The living God gave His wisdom authority over creation, and when creation was finished, it was this same Word who fulfilled the saying, "God blessed the seventh day, and sanctified it."[1499] This creating Word found its self in *man's* flesh, and concerning this word, "flesh," it is not literal or physical flesh.

1495 Hebrews 9:14
1496 Hebrews 9:9
1497 John 1:14
1498 John 1:1
1499 Genesis 2:3

19. "The Word of life"[1500] is "the Spirit of life,"[1501] so when hearing that the Word was "God," it is that we are hearing that the living God's Spirit is the God of creation. Seeing as how "a spirit hath not flesh and bones,"[1502] this Spirit must inhabit a *body* within man that is similar to it, wherefore it is well to know and remember that "there is a natural body, and there is a spiritual body."[1503]

20. The "body" of the spirit of the mind is the only "flesh" that the Word can inhabit, which is why this Spirit's man teaches, "That which is born of the Spirit is spirit."[1504] For the Word to dwell in "flesh," it is for "the law of the Spirit of life"[1505] to direct the personal religious conversation, and if this Word is that same Spirit blessing the seventh day; and this Spirit is that God; then it is an indisputable fact that the conversation of this LORD's man did not exist without the seventh-day Sabbath of His Word.

21. Again, how can we say such a thing? "Having abolished in his flesh the enmity, even the law of commandments contained in ordinances,"[1506] this man has for ever separated "sin" from creation's Faith, "and the strength of sin is the law."[1507]

22. The Jews took Moses' religious law to be the end of the Word's Faith, and in so doing, created to themselves a creed after the inspiration of their hero; the serpent; which religious philosophy the LORD's man condemns by saying, "Full well ye reject the commandment of God, that ye may keep your own tradition."[1508] Today, we understand that false *Christ* by the spirit of his doctrine, which spirit teaches, "Righteousness come by the law,"[1509] yet "if righteousness come by the law, then Christ is dead in vain."[1510]

1500 1 John 1:1
1501 Revelation 11:11
1502 Luke 24:39
1503 1 Corinthians 15:44
1504 John 3:6
1505 Romans 8:2
1506 Ephesians 2:15
1507 1 Corinthians 15:56
1508 Mark 7:9
1509 Galatians 2:21
1510 Galatians 2:21

23. The passing of this LORD's man on the tree signifies the end of what halts faith's experimental exercise for knowledge to live by, wherefore it is well to know that "whatsoever is not of faith is sin,"[1511] and that "the law is not of faith."[1512] To hear a *Christ* preaching, "You are justified by the law";[1513] that is, *you* are *perfect* by the handwritten religious law of priests and elders; is to observe a message blatantly transgressing the new covenant doctrine of creation's science, and "whosoever transgresseth, and abideth not in the doctrine of Christ, hath not God."[1514] Being without God; who is the Word; the religious conversation is without the doctrine and commandments of that Word, meaning that it does not love the LORD of that Word, "and this is love, that we walk after his commandments."[1515]

24. "He that saith, I know him, and keepeth not his commandments, is a liar, and the truth is not in him."[1516] And concerning the "truth," we read, "Thy word is truth,"[1517] and, "Thy law is the truth."[1518]

25. The Spirit's Word is the Spirit's law of creation. Without learning of and doing "the law of truth,"[1519] the conversation will not find any harmony with the commandments of the living God's throne. This is why the LORD's man said, and still says, to the fraudulent, "Full well ye reject the commandment of God, that ye may keep your own tradition,"[1520] for by failing to examine creation's commandment, respect to creation's Word, and to the will of that counsel, is not given.

26. According to the Spirit's law, every doer of it should confess, "The law of the Spirit of life in Christ Jesus hath made me free from the law of sin and death,"[1521] opening up the conscience to every word spoken by the living God's Spirit. Should we therefore think that,

---

1511 Romans 14:23
1512 Galatians 3:12
1513 Galatians 5:4
1514 2 John 1:9
1515 2 John 1:6
1516 1 John 2:4
1517 John 17:17
1518 Psalm 119:142
1519 Malachi 2:6
1520 Mark 7:9
1521 Romans 8:2

with creation's wisdom operating within the conversation of His man, that this man should speak any thing contrary to this wisdom? This man can do no thing but return the mind to creation when questions surrounding the Word's Faith arise, for this is that Spirit of creation, and concerning its voice, it says, "The word of God, which liveth and abideth for ever."[1522]

27. We are therefore without excuse when failing to know this Word's Sabbath, for, "this is the commandment, That, as ye have heard from the beginning, ye should walk in it."[1523]

28. There is no thing heard or spoken from the beginning against the seventh day, meaning that all speech revolving around another *sabbath* is a handwritten religious law of priests and elders, making any other *sabbath* "sin" to entertain, seeing as how "the strength of sin is the law."[1524] We may therefore understand that our conversation is "sinful" or erroneous by what influences it, for, "having abolished in his flesh the enmity, even the law of commandments contained in ordinances,"[1525] there are today only two routes we can take: we can accept a conversation under the rule of "philosophy and vain deceit, after the tradition of men";[1526] which rule is "sin"; or we can embrace a conversation learning of and doing the words of the Spirit, even as it says, "Live according to God in the spirit."[1527]

29. A mind blessed by creation's mind is the only means knowledge of creation consumes our being to respect that Word of creation, for this learning is based upon an experimental faith for knowledge to live by, and this wisdom says, "By his knowledge shall my righteous servant justify many."[1528] It is therefore plainly wrong to take *righteousness* and *sanctification* by the religious law. Heaven's baptism is "with the

---

1522 1 Peter 1:23
1523 2 John 1:6
1524 1 Corinthians 15:56
1525 Ephesians 2:15
1526 Colossians 8:2
1527 1 Peter 4:6
1528 Isaiah 53:11

washing of water by the word,"[1529] making this creation that "salvation through sanctification of the Spirit and belief of the truth."[1530]

30. With the conversation's conscience sanctified by the law and commandment of creation's commandment, knowledge that "God blessed the seventh day"[1531] will not escape the conversation's conscience. Concerning this LORD's Word, it says, "I am the LORD, I change not,"[1532] therefore any change that causes doubts or divisions to arise, we may understand that it is not of this LORD's Spirit, but is of that spirit preaching, "Righteousness come by the law."[1533]

31. We may understand this spurious spirit because the living God's "Christ hath redeemed us from the curse of the law,"[1534] liberating the conscience of the conversation to soberly know the living God without flesh-based constraints. Any other commandment than that established at creation by Eden's Word is therefore become religious error, and with the His man "blotting out the handwriting of ordinances"[1535] crafted by every *Moses* "not only in this world, but also in that which is to come,"[1536] we may plainly understand whether or not we cling to "sin" against heaven's new covenant will.

32. A first day *sabbath* is therefore no work of the living God's man, whose ministry was blessed, and still is blessed, "to redeem them that were under the law."[1537] Being a religious law of priests and elders, a contrary *sabbath* spoken in devotion to *the LORD* and *Word* of *the Bible* is herein understood to be open "sin" against the living Wisdom and Word of the Bible.

1529 Ephesians 5:26
1530 2 Thessalonians 2:13
1531 Genesis 2:3
1532 Malachi 3:6
1533 Galatians 2:21
1534 Galatians 3:13
1535 Colossians 2:14
1536 Ephesians 1:21
1537 Galatians 4:5

18

An Ever-Lasting Commandment

1. "The everlasting God, the LORD, the Creator of the ends of the earth, fainteth not, neither is weary,"[1538] and it is wrong to think otherwise. It is wrong to assume any end or halting of His throne's rule, for, due to the illustration of His man suffering the tree, "every tongue should confess that Jesus Christ is Lord, to the glory of God the Father."[1539]

2. "Having abolished in his flesh the enmity, even the law of commandments contained in ordinances,"[1540] this LORD's man purged the spirit and philosophy of the serpent from his LORD's Word, opening up the opportunity for the doer of that Word to love the LORD of that Word, "and this is love, that we walk after his commandments."[1541] It is

---

[1538] Isaiah 40:28
[1539] Philippians 2:11
[1540] Ephesians 2:15
[1541] 2 John 1:6

therefore well for us to understand just what "world" the LORD's man delivered from the serpent's spirit, and His man explains this "world" by saying, "I spake openly to the world; I ever taught in the synagogue, and in the temple, whither the Jews always resort."[1542]

3. The "world" that this man is savior of is that religious world of the Jewish religion, which world does not begin with the Jews, but with the host of Eden, for "the LORD God planted a garden eastward in Eden."[1543] The error committed by Eden's host caused the Word's name to suffer a "death," and "the sting of death is sin; and the strength of sin is the law."[1544] The serpent's persuasion is a conversation fastened by "the handwriting of ordinances,"[1545] but by the offering and heavenly mediation of creation's law and doctrine, such a rule is become "sin," returning the conversation's mind to Eden's liberty, and to the worship and service of Eden's LORD and Wisdom by that liberty.

4. The LORD's Word or Wisdom is that Savior and Deliverer of the living God's religious character from the religious world's spiritual philosophy, separating that religion of His heavenly throne from the serpent's mind of service, and that separation understood by how it says, "I will put enmity."[1546] Therefore "having abolished in his flesh the enmity, even the law of commandments contained in ordinances,"[1547] it is that this enmity, being removed from the Spirit's Faith and nailed to the tree, is become a wall dividing spiritual fact from religious fiction.

5. We may understand the living God's man from the serpent's *Christ* by this enmity, for the serpent's creed gravitates towards what is doctrinally accursed, teaching, "You are justified by the law,"[1548] when the LORD's "Christ hath redeemed us from the curse of the law, being made a curse for us: for it is written, Cursed is every one that hangeth on a tree."[1549] The Spirit's man on the tree means the absolute annihi-

---

1542 John 18:20
1543 Genesis 2:8
1544 1 Corinthians 15:56
1545 Colossians 2:13
1546 Genesis 3:15
1547 Ephesians 2:15
1548 Galatians 5:4
1549 Galatians 3:13

lation of the pen of priests and elders from the living God's religious character. This man's flesh represents an ideology come under condemnation by creation's science, which is why His man was "made under the law, to redeem them that were under the law."[1550]

6. The redemption explained by this man is one where the conversation's conscience is resurrected from religious laws and traditions of priests and ministers to experience regeneration and reform within the heart of the conversation's mind by "the law of the Spirit of life."[1551] Herein is the reason why he said, before passing away, "Father, into thy hands I commend my spirit."[1552]

7. His man witnesses to a reform in personal manners of devotion to the living God's name when found on the tree. With His flesh nailed to and passed away on the tree, the saying is fulfilled, "Put off concerning the former conversation the old man...and be renewed in the spirit of your mind; and that ye put on the new man, which after God is created in righteousness and true holiness."[1553]

8. What His man preaches is the revival and reform of the conversation's conscience to fully experience the Word's righteousness for a perfect *body* of faith, and "perfect, as pertaining to the conscience."[1554] By preaching, "Righteousness come by the law,"[1555] and not, "Through the Spirit wait for the hope of righteousness by faith,"[1556] the spirit of religious error forwards a persuasion that is absent of an experimental faith for benevolent knowledge, compelling the person to take faith in the handwriting of *men*. There is no faith or knowledge in the pen of men to soberly encourage the person to care for self, allowing us to understand that "whatsoever is not of faith is sin,"[1557] and that "the law is not of faith."[1558]

1550 Galatians 4:4,5
1551 Romans 8:2
1552 Luke 23:46
1553 Ephesians 4:22-24
1554 Hebrews 9:9
1555 Galatians 2:21
1556 Galatians 5:5
1557 Romans 14:23
1558 Galatians 3:12

9. With the LORD's man abolishing "the enmity, even the law of commandments contained in ordinances"[1559] from creation's new covenant law, faith's right learning and exercise is become the key to receive knowledge of the living God to sincerely love His voice. This love is witnessed by our willing service to His throne's ten laws, seeing as how Moses once said of them, "I stood...to shew you the word of the LORD."[1560]

10. The commandment of the LORD's Faith is drawn from His Ten Commandments, and He tells us this by saying, "A law shall proceed from me, and I will make my judgment to rest for a light of the people."[1561] The Spirit promised that, from out of His Ten Commandments, a law or a judgment would come, and it did, for His man preached it, saying, "For judgment I am come into this world,"[1562] and, "I have not spoken of myself; but the Father which sent me, he gave me a commandment, what I should say, and what I should speak."[1563]

11. This man passed away on the tree means the absolute condemnation of that spirit and philosophy preaching, "Righteousness come by the law,"[1564] and the absolute reign of righteousness by an experimental faith on "the law of the Spirit of life,"[1565] for by him, the saying is fulfilled, "By his knowledge shall my righteous servant justify many."[1566] The deliverance and salvation preached by this man is ordained to resurrect the mind from religious "philosophy and vain deceit, after the tradition of men, after the rudiments of the world,"[1567] by the knowledge obtained from learning of and doing the Spirit's will and law, teaching us that "through knowledge shall the just be delivered."[1568]

12. The serpent and his host preach *righteousness* by their pen, but the conversation is to be "written not with ink, but with the Spirit of the

---

1559 Ephesians 2:15
1560 Deuteronomy 5:5
1561 Isaiah 51:4
1562 John 9:39
1563 John 12:49
1564 Galatians 2:21
1565 Romans 8:2
1566 Isaiah 53:11
1567 Colossians 2:8
1568 Proverbs 11:9

living God."[1569] This opens us up to understand that "that which is born of the Spirit is spirit,"[1570] and that it is the Spirit's intention to "purge your conscience from dead works to serve the living God."[1571]

13. Therefore through the passing, regenerating, and high priestly appointment of the living God's law of creation; for "we have such an high priest, who is set on the right hand of the throne of the Majesty in the heavens";[1572] creation's science is magnified, establishing the fact that "the LORD is the true God, he is the living God, and an everlasting king."[1573] This is the entire point behind the offering of His man, even that like as by one man an erroneous conversation was shared to uphold the wisdom and spirit of error, so too by one man a right conversation is shared to uphold the wisdom and spirit of creation's fact, for it says of this man, "The spirit of the LORD shall rest upon him, the spirit of wisdom and understanding, the spirit of counsel and might, the spirit of knowledge and of the fear of the LORD."[1574]

14. This man, through his doctrine's offering and mediation, shares with us the conversation that He consecrated to the hands of his Father, to the end that like as the first Adam shared with us, by one act, a conversation of spiritual negligence, so by the second and last Adam a conversation of everlasting spiritual regeneration and reform is shared with the doer of that Faith's Spirit, which is why it says, "Be ye doers of the word."[1575] He or she failing to examine and do the Spirit's law will not know the benevolence decreed for their conversation, for "we might be justified by the faith of Christ, and not by the works of the law: for by the works of the law shall no flesh be justified."[1576]

15. Paul's language is specific, for the LORD's man, in abolishing the spirit of error from His LORD's Word, replaced that spirit and error with that Faith hiding within the spirit of His conversation.

1569 2 Corinthians 3:3
1570 John 3:6
1571 Hebrews 9:14
1572 Hebrews 8:1
1573 Jeremiah 10:10
1574 Isaiah 11:2
1575 James 1:22
1576 Galatians 2:16

Justification; which is another term for sanctification; is only through exercising faith on His man's doctrine, allowing us to understand that it is not enough to say, "*Jesus, Jesus.*" True and sober belief is born by comprehending the Faith "of" the living God's man, which means that unless we would hear and do the counsel, "Be ye transformed by the renewing of your mind, that ye may prove what is that good, and acceptable, and perfect, will of God,"[1577] we will not know the salvation of the Spirit's Word, and worse, our conversation will remain within the spirit of the first Adam's error.

16. Scripture does not say that Adam's spirit of error is abolished from existence, but that it is only removed from the living God's religious character; we need to be careful. Adam's religion is understood by its confidence on what is nailed to the tree, making that tree the confidence of its conversation, when it is that "he that is hanged is accursed of God."[1578] What is found on the tree is no man, but is, in reality, a religious ideology. Adam's transgression magnifies this ideology, but the LORD's man wounded it, taking it out of the way of heaven's will and doctrine. By His man, we understand that "the strength of sin is the law,"[1579] and that every conversation under Adam's error will invent and employ the religious law and tradition.

17. Thus, by the LORD's man, all praise returns to the One by whom salvation's law and science comes from, even as it says, "Therefore are they before the throne of God, and serve him day and night in his temple: and he that sitteth on the throne shall dwell among them."[1580] Thus, "the LORD hath prepared his throne in the heavens,"[1581] even within that Building where He "hath raised us up together, and made us sit together in heavenly places in Christ Jesus."[1582]

18. The "heavens" of the living God represent the two rooms of His heavenly Sanctuary, for, since brining up His man's conversation

---

1577 Romans 12:2
1578 Deuteronomy 21:23
1579 1 Corinthians 15:56
1580 Revelation 7:15
1581 Psalm 103:19
1582 Ephesians 2:6

into His Temple, we have "a minister of the sanctuary, and of the true tabernacle, which the Lord pitched, and not man."[1583] This conversation fled into this Building upon its ascension to fulfill the saying, "Blessed is he that cometh in the name of the Lord."[1584]

19. There is only one given the responsibility to appear before the people in the LORD's name, and such an office belonged to Aaron, of whom it says, "Aaron was separated...to minister unto him, and to bless in his name for ever."[1585] Therefore, being found next to the LORD's throne within His heavenly Temple, the saying is for ever fulfilled, "He shall stand and feed in the strength of the LORD, in the majesty of the name of the LORD his God."[1586] This mind of devotion within the heavenly Sanctuary for ever preserves the name and throne of its LORD, making it a binding responsibility for every one within His congregation to "keep the commandments of God, and the faith of Jesus."[1587]

20. This is truly a blessed revelation, for we today may know that Scripture does not lie when saying of the living God's wisdom, "Thy years are throughout all generations,"[1588] and, "Thou art the same, and thy years shall have no end."[1589]

21. With His man's conversation purged from the tree and found in His Spirit's direct presence; "for Christ is not entered into the holy places made with hands, which are the figures of the true; but into heaven itself, now to appear in the presence of God for us";[1590] as that High Priest of this wisdom's name and doctrine, every one of this doctrine's commandments are become the lot of "the general assembly and church of the firstborn, which are written in heaven."[1591] This is that conversation whose offering witnesses to the fact that "God is the

---

1583 Hebrews 8:2
1584 Luke 13:35
1585 1 Chronicles 23:13
1586 Micah 5:4
1587 Revelation 14:12
1588 Psalm 102:24
1589 Psalm 102:27
1590 Hebrews 9:24
1591 Hebrews 12:23

LORD,"[1592] and that since, in the beginning "the Word was with God, and the Word was God,"[1593] the Word is still today God.

22. With creation occurring through the heavenly mediation of His man's conversation, we may today know that creation's emblem has not been changed or altered, "for in six days the LORD made heaven and earth, the sea, and all that in them is, and rested the seventh day: wherefore the LORD blessed the Sabbath day, and hallowed it."[1594] The Spirit's Sabbath commandment, because the LORD's throne has no end, and because the LORD's man verifies the everlasting condition of this throne, is a perpetual law and covenant between His Spirit and the spirit of His creation.

23. The seventh day's refreshing seals our involvement with salvation's science. If after the first creation "God blessed the seventh day, and sanctified it,"[1595] then there should be no reason for creation's Sabbath to fail among conversations created by His voice, seeing as how "of his own will begat he us with the word of truth, that we should be a kind of firstfruits of his creatures."[1596] If it is that we are doers of His Word, and are patiently and temperately proving that spiritual understanding, it is that we are blessed to experience the promised sanctification, which is why it says, "By his knowledge shall my righteous servant justify many."[1597]

24. The mind must individually spend the power of its organs in order to discern the Spirit's voice, to do it; this is right learning. Our faith's higher education will inform us of what "sin" today is, and being doers of the Spirit's will, we will confess, "The law of the Spirit of life in Christ Jesus hath made me free from the law of sin and death."[1598] Being free from the pen of priests and elders to handle the Spirit's law without restriction, the spirit of the mind has the opportunity to become a subject of creation, and as such, is one blessed to receive "the

---

1592 Psalm 118:27
1593 John 1:1
1594 Exodus 20:11
1595 Genesis 2:3
1596 James 1:18
1597 Isaiah 53:11
1598 Romans 8:2

sign of circumcision, a seal of the righteousness of the faith,"[1599] even as the earth received in the beginning.

25. The operation of the living God does not change; every creation of His Spirit will know that "the seventh day is the Sabbath."[1600] If it is that we do not know the seventh day is the appointment for His Word's Sabbath, it is because our conversation is fashioned after the manner of Adam's "death," and "the sting of death is sin; and the strength of sin is the law."[1601]

26. "Death's" estate is governed by "sin's" wisdom, which spirit is forwarded by "the law of commandments contained in ordinances."[1602] With His man abolishing such *wisdom* from His religious character, this train of thought is today become "sin" against this Word's science. We may therefore understand that we are "sinners" before the Word by our willing adherence to what is nailed to the tree, which is a spirit and religious ideology preaching *righteousness* and *salvation* by doctrines, laws, ceremonies, baptisms, degrees, and *sabbaths*.

27. With this Spirit condemning, through the offering of His man, the pen of priests and elders; and "not only in this world, but also in that which is to come";[1603] to hear of a *Christ*, and the minister of that *Christ*, preaching any religious law or commandment contrary to Him whose "years shall have no end,"[1604] is to hear of religious error against His man's conversation, for His "Christ hath redeemed us from the curse of the law."[1605] Any other *sabbath* than that of His seventh day is herein understood to be fraudulence concocted by "the handwriting of ordinances,"[1606] making it "sin" against creation's science, and our conversation, by our consent to it, "sinful" before the Spirit and High Priest of that science.

1599 Romans 4:11
1600 Exodus 20:10
1601 1 Corinthians 15:56
1602 Ephesians 2:15
1603 Ephesians 1:21
1604 Psalm 102:27
1605 Galatians 3:13
1606 Colossians 2:14

28. With the LORD's man "having abolished in his flesh the enmity, even the law of commandments contained in ordinances,"[1607] all commandments contrary to his LORD's ten laws are become accursed of the blessing constrained to his doctrine's intercession. This man on the tree, and then removed from the tree "that he might be a merciful and faithful high priest in things pertaining to God, to make reconciliation for the sins of the people,"[1608] preaches service to every one of his Father's commandments through the course of their faith's learning. Whosoever will pick up the saying of this man will therefore know his wisdom's present love, "and this is love, that we walk after his commandments."[1609]

29. The Spirit's law is born from His ten laws so that the doer of them may wholeheartedly return to them. If we are not doers of His will and judgment of creation then our mind cannot return to His voice, "and hereby we do know that we know him, if we keep his commandments."[1610]

30. "We have received a commandment from the Father"[1611] so that we may know His name, that His intention is for the good of our conversation's conscience, seeing as how "the end of the commandment is charity out of a pure heart, and of a good conscience, and of faith unfeigned."[1612] This is the only Savior and God in existence, and if it is that we joy in the liberty purchased for our conversation through His man's offering, we will delight in the hope of a sound mind to govern the *body* of our faith, and also in that seventh-day Sabbath sanctified to celebrate that joy.

1607 Ephesians 2:15
1608 Hebrews 2:17
1609 2 John 1:6
1610 1 John 2:3
1611 2 John 1:4
1612 1 Timothy 1:5

19

The Jewish Roman Mystery

1. We understand that the conversation of the living God's man is that "Christ" because it preaches against the wisdom of the religious world. Therefore "having abolished in his flesh the enmity, even the law of commandments contained in ordinances,"[1613] this man condemned the wisdom of the religious world as "sin," making it an everlasting fact that "the strength of sin is the law."[1614]

2. The handwritten religious law of priests and elders is understood to be the definition of "sin" against heaven's will and doctrine because it halts faith's free exercise for knowledge to live by, "for whatsoever is not of faith is sin,"[1615] "and the law is not of faith."[1616]

1613 Ephesians 2:15
1614 1 Corinthians 15:56
1615 Romans 14:23
1616 Galatians 3:12

3. When His man says, "I came not to call the righteous, but sinners to repentance,"[1617] he opens up before us two classes of worshippers, namely, them believing that "righteousness come by the law,"[1618] and them understanding that "we through the Spirit wait for the hope of righteousness by faith."[1619]

4. Them that he calls *righteous*, these are, in reality, them that "hold the truth in unrighteousness,"[1620] and "all unrighteousness is sin,"[1621] "and the strength of sin is the law."[1622] Them He calls *righteous* are them that mishandle the living God's name by the philosophy of the religious law, and it is blatantly an issue of mishandling because His "Christ hath redeemed us from the curse of the law."[1623] Therefore where we find a *Christ* preaching, "You are justified by the law,"[1624] we observe counterfeit speech blaspheming the living God's new covenant commandment.

5. And this we may affirm because, when found failing to adhere to the rule of elders, they said to him, "Why do thy disciples transgress the tradition of the elders?"[1625]

6. "The handwriting of ordinances"[1626] meant very little to the living God's man because they represent that enmity against his Father's religious character. The saying, "Having abolished in his flesh the enmity, even the law of commandments contained in ordinances,"[1627] fully portrays the Godhead's attitude towards the traditions and commandments of priests and elders. With this man passed away on the tree, what is preached to us is the complete annihilation of the hand of whatever *Moses*; "not only in this world, but also in that which is to come";[1628] from creation's present will and course of learning.

1617 Mark 2:17
1618 Galatians 2:21
1619 Galatians 5:5
1620 Romans 1:18
1621 1 John 5:17
1622 1 Corinthians 15:56
1623 Galatians 3:13
1624 Galatians 5:4
1625 Matthew 15:2
1626 Colossians 2:14
1627 Ephesians 2:15
1628 Ephesians 1:21

7. It is therefore become religious error to invent and employ religious laws, and to associate such laws to the name of the Word and His wisdom. The Spirit prophesied of this negligence by saying, "He that killeth an ox is as if he slew a man; he that sacrificeth a lamb, as if he cut off a dog's neck; he that offereth an oblation, as if he offered swine's blood; he that burneth incense, as if he blessed an idol,"[1629] and, "I will also cause all her mirth to cease, her feast days, her new moons, and her sabbaths, and all her solemn feasts."[1630] Not only are physical religious offerings of animals, of washings, and of drinks passed away by His man, but also all other forms of laws and oblations according to the same spirit of error.

8. We understand the LORD's man is that man because his doctrine's heavenly ministry is already bound to laws, judgments, and ordinances of the living God's throne, and as that High Priest of this LORD's name; as it says, "A minister of the sanctuary, and of the true tabernacle, which the Lord pitched, and not man";[1631] this doctrine would be in the wrong for inventing and employing religious laws of its own. If Aaron blessed the congregation in his own name and knowledge, then we ought to accept such actions from that conversation acting as Aaron's true fulfillment, but since it says of Aaron, "Aaron was separated...to burn incense before the LORD, to minister unto him, and to bless in his name for ever,"[1632] we must conclude that "no man taketh this honour unto himself, but he that is called of God, as was Aaron. So also Christ glorified not himself to be made an high priest."[1633]

9. If the living God's man was a minister unto his own name, then we ought to call him fraudulent or coarse, for he has resurrected himself, anointed himself, and blessed his ministry unto himself. Since this is not the case, but that it was "God the Father, who raised him from the dead,"[1634] and that "it pleased the Father that in him

---

1629 Isaiah 66:3
1630 Hosea 2:11
1631 Hebrews 8:2
1632 1 Chronicles 23:13
1633 Hebrews 5:4,5
1634 Galatians 1:1

should all fulness dwell,"¹⁶³⁵ "when he saith all things are put under him, it is manifest that he is excepted, which did put all things under him."¹⁶³⁶

10. Paul has written this fact of creation's present office for our consolation, to the end we may understand that the role of its conversation is strictly ecclesiastical, and that it is subject to the religious and kingly rule of a throne above it, and that as a chief priest subject to that throne, every member of his conversation's congregation is become subject to the LORD of that same Church and State of its mediation.

11. It therefore does us well to understand that, after being taken of the LORD into His heavenly Sanctuary, being brought before this LORD's throne; which throne sits in this same Sanctuary; that this LORD consecrated His man's spiritual understanding to "be a merciful and faithful high priest in things pertaining to God."¹⁶³⁷ This means that every law and judgment of his conversation's ministry is that commandment of his LORD and Father's throne, and as Aaron's true fulfillment, it is this doctrine's responsibility to bless the assembly of this LORD's Spirit in the name of this LORD's Spirit, even as it says of him, "He shall stand and feed in the strength of the LORD, in the majesty of the name of the LORD his God."¹⁶³⁸

12. Herein is the reason why His man did not adhere to the rule of priests and elders, for while they subscribed to "sin's" strength for *righteousness*, he subscribed to the strength of his LORD's wisdom for "the kindness and love of God our Saviour toward man,"¹⁶³⁹ seeing as how "the righteousness of God without the law is manifested."¹⁶⁴⁰ It is therefore become evident that this "Christ" of the Bible will not go against or contradict any commandment of his LORD's Spirit, for, "having abolished in his flesh the enmity, even the law of commandments contained

---

1635 Colossians 1:19
1636 1 Corinthians 15:27
1637 Hebrews 2:17
1638 Micah 5:4
1639 Titus 3:4
1640 Romans 3:21

in ordinances,"[1641] the statement is made that "the strength of sin is the law."[1642]

13. Now, if this man should invent to himself what his own flesh abolished, is he not become a transgressor of the Spirit's doctrine? Isn't it written, "Whosoever transgresseth, and abideth not in the doctrine of Christ, hath not God"?[1643] Isn't it written, "If I build again the things which I destroyed, I make myself a transgressor"?[1644] If this man should pick up what his doctrine dismantles, then truly *righteousness* appears by the religious law, but "if righteousness come by the law, then Christ is dead in vain,"[1645] for it is written, "Made under the law, to redeem them that were under the law."[1646]

14. To observe a *Christ* doing contrary to redeeming from the religious law, but subjecting the conversation under the religious law, is to observe a *Christ* uttering a contrary doctrine to the living God's religious character. And again, if they did not say, "Why do thy disciples transgress the tradition of the elders?"[1647] but said, "Now thy disciples keep the tradition of the elders," then we ought to invent and bless whatever religious law and tradition we would, but since this man refrained from the mindless judgment of priests and elders; that is, from "Jewish fables, and commandments of men, that turn from the truth";[1648] he has set the example that there is no counsel above the living God's Spirit.

15. There is therefore no greater Jewish fable than a *sabbath* contrary to the living God's seventh-day Sabbath. Because there is no witness for such a *sabbath* in the Bible, it is wholeheartedly a religious law or tradition of elders, and, according to the wisdom and commandment of the living God, is "sin" against His doctrine, seeing as how "the strength of sin is the law."[1649]

1641 Ephesians 2:15
1642 1 Corinthians 15:56
1643 2 John 1:9
1644 Galatians 2:18
1645 Galatians 2:21
1646 Galatians 4:4,5
1647 Matthew 15:2
1648 Titus 1:14
1649 1 Corinthians 15:56

16. This Spirit does not mince words when it comes to His Sabbath, for, "in the end of the Sabbath, as it began to dawn toward the first day of the week,"[1650] it was this same Spirit that brought up His man's conversation to Himself. If this man, on the first day, did bring up himself after his passing, then we ought to think that creation's Sabbath is passed away. If the LORD's Spirit brought up His Faith to Himself during the second day after his passing, then we ought to think that the LORD Himself has put His own Sabbath away. But if the Spirit of the living God did resurrect His *Son* on the third day after his passing, and not even during the day, but rather "very early in the morning the first day of the week,"[1651] "when the Sabbath was past,"[1652] then we ought to understand that the living God, by refraining from working on His Sabbath, has for ever linked His seventh day Sabbath to His man's Faith.

17. "Upon the first day of the week, very early in the morning,"[1653] the LORD's Spirit acted, and this He did to more fully pronounce the fact that "the seventh day is the Sabbath of the LORD."[1654] The LORD's man, by his conversation's passing, regenerating, and high priestly consecration, preaches that there is only one God of *heaven* and *earth*, and that "God is the LORD."[1655] Such a testimony moves the mind to think on creation, where there is more than one God at work, for, "in the beginning was the Word, and the Word was with God, and the Word was God."[1656]

18. In the beginning, it was the living God and His Word, and the Word of this living God created every thing that He thought up; "all things were made by him; and without him was not any thing made that was made."[1657] At the end of creation, it is this same Word of this same living God who is that Spirit blessing the seventh day with the seal

---

1650 Matthew 28:1
1651 Mark 16:2
1652 Mark 16:1
1653 Luke 24:1
1654 Exodus 20:10
1655 Psalm 118:27
1656 John 1:1
1657 John 1:3

of His creative power and wisdom, even as it says, "God blessed the seventh day, and sanctified it."[1658]

19. This Word is that same God who resurrected His man's name after His Sabbath, for if the God of creation should transgress His own commandment, what God is He? The LORD's man could not rise at any other hour than the third day because the time of his passing occurred before and during the Sabbath. If passed away on a Tuesday, surely that afternoon the LORD's man should be risen; if on a Thursday, the same would occur; but the Spirit would not disturb His seventh day, for it is a perpetual covenant between He and His creation spoken in to existence by His own mouth. And concerning that covenant passing out of His mouth, He says, "My covenant will I not break, nor alter the thing that is gone out of my lips."[1659]

20. Where we observe a *Christ* breaking or altering what the Word has spoken, we may understand that we are observing Barab'bas, who cares for no thing more than insurrection against the living God's religious character. This spirit of quitting the Word's voice, and of saying, "Ye shall not surely die,"[1660] when the Spirit says, "In the day that thou eatest thereof thou shalt surely die,"[1661] is that spirit and philosophy not only nailed to the tree and condemned by creation's counsel, but completely purged and separated from the living God's spiritual understanding. This allows us to understand that whatever *Christ* should subscribe to "the enmity, even the law of commandments contained in ordinances,"[1662] is a *Christ* conceived after the imagination of priests and elders, and whose rule goes no higher than the clouds.

21. And this is certainly true, for the tradition of a first day *sabbath* is not of the Hebrew, but of the sun-worshipping Roman, who says, "These men, being Jews, do exceedingly trouble our city, and teach customs, which are not lawful for us to receive, neither to observe, being

---

1658 Genesis 2:3
1659 Psalm 89:34
1660 Genesis 3:4
1661 Genesis 2:17
1662 Ephesians 2:15

Romans."[1663] It is the Roman Jews that helped invent a Greco-Roman *Christ*, who, in reality, is that "image which fell down from Jupiter,"[1664] who the Romans honored; and still honor; every first day of the week.

22. If news of Paul's trial did not reach these Roman Jews; for they said to Paul, "We neither received letters out of Judaea concerning thee, neither any of the brethren that came shewed or spake any harm of thee";[1665] then it is fair to conclude that the doctrine put forth by the LORD's man, and every thing surrounding his conversation's death and regeneration, also had no great effect on the Jews of Rome. The Jews of Rome were utterly disconnected from the events occurring in Jerusalem against Paul, wherefore it is fair to conclude that, at the time of "Christ's" ministry; from the beginning to the end; they were also subtly disconnected from the things transpiring within the land of the Jews.

23. But upon seeing Paul, and hearing of what had fallen against him, at this time the Christian tribe had taken root and spread from out of Syria of An'tioch, and they said to him, "We desire to hear of thee what thou thinkest: for as concerning this sect, we know that every where it is spoken against."[1666] Paul then preached the Word's Faith "both out of the law of Moses, and out of the prophets, from morning till evening. And some believed the things which were spoken, and some believed not."[1667] But after Paul rebuked the Jews for their hardheartedness, and they had their conscience pricked by what was said to them by Paul, "when he had said these words, the Jews departed, and had great reasoning among themselves."[1668]

24. From this communion, these Jews of Rome said, "It is expedient for us, that one man should die for the people, and that the whole nation perish not."[1669]

25. The living God's man was again crucified, albeit not physically, but rather spiritually, through the *body* of his doctrine. No longer would

---

1663 Acts 16:20,21
1664 Acts 19:35
1665 Acts 28:21
1666 Acts 28:22
1667 Acts 28:23,24
1668 Acts 28:29
1669 John 11:50

the Romans say, "These men, being Jews, do exceedingly trouble our city, and teach customs, which are not lawful for us to receive, neither to observe, being Romans,"[1670] for they would come to reverence a *Christ* moving Paul to write, "There be some that trouble you, and would pervert the gospel of Christ. But though we, or an angel from heaven, preach any other gospel unto you than that which we have preached unto you, let him be accursed."[1671]

26. This other *Christ* is the preaching of an accursed religious philosophy, directing our mind to how it is written, "He that is hanged is accursed of God."[1672] Through these Roman Jews, an odd mystery began to form around *the LORD's Christ* to preserve the spirit of "sin" and religious error, for the tree, instead of preaching, "Seek those things which are above, where Christ sitteth on the right hand of God,"[1673] began preaching that philosophy nailed it, teaching, "Righteousness come by the law."[1674]

27. Therefore, to celebrate that "image which fell down from Jupiter,"[1675] the Jews of Rome invoked the spirit of the serpent, becoming "inventors of evil things,"[1676] exchanging heaven's Faith and Sabbath for the spirit and persuasion of the sun.

1670   Acts 16:20,21
1671   Galatians 1:7,8
1672   Deuteronomy 21:23
1673   Colossians 3:1
1674   Galatians 2:21
1675   Acts 19:35
1676   Romans 1:30

20

A Risen Appointment

1. When hearing of the LORD's man, "He is risen,"[1677] it is a message directing our mind to consider the manner of this resurrection. Our understanding of this regeneration comes from how one, when hearing the voice of the LORD's man, said of John, "That John the Baptist was risen from the dead."[1678] It is not that John was literally raised up from the grave and physically among the people, but this one observing the doctrine of the living God's man said, "That John the Baptist was risen from the dead, and therefore mighty works do shew forth themselves in him."[1679]

2. What was raised from the dead was not the man John, but rather the works of John. Concerning these "works," others, when hearing

---

1677 Mark 16:6
1678 Mark 6:14
1679 Mark 6:14

the speech of the Spirit's man, said, "From whence hath this man these things? and what wisdom is this which is given unto him, that even such mighty works are wrought by his hands?"[1680] And again, "What thing is this? what new doctrine is this?"[1681]

3. John, the man, was not raised from the dead, but when they heard his voice through the speech of the Spirit's man, it was that John's doctrine was resurrected and given life by the wisdom of his speech. It is also well to note where the demonstration of these "works" of wisdom and doctrine occurred, for in every case "he entered into the synagogue, and taught. And they were astonished at his doctrine."[1682]

4. This rising of *John* is through teaching, for, when hearing of the living God's man, "That John the Baptist was risen from the dead, and therefore mighty works do shew forth themselves in him,"[1683] it is well to compare the language of this statement with how it says, "When the Sabbath day was come, he began to teach in the synagogue: and many hearing him were astonished, saying, From whence hath this man these things? and what wisdom is this which is given unto him, that even such mighty works are wrought by his hands?"[1684]

5. John is raised from the dead in no natural sense; that is, in no physical or tangible manner; but by the wisdom of his understanding. What was *raised* before the people was no literal appearance of a man called John, but rather the name or doctrine of a man, even as it says, "John came unto you in the way of righteousness."[1685]

6. The doctrine of the Spirit's manner of righteousness shone through the *face* of the living God's man, and so the wisdom of John was elevated before the people through the law and commandment of His voice. This elevation, this awakening, this surfacing, this rousing, this quickening of *John*, is through teaching and demonstration to the mind of the hearer, even as it says, "By manifestation of the

---

1680 Mark 6:2
1681 Mark 1:27
1682 Mark 1:21,22
1683 Mark 6:14
1684 Mark 6:2
1685 Matthew 21:32

truth commending ourselves to every man's conscience in the sight of God."[1686]

7. If the one observing the LORD's man had not stated mighty works through him of *John*, and if these mighty works were not associated to the synagogue; in that the works mentioned is heaven's wisdom demonstrated through knowledge and understanding; then the manner of John's raising from the dead would not be a continuation of his spiritual wisdom, but rather some superstitious interpretation of the man. *John* is "raised" only through demonstration to the conscience, and this is why Paul counsels, "My speech and my preaching was not with enticing words of man's wisdom, but in demonstration of the Spirit and of power: that your faith should not stand in the wisdom of men, but in the power of God."[1687]

8. *John's* confirmation and manifestation appeared through the preaching of his wisdom and confidence through the Spirit's understanding, for "that which is born of the Spirit is spirit."[1688] Only the spirit of the conversation's mind benefits from the Spirit's impression, which impression is secured to the person according to how it says, "I am full of power by the spirit of the LORD, and of judgment, and of might,"[1689] and, "I have filled him with the spirit of God, in wisdom, and in understanding, and in knowledge."[1690]

9. All demonstration of the Spirit is through the knowledge and judgment of His doctrine, which "judgment" is understood by how He says, "A law shall proceed from me, and I will make my judgment to rest for a light of the people."[1691]

10. The Spirit's power is the Spirit's understanding, and this Faith is known as "the law of the Spirit of life."[1692] John's message only prepared the way for the Spirit's law, for John preached the act and effect of

---

1686 2 Corinthians 4:2
1687 1 Corinthians 2:4,5
1688 John 3:6
1689 Micah 3:8
1690 Exodus 31:3
1691 Isaiah 51:4
1692 Romans 8:2

righteousness through repentance, but the living God's man preached the perfection to appear after that righteousness and repentance.

11. "Righteousness" is the living God's praise and benevolence, for it is His doctrine's intention to "purge your conscience from dead works to serve the living God."[1693] His new covenant commandment's will and law is for regeneration and reformation of the conversation's conscience; this is His kingdom and righteousness; but in order to successfully capture the person, the heart of the conversation must quit "sin" against this science and learning.

12. "Having abolished in his flesh the enmity, even the law of commandments contained in ordinances,"[1694] the LORD's man has today openly defined "sin," "and the strength of sin is the law."[1695] This commandment's intention cannot be realized if the mind is not singular to its course, wherefore it is necessary to quit the religious law of priest and elder to take full knowledge; both mentally and spiritually; of the Spirit's law.

13. Herein is the reason why it says, "Be dead with Christ from the rudiments of the world."[1696]

14. The illustration drawn by the LORD's man passed away on the tree is of a religious philosophy abolished from the living God's Faith, seeing as how "he that is hanged is accursed of God."[1697] What is accursed on the tree is not a man, but rather what the flesh of that man symbolizes. The flesh of the LORD's man illustrates; because He was "made under the law"[1698] of a religious tradition; the perpetual condemnation of every "vain conversation received by tradition,"[1699] and "not only in this world, but also in that which is to come."[1700] With the ghost of this man's *body* removed from him on the tree, it is that the spirit empowering the religious law is utterly taken away from the

---

1693 Hebrews 9:14
1694 Ephesians 2:15
1695 1 Corinthians 15:56
1696 Colossians 2:20
1697 Deuteronomy 21:23
1698 Galatians 4:4
1699 1 Peter 1:18
1700 Ephesians 1:21

Word's Faith, for the man on the tree is become separated from it, cursing it as "sin" to his God's Word.

15. And if this were the end of the illustration we might embrace a perplexed mind, for there is no statement of Faith in that routine held to the tree, but only complete division from the living God's religious character. But when we hear him say, before passing away, "Father, into thy hands I commend my spirit,"[1701] it is that a law of creation for a new conversation is opened up to us, for with his natural conversation bound to the philosophy of the religious law and passed away, a new and perfect manner of devotion is born, and "perfect, as pertaining to the conscience."[1702]

16. If he had not consecrated his conversation's spirit to his Father, that spirit and philosophy nailed to the tree might be taken for our confidence, but what is nailed to the tree is absolutely forgotten and annihilated through the offering of his spirit, verifying the fact that this "Christ hath redeemed us from the curse of the law, being made a curse for us: for it is written, Cursed is every one that hangeth on a tree: that the blessing of Abraham might come on the Gentiles through Jesus Christ; that we might receive the promise of the Spirit through faith."[1703]

17. Now, the blessing of Abraham is without the use of the religious law, "for if the inheritance be of the law, it is no more of promise: but God gave it to Abraham by promise."[1704] The LORD's man abolished the invention and employment of the religious law and tradition from his Father's Faith that His spiritual understanding may be the Father of our conversation, even as the same Spirit was, and still is, the Father of his.

18. Abraham's blessing appeared "through the righteousness of faith,"[1705] for he was given a promise, and by consistently exercising faith on that promise, and growing up in heart and mind by that promise, it

---

1701 Luke 23:46
1702 Hebrews 9:9
1703 Galatians 3:13,14
1704 Galatians 3:18
1705 Romans 4:13

was then said of him, "Abraham obeyed my voice, and kept my charge, my commandments, my statutes, and my laws."[1706] Abraham did not obey any promise "through the law, but through the righteousness of faith,"[1707] and with the living God's man magnifying Abraham's mind of devotion, our route to creation and edification is today through Abraham's manner of worship and learning.

19. The religious law is error because it halts faith's right exercise, allowing us to understand that "whatsoever is not of faith is sin,"[1708] and that "the law is not of faith."[1709] "Having abolished in his flesh the enmity, even the law of commandments contained in ordinances,"[1710] the LORD's man purged the Word's doctrine of the pen of priests and elders, making it an eternal fact that our conversation's conscience is to be "written not with ink, but with the Spirit of the living God."[1711] Henceforward a new nature should capture the doer of the Spirit's law, seeing as how His man "took not on him the nature of angels; but he took on him the seed of Abraham."[1712]

20. The "nature" is the religious conversation, and the nature of the "angel," or of the priest and minister, is according to the saying, "Full well ye reject the commandment of God, that ye may keep your own tradition."[1713] The "nature" of the minister or pastor is a conversation governed by religious laws and traditions, for they preach and believe that "righteousness come by the law."[1714]

21. This is an innately erroneous nature because it maintains "unrighteousness," and since "all unrighteousness is sin,"[1715] we cannot escape the fact that "the strength of sin is the law."[1716] The nature of the "ungodly" or "unrighteous" conversation therefore honors the

---

1706 Genesis 26:5
1707 Romans 4:13
1708 Romans 14:23
1709 Galatians 3:12
1710 Ephesians 2:15
1711 2 Corinthians 3:3
1712 Hebrews 2:16
1713 Mark 7:9
1714 Galatians 2:21
1715 1 John 5:17
1716 1 Corinthians 15:56

tradition of flesh for *righteousness*, but that right or sober nature honors the Spirit's commandment without the religious law, for, through His man suffering the tree, "the righteousness of God without the law is manifested."[1717]

22. With the LORD's man "blotting out the handwriting of ordinances"[1718] invented by *Moses*; and by *Moses* "not only in this world, but also in that which is to come";[1719] all that remains is an experimental faith on the Spirit's voice for "the kindness and love of God our Saviour toward man."[1720] With the living God's man passed away on the tree and offering to his LORD not that slain "body," but rather the spirit of his conversation's heart, it is that the seed and nature of Abraham is for ever shared with whoever should hear and do the counsel, "Be ye transformed by the renewing of your mind, that ye may prove what is that good, and acceptable, and perfect, will of God."[1721]

23. With the nature of Abraham ratified for the one doing the Word's will, the new covenant promise of that will is shared with them also, which promise is, "I will put my law in their inward parts, and write it in their hearts; and will be their God, and they shall be my people."[1722] As Abraham believed that promise and exercised his mind on that promise by faith, acting out the confidence obtained from spiritually discerning that promise to receive that confidence's circumcision for his faith, so too it is our responsibility to "believe on him that raised up Jesus our Lord from the dead,"[1723] and it was "God the Father, who raised him from the dead."[1724] Thus, "if the Spirit of him that raised up Jesus from the dead dwell in you, he that raised up Christ from the dead shall also quicken your mortal bodies by his Spirit that dwelleth in you."[1725]

1717 Romans 3:21
1718 Colossians 2:13
1719 Ephesians 1:21
1720 Titus 3:4
1721 Romans 12:2
1722 Jeremiah 31:33
1723 Romans 4:24
1724 Galatians 1:1
1725 Romans 8:11

24. The LORD's man was raised up from the dead according to the same manner that *John* was raised up from the dead, for it says, of His chief apostle, "Put to death in the flesh, but quickened by the Spirit."[1726] This allows us to understand that what was "risen" by the Spirit is no literal or physical body, for it was that when king Herod heard of the living God's man, "he said, That John the Baptist was risen from the dead, and therefore mighty works do shew forth themselves in him."[1727]

25. It is not that the man John was resurrected in the form of another man called Jesus, but the name of John had risen up by the name and spiritual commandment of creation's chief witness. It was the "name" of the LORD's man that captured audiences, and concerning the definition of "name," we read, "And hast kept my word, and hast not denied my name,"[1728] and, "Thou holdest fast my name, and hast not denied my faith."[1729]

26. The "name" of the Spirit's man is the Word and Faith of the Spirit's man. What the king beheld was the resurrection of John's name through the name of the Spirit's chief minister, and when hearing, of this same man, "He is risen, as he said,"[1730] it is that the name of the LORD's man is risen from the "dead," wherefore it is well to know and understand that "the sting of death is sin; and the strength of sin is the law."[1731]

27. To be risen from the "dead" is to no longer "be delivered into the hands of sinful men,"[1732] which men of "sin" are understood by how it says, "The Son of man must suffer many things, and be rejected of the elders and chief priests and scribes, and be slain."[1733]

28. The "dead" are them that reverence the spirit and philosophy of the tree, but the *living* are them that are turned away from that persuasion nailed to the tree for executing the counsel, "Worship God

---

1726 1 Peter 3:18
1727 Mark 6:14
1728 Revelation 3:8
1729 Revelation 2:13
1730 Matthew 28:6
1731 1 Corinthians 15:56
1732 Luke 24:7
1733 Luke 9:22

in the spirit,"[1734] which is why they confess, "The law of the Spirit of life in Christ Jesus hath made me free from the law of sin and death."[1735] As John's "name" was risen from the dead by the wisdom and spirit witnessed by the LORD's man, so the "name" of the LORD's man was resurrected by the LORD's Spirit from "philosophy and vain deceit, after the tradition of men, after the rudiments of the world."[1736] Because "name" is not physical, and because "a spirit hath not flesh and bones,"[1737] it is that the wisdom and knowledge of salvation's science found itself raised from the religion of the ministers of "death."

29. Truly the "Lord" of salvation's science was risen from the grave by the LORD's Spirit, which "Lord" is understood by how it says, "Blessed be the Lord, who daily loadeth us with benefits, even the God of our salvation,"[1738] and, "Bless ye God in the congregations, even the Lord, from the fountain of Israel."[1739]

30. This "Lord" who is "God" of the Spirit's assembly is that God fulfilling the saying, "The God of Israel is he that giveth strength and power unto his people."[1740] The "Lord" and "God" of salvation is the LORD's power and strength, and it is well to remember that "wisdom strengtheneth."[1741]

31. The "Lord" and "God" of salvation is no literal or physical entity, but is, in reality, the wisdom and knowledge of the living God's Spirit. It is therefore well to understand that "Jesus Christ," as the phrase is used, is but a term denoting the name or doctrine of the LORD's man, for "the Lord Jesus Christ our Saviour"[1742] is, in right context of language, "the commandment of God our Saviour."[1743]

1734 Philippians 3:3
1735 Romans 8:2
1736 Colossians 2:8
1737 Luke 24:39
1738 Psalm 68:18
1739 Psalm 68:26
1740 Psalm 68:35
1741 Ecclesiastes 7:19
1742 Titus 1:4
1743 Titus 1:3

32. What Herod observed when hearing the voice of the LORD's man was the perfected commandment of John's ministry. When hearing that the LORD's man is raised from the "dead," the application constrained to John's name cannot escape the tense used to pronounce the rising of the name of the living God's man.

33. What is risen from the "dead" is a commandment of perfect regeneration relaying the wisdom of the living God's will for every conversation willing to bring their conversation "above, where Christ sitteth on the right hand of God."[1744] What was risen from the "dead" was the law and doctrine the heavenly Sanctuary's Faith, and as, of old, the LORD's man taught the wisdom of this judgment in the synagogues, so today this wisdom is removed from the religious world and found only in the heavenly Sanctuary, which is why it says, "They have seen thy goings, O God; even the goings of my God, my King, in the sanctuary."[1745]

34. That "God" within the LORD's heavenly Sanctuary is "the spirit of wisdom and understanding, the spirit of counsel and might, the spirit of knowledge and of the fear of the LORD,"[1746] for he said, "Father, into thy hands I commend my spirit."[1747] This allows us to understand that the living God has, for the second and last time, made His Word the author of modern-day creation.

35. With the LORD's man condemning that philosophy held to the natural conversation, but magnifying that law regenerating the spirit of the mind from that accursed philosophy, the doctrine of this man's mind is become that "Lord" and "God" of our conversation's conscience, which is why we are counseled, "Put off concerning the former conversation...and be renewed in the spirit of your mind."[1748] It is therefore become evident that, like as Abraham obeyed the living God's voice and received the sign of his faith's service, so also every mind examining and doing creation's present voice; and He "hath in

---

1744 Colossians 3:1
1745 Psalm 68:24
1746 Isaiah 11:2
1747 Luke 23:46
1748 Ephesians 4:22-24

these last days spoken unto us by his Son,"[1749] that is, by "the knowledge of the Son of God";[1750] will not be void of that emblem representing their course in His Spirit's righteousness.

36. With that "Lord" and "God" of salvation's science being the same Word and Spirit of creation, the Sabbath of this "Lord" and "God" of creation's present commandment is become a witness to the living God's righteousness, making the day of the "Lord" and "Wisdom" of resurrection the same day of the Spirit's Word and Faith. This same God, in the beginning, "blessed the seventh day, and sanctified it."[1751]

37. To hear that "the Lord Jesus Christ our Saviour"[1752] is risen from the "dead"; which "Lord" and "Savior" is "the commandment of God our Saviour";[1753] is to hear of the Word's will and law separated from the *righteousness* of *men* for the righteousness of its LORD's Spirit. The *righteousness* of ministers is "sin" against the Spirit's righteousness, for "the strength of sin is the law."[1754] With the philosophy of the religious law condemned by the spirit of the LORD's man, all that remains is for the Spirit's creation to "keep the commandments of God, and the faith of Jesus."[1755]

38. With the Faith of the LORD's man risen from them that invent and practice "death," it is become a fact "that we might be justified by the faith of Christ, and not by the works of the law: for by the works of the law shall no flesh be justified."[1756] This justification, or sanctification, being without works of the religious law, is of the works of an exercised faith on the Spirit's wisdom, which labor preaches the creation of newness within the conversation's conscience to better keep the body of that conversation's faith. Thus, the confession of that spirit advancing in the Godhead's science is, "The law of the Spirit of life in

---

1749   Hebrews 1:2
1750   Ephesians 4:13
1751   Genesis 2:3
1752   Titus 1:4
1753   Titus 1:3
1754   1 Corinthians 15:56
1755   Revelation 14:12
1756   Galatians 2:16

Christ Jesus hath made me free from the law of sin and death,"[1757] for that "Lord" escaping the "dead" is that wisdom bringing its doer out of "death" with it, and into the Great Building of its LORD and Spirit.

39. Our conversation will realize its higher education in this heavenly Building, and that to such a learning is blessed a Sabbath of resurrection's righteousness; "having abolished in his flesh the enmity, even the law of commandments contained in ordinances,"[1758] the LORD's man has made it an ever lasting fact that "the seventh day is the Sabbath of the LORD."[1759] So then are we risen with this God? Does this Word's "Lord" bless our conversation? Is the *body* of our faith wearing that sacrificed "divine nature, having escaped the corruption that is in the world through lust"?[1760]

40. We understand that we honor the religious world's spiritual corruption by our sufficiency on the "sin" of ministers, and with the LORD's man perpetually "blotting out the handwriting of ordinances"[1761] devised by priests and elders, it is become known that "the strength of sin is the law."[1762] To hear of the Spirit's risen wisdom is to therefore hear of that law's seal and joy of righteousness, for this Spirit's man, by his offering, has for ever fixed the Sabbath of this same Spirit of creation to the charge of this Spirit's new covenant commandment.

41. By one offering, the LORD's man not only put away the spirit and philosophy of the serpent from the living God's religious character, but also reinstated Eden's original higher learning to that mind willing to venture in to the heavenly Sanctuary for knowledge of that counsel. Today, if our conversation is raised with salvation's science, we will possess the mind of that doctrine's God, which "God" is a law and doctrine of creation, which creation is celebrated every week on the seventh day.

1757 Romans 8:2
1758 Ephesians 2:15
1759 Exodus 20:10
1760 2 Peter 1:4
1761 Colossians 2:14
1762 1 Corinthians 15:56

21

That Required Offering

1. If it is written that "the LORD had respect unto Abel and to his offering: but unto Cain and to his offering he had not respect";[1763] must we today believe that we can offer to this same LORD God any thing contrary to what He asks?

2. If this LORD's Spirit has decreed a commandment to be observed, does it make sense to do less or more than that commandment demands?

3. If we know some one who specifically told us some thing that they need, to get it for them, would it make sense to buy them what we think they need? If we should think to bring them what we think they need, and not what they know they need, shouldn't we receive their displeasure?

1763 Genesis 4:4,5

4. If we were hungry and wanted food, would we bring to our stomach material that we cannot eat; like wood, cloth, dirt, hair, or soap; or would we not rather offer good and edible food to our stomach? If we knew that we needed a good grade to pass for the semester, hoping to excel in our major, would we not bring our mind to do what needed to be done for a good grade? In every case we would bring what is asked for; circumstance demands our attention to what is necessary; therefore when creation's present circumstance is outlined by the Word's man, isn't it that we rise to the present circumstance to meet the outlined standard? If we should not, must we think that our offering is *blessed* of the living God, especially when it is witnessed, from the beginning, that such stubbornness is not respected?

5. The wisdom of Eden is the same Spirit of Eden, and that same Spirit of Eden is that same Word today; "I am the LORD, I change not,"[1764] says His Spirit. Cain's example is for our learning and correction, for this man invented to his self a religious law and ordinance to honor *the Word* by, and was rejected in his service; "do they not err that devise evil?"[1765] Cain's "works were evil, and his brother's righteous,"[1766] wherefore we may understand that what is "evil" is "unrighteous," and that "all unrighteousness is sin."[1767]

6. Cain does define "sin" for us as not only doing contrary to what the Spirit's voice demands, but doing contrary to what the Spirit requires by an invention of the hands. For, who told Cain to bring "of the fruit of the ground an offering unto the LORD"?[1768]

7. Who told Cain that this was an acceptable offering? Abel's offering matches the Spirit's mind, for "unto Adam also and to his wife did the LORD God make coats of skins, and clothed them."[1769] It makes sense for Abel to bring "of the firstlings of his flock and of the fat thereof,"[1770] for the LORD's Spirit established this standard. What

---

1764 Malachi 3:6
1765 Proverbs 14:22
1766 1 John 3:12
1767 1 John 5:17
1768 Genesis 4:3
1769 Galatians 3:21
1770 Genesis 4:4

good, then, is fruit to blood? What good is any thing other than the Spirit's decreed judgment? There is no valuable thing outside of the LORD's voice, and yet Cain thought it well to not only do contrary to the commandment, but to invent to his self a law prescribing *righteousness* for his own spiritual understanding.

8. Cain's process of thinking is similar to his mother's, who was persuaded to violate the Spirit's then commandment, taking the tree for a religious law establishing *righteousness*. The same spirit and philosophy motivating Eve now moved Cain to act, for he brought what was contrary as though it wasn't. Cain then grew angry with his brother because the "God" that he offered to was not that God of the offering, for Cain subscribed to the "God" of "sin," "and the strength of sin is the law."[1771]

9. The wisdom of "sin" preaches that "righteousness come by the law,"[1772] but hearing that the Spirit had no respect for Cain's offering, "that no man is justified by the law in the sight of God, it is evident: for, The just shall live by faith."[1773] Now, the religious "law is not of faith,"[1774] and "whatsoever is not of faith is sin,"[1775] therefore "the law of commandments contained in ordinances"[1776] is "sin" against the living God's will and wisdom.

10. The LORD formed and accepted the sacrifice of fat and blood because it illustrated the offering to appear for amending the error within the philosophy of the religious law. "Fat" is a symbol of pride, as it says, "They are inclosed in their own fat: with their mouth they speak proudly."[1777] The "fat" within the offering of the LORD's man is his flesh, which is a figurative illustration of a religious spirit and ideology. "Having abolished in his flesh the enmity, even the law of commandments contained in ordinances,"[1778] it is that the "fat" or "pride" of

---

1771 1 Corinthians 15:56
1772 Galatians 2:21
1773 Galatians 3:11
1774 Galatians 3:12
1775 Romans 14:23
1776 Ephesians 2:15
1777 Psalm 17:10
1778 Ephesians 2:15

a religious conversation supported by religious laws and traditions is become abolished and condemned from the living God's religious character, and from the conversation learning of and doing that religious character's new covenant commandment.

11. Cain spoke proudly against the LORD's voice; as did his parents; by inventing to his conversation a religious law for his conversation's *righteousness*. Abel's offering testified to his acknowledging the fact that his natural conversation received by his parents is innately prideful against the living God, and so he burned the fat to burn the flesh of that pride, which is the fulfilling of the saying, "Put off concerning the former conversation...and be renewed in the spirit of your mind; and that ye put on the new man, which after God is created in righteousness and true holiness."[1779]

12. The burning of the fat illustrates the complete annihilation of "the law of commandments contained in ordinances"[1780] from the personal religion, but the blood offered illustrates the active ratification of heaven's new covenant will and law to regenerate and reform the conversation from its former estate. Abel truly deserves all respect, for "by faith Abel offered unto God a more excellent sacrifice than Cain, by which he obtained witness that he was righteous,"[1781] wherefore we may understand Cain's offering to be "unrighteousness," and "all unrighteousness is sin,"[1782] "and the strength of sin is the law."[1783]

13. Cain despised his brother because Abel would not subscribe to the spirit and philosophy of their mother, who is still the mother and doctrine of every living and stout mind. Cain was moved to offer foreign *wine* to the living God, even as two men of his mind would afterwards do, and when they did, "there went out fire from the LORD, and devoured them, and they died before the LORD."[1784]

1779   Ephesians 4:22-24
1780   Ephesians 2:15
1781   Hebrews 11:4
1782   1 John 5:17
1783   1 Corinthians 15:56
1784   Leviticus 10:2

14. Through Cain, the religion of the serpent had a son to herald it, which is why, after Cain slew his brother for his own disobedience and bullheadedness, it was told him, "Now art thou cursed from the earth."[1785] As his parents had been driven out of Eden's benevolence for their error, so Cain, and the spirit attached to his conversation, was removed from that *earth* established by that doctrine preached through the fat and blood of the firstling. Henceforward an unrighteous religion professing *the Word of Eden* would find itself magnified by Cain's mind, who swallowed up that practice with "sin's" wisdom, further distorting the living God's name through the philosophy impressed upon his conversation by his mother.

15. Herein is a very important lesson for us, that whether alive today or anciently, at all periods of time under the heavens, "the sting of death is sin; and the strength of sin is the law."[1786] We may therefore understand that we are of Cain's line of devotion by the support of our conversation: is our faith *blessed* by "the enmity, even the law of commandments contained in ordinances,"[1787] or is our "service perfect, as pertaining to the conscience"?[1788]

16. Do we not remember how the Spirit said to the serpent's philosophy, "I will put enmity between thee and the woman"?[1789] "Having abolished in his flesh the enmity, even the law of commandments contained in ordinances,"[1790] the LORD's man has fulfilled this promise, for, today, what separates creation's will from the serpent's intention is the philosophy of the religious law. While the Spirit's Faith exists without the religious law; for it is a doctrine ordained "to redeem them that were under the law";[1791] the creed of the serpent gravitates towards it, moving his ministers to invent and employ religious traditions and doctrines professedly in service to *the LORD* and *Word* of *the*

1785 Genesis 4:11
1786 1 Corinthians 15:56
1787 Ephesians 2:15
1788 Hebrews 9:9
1789 Genesis 3:15
1790 Ephesians 2:15
1791 Galatians 4:5

Bible, but that are, in reality, in devotion to the *God* of "sin" against the Father and Counsel of *heaven's* will and science.

17. The living God's "Christ hath redeemed us from the curse of the law,"[1792] wherefore to hear any *Christ* saying, "Righteousness come by the law,"[1793] is to hear a false spirit saying, "It is vain to serve God: and what profit is it that we have kept his ordinance, and that we have walked mournfully before the LORD of hosts?"[1794] The spirit of the serpent is carnal and flesh-based, for it is wholly against exercising faith for knowledge to bless and reform the conversation. It is therefore well to understand that "whatsoever is not of faith is sin,"[1795] and that "the law is not of faith,"[1796] "for to be carnally minded is death,"[1797] and "the sting of death is sin; and the strength of sin is the law."[1798]

18. Religious laws and doctrines strengthen the carnal religious conversation, and being fleshy and not mental or spiritual, it is against the development of the mind for right care of our faith's *body*. To the carnal conversation, a *right* conversation is through restricting the heart by handwritten laws and judgments, for, to the carnal, all that exists is physical, and, to their mind, what can bind the flesh but the flesh? But to them that are mental and spiritual, a right conversation is by the development of the organs of the conversation's conscience, and these "are the circumcision, which worship God in the spirit,"[1799] who also please the Spirit's law, because "that which is born of the Spirit is spirit."[1800] Therefore Cain is right to kill Abel, for his "God" is entirely sensual, but the God to whom the offering is for; then and now; is not that carnal pestilence of Cain.

1792 Galatians 3:13
1793 Galatians 2:21
1794 Malachi 3:14
1795 Romans 14:23
1796 Galatians 3:12
1797 Romans 8:6
1798 1 Corinthians 15:56
1799 Philippians 3:3
1800 John 3:6

19. Two God's are in controversy with one another through Cain and Abel, pointing us to how it is said, "Whether is easier, to say, Thy sins be forgiven thee; or to say, Rise up and walk?"[1801]

20. In all honesty, and most certainly, all do agree; due to the ancient and still popular subscription to Cain's "God"; that if all that is told us is, "Your sins are forgiven," then that it is a very easy route. It is easy to have flesh say to flesh, "Your sins are forgiven," to then have flesh walk away from flesh sensually puffed up by flesh to continue in what is ultimately wrong against the living God's name, self, and one another. There is no thing hard against being told, "Your sins are forgiven," for by this saying, *righteousness* is imputed where righteousness is nonexistent, even as the Spirit says to the ministers of the "God" of religious error, "I am against your pillows,"[1802] and, "With lies ye have made the heart of the righteous sad, whom I have not made sad; and strengthened the hands of the wicked, that he should not return from his wicked way, by promising him life."[1803]

21. These "pillows" are as the same "aprons" that *man* made; and still concocts; when in religious error. These "pillows" of "aprons" are "the enmity, even the law of commandments contained in ordinances,"[1804] and from the beginning of time, the Spirit and wisdom of the heavenly Sanctuary has been against them.

22. Who is it that says, "Thy sins be forgiven thee"?[1805] If the LORD's man says, "Rise up and walk,"[1806] then the spirit saying, "Your sins are forgiven," is not that full doctrine of the living God's religious character. This saying, "Your sins are forgiven you," is an invention of *men* and not of the living God.

23. *Sin* to priests and elders is, by this saying of forgiveness, outward, and cannot be controlled by the inwards, therefore a chain on the flesh is, to them, the route to *righteousness*. In essence, the nature of this

---

1801 Luke 5:23
1802 Ezekiel 13:20
1803 Ezekiel 13:22
1804 Ephesians 2:15
1805 Luke 5:23
1806 Luke 5:23

saying is one endorsing evolution and atheism, for if by the commandment I am told that my sins are forgiven, then by the commandment I am *righteous*, and being *righteous*, I need not give any thought to the root of my error. But for this cause a continual bout of repentance and *sin* holds the conversation in limbo, for, whether today or anciently, the serpent's philosophy "could not make him that did the service perfect, as pertaining to the conscience."[1807]

24. Now, that wisdom saying, "Rise and walk," this is a course defining "sin" to the conversation to "purge your conscience from dead works to serve the living God."[1808] To the Spirit of creation, "sin" against the Word, self, or the spirit of another, begins inwardly, and "sin" can be controlled and extinguished, albeit through a certain learning and baptism, which is why it says, "Be not conformed to this world: but be ye transformed by the renewing of your mind, that ye may prove what is that good, and acceptable, and perfect, will of God."[1809] Thus, to the natural ear, it is easier to hear that your sins are forgiven, for such a saying appeases the flesh to continue its ignorance, but to the mind of the Spirit, it is infinitely easier to hear, "Rise and walk."

25. Personal and spiritual wrong is not a light issue, but is innately confined to the human being. To the one tired of self's irrational estate, and to the one conscious of wrong against self, others, and the Word by self's appetite and negligent passion, there is no thing better than hearing, "Rise up," for the mind is now empowered to watch self for obtaining knowledge on how to benevolently forgive and care for self.

26. There are no pillows in the Spirit's Faith. The soul is meant to receive wounds, and the mind is meant to mentally and spiritually examine and do the Spirit's voice, so that the knowledge retained may care for the wounds suffered on the soul, to help the person forgive their ignorance. This occurs so that our conversation may have scars to remind our heart what and what not to know, which is why it says,

---

1807 Hebrews 9:9
1808 Hebrews 9:14
1809 Romans 12:2

"Guide thine heart in the way,"[1810] and, "Let thine heart retain my words: keep my commandments, and live."[1811]

27. To the living God's mind, error must be broken off and not ignorantly coddled, which is why it says, "Break off thy sins by righteousness."[1812] To hear, "Rise and walk," is to hear the true and unadulterated doctrine of the Spirit's righteousness, which righteousness is understood by the confession, "The law of the Spirit of life in Christ Jesus hath made me free from the law of sin and death."[1813]

28. The Spirit's intention, after "having abolished in his flesh the enmity, even the law of commandments contained in ordinances,"[1814] is to resurrect the spirit of the conversation's conscience from religious error to understand that "the strength of sin is the law."[1815] This is important to understand because no offering tainted by what the LORD's man has abolished will be accepted, and further, if ever presenting what is abolished, it is that "God shall send them strong delusion, that they should believe a lie: that they all might be damned who believed not the truth, but had pleasure in unrighteousness."[1816]

29. Again, "all unrighteousness is sin,"[1817] "and the strength of sin is the law,"[1818] therefore any offering of the philosophy of the religious law is "sin" before the living God's commandment and deserving of Cain's lot. To help still this tide of the living God's "wrath" against the heart and mind of whoever should care to comprehend the knowledge of His name, His "Christ hath redeemed us from the curse of the law, being made a curse for us: for it is written, Cursed is every one that hangeth on a tree."[1819] Thus, whether invented of self or of a *Moses*, the religious law and tradition is religious error against the Word's Faith,

---

1810 Proverbs 23:19
1811 Proverbs 4:4
1812 Daniel 4:37
1813 Romans 8:2
1814 Ephesians 2:15
1815 1 Corinthians 15:56
1816 2 Thessalonians 2:11
1817 1 John 5:17
1818 1 Corinthians 15:56
1819 Galatians 3:13

wherefore it well to understand that if what is brought is contrary to what is decreed, that offering is of no value.

30. The LORD's man, by one sacrifice, has shed light on the right Word and Wisdom of *heaven* and *earth*, and with his flesh "blotting out the handwriting of ordinances,"[1820] what remains for his assembly to do is to "fear God, and keep his commandments."[1821] That wisdom hidden for ages and for generations is that Word of creation, and with the Spirit's sacrifice condemning the religious law and tradition to a perpetual slaughter, through this man we have the pure will and commandments of the living God pronounced to us. And because the Spirit wrought this benevolence "to make in himself of twain one new man,"[1822] the aim of creation's present endeavor shines forth through His man's name, and also that Sabbath of the Creator in beautiful brilliance.

31. Salvation's science, by the act of salvation's Captain, is for ever linked to the Word's seventh-day Sabbath. This man, having purged the Word's Faith from the pen of priests and elders, has secured his doctrine to the ten laws of His Father's throne, letting us know that "we do know that we know him, if we keep his commandments."[1823]

32. If we know his voice, "The law of the Spirit of life in Christ Jesus hath made me free from the law of sin and death,"[1824] we will say. Being made free from the religious law, it is that the mind may exercise itself on the Bible's spiritual understanding, to know whether it is of the living God or not. Such a mind released from "sin" by the Spirit's law will learn creation's confidence, and by that experience, will understand why "the seventh day is the Sabbath of the LORD."[1825]

33. The Word's man has clearly pronounced, by his passing on the tree, that there is only one charge of one Spirit in existence, and that this charge is that wisdom fulfilling the saying, "In the beginning was the Word, and the Word was with God, and the Word was God."[1826] The

---

1820 Colossians 2:14
1821 Ecclesiastes 12:13
1822 Ephesians 2:15
1823 1 John 2:3
1824 Romans 8:2
1825 Exodus 20:10
1826 John 1:1

Word of creation's science; both former and present; is that same God from the beginning, and every spirit educated by the knowledge and judgment of this Spirit will understand that this same "God blessed the seventh day, and sanctified it."[1827] When therefore thinking to offer any thing to this God on any other *sabbath* than that Sabbath of the seventh day, must we expect it to be accepted, and when this same Spirit cursed Cain, Na'dab, and Abi'hu, for their blatant religious error?

34. Through the slain flesh of His man, salvation's Sabbath is eternally established, allowing us to understand that any other *sabbath* is "sin" against His will and wisdom, for it is but a religious law and tradition, "and the strength of sin is the law."[1828] If there is a subscription to the religious law, then there is a violation of the living God's doctrine, which counsel preaches edification upon the conversation's inwards by an experimental faith on heaven's new covenant will. It is therefore a fact that "whosoever transgresseth, and abideth not in the doctrine of Christ, hath not God,"[1829] and if without this doctrine, the conversation is without that Sabbath magnifying the name of the living God's throne, and His wisdom's intercession, on the seventh day.

1827 Genesis 2:3
1828 1 Corinthians 15:56
1829 2 John 1:9

22

No Sign Given

1. The only way the LORD's man could have secured a popular favor with priests and elders would be if he became as "them that prophesy out of their own hearts."[1830] We understand this from how they said to him, "What sign shewest thou then, that we may see, and believe thee? what dost thou work? Our fathers did eat manna in the desert,"[1831] and by how, upon one occasion, "the Pharisees came forth, and began to question with him, seeking of him a sign from heaven, tempting him. And he sighed deeply in his spirit, and saith, Why doth this generation seek after a sign? verily I say unto you, There shall no sign be given unto this generation."[1832]

2. The "sign" that these people looked for was a "work" or "witness" of *righteousness*, which *righteousness* is understood by them

---

1830 Ezekiel 13:2
1831 John 6:30,31
1832 Mark 8:11,12

mentioning the bread in the wilderness, which witness this man states by saying, "Moses therefore gave unto you circumcision; (not because it is of Moses, but of the fathers;)."[1833] The sign that this people wanted from the living God's man was a carnal or flesh-based commandment similar to that act in the wilderness, or to the circumcision of flesh. This they desired of him because their "God" required it of them, educating them that, if a doctrine is without "the law of commandments contained in ordinances,"[1834] then it is an erroneous understanding, and of the one preaching it, that "he hath Beel'zebub, and by the prince of the devils casteth he out devils."[1835]

3. In this world of the Jewish religion, the living God's Word and Spirit is a false God. The LORD's Spirit is not that *God* of the religious world, and we may understand this by the testimony given of this Spirit at creation.

4. The LORD's Word is that God and Spirit of creation; "in the beginning was the Word, and the Word was with God, and the Word was God."[1836] When creation commenced, all that mattered was the Word's Spirit educating the elements of the atmosphere. In the beginning, there was no religious law used to intercede on behalf of creation; there was no handwritten ordinance to purchase *righteousness* for heaven and earth; there was no other commandment than that spoken of the Word for regenerating and reforming heaven and earth. There was no Moses at creation; there was no "handwriting of ordinances"[1837] "to make the Gentiles obedient, by word and deed";[1838] but "he spake, and it was done; he commanded, and it stood fast."[1839]

5. Creation's law is clearly defined for us, for if all that wrought creation was a voice; for, quite simply, "he commanded, and they were created";[1840] then it is a fact that the Word's manner of righteousness

---

[1833] John 7:22
[1834] Ephesians 2:15
[1835] Mark 3:22
[1836] John 1:1
[1837] Colossians 2:14
[1838] Romans 15:18
[1839] Psalm 33:9
[1840] Psalm 48:5

is through an experimental faith on His voice. Creation took six days, instead of less than a second, because the elements of the world had to examine and do the commandment given to them, and without any help from outside of creation's commandment. If creation did not receive any help from outside of creation's law; and it did not; then it is that creation had to wait on creation's commandment to properly comprehend it; this is why we today are counseled, concerning the doctrine of the LORD's Spirit, "Wait for his law."[1841]

6. This "waiting" is evidently not a literal lethargic waiting, as being idle, but rather as one waits on a table, so the mind is to wait on creation's law. Creation, having only the Word as an intercessor between its spirit and the living God's Spirit, had to press its intelligence to soberly discern His Word's voice; this is why it says of His faithful, "In his law doth he meditate day and night."[1842]

7. Creation had to tax its mind to understand just what was expected of it, and after taking knowledge of the commandment, creation's consciousness experienced a new state of being, opening it up to form, from invisible matter stimulated by the vibration of a voice, a living and breathing realm for cultivating and sustaining life; this is why we are counseled, "Be ye transformed by the renewing of your mind, that ye may prove what is that good, and acceptable, and perfect, will of God."[1843] There is therefore an express correlation between that Word from creation and that Word of creation's present new covenant science, and this is apparent because this Word is that "God, who quickeneth the dead, and calleth those things which be not as though they were."[1844] Amen.

8. Creation is the only thing on the mind of the living God's Spirit, and if creation is not forwarded by an experimental faith on His voice, then whatever halts faith's exercise, to the Spirit's mind, is "sin" against

---

1841 Isaiah 42:4
1842 Psalm 1:2
1843 Romans 12:2
1844 Romans 4:17

creation. This helps us to remember that "whatsoever is not of faith is sin,"[1845] "and the law is not of faith."[1846]

9. The religious law is not of faith because it does not take faith to exercise faith on what the flesh, or on what the body of our faith, can touch. The "God" of "sin" demands that "righteousness come by the law,"[1847] but, according to the God of creation; who is the Word of creation; "the righteousness of God without the law is manifested,"[1848] allowing us to know that the *righteousness* of that "God" or *wisdom* within the religious law is not that righteousness of the living God's Word.

10. And this is a fact of creation's law, for, if the Spirit's voice should impress the mind, that mind must have an eye only towards His voice, and not towards the influence of other voices telling it how to do what only an exercised faith can do. Do we tell our heart to beat? Can we consciously create bile? These things exist without our active consciousness, for our systems exercise faith on their order for their government. Our conversation's faith is the same; it needs to be unconsciously exercised to rightly bless and govern the conversation.

11. How do we exercise faith unconsciously? As the heart exercises faith on its various systems to keep beating, so our faith needs material to exercise if it should live freely to the Spirit's voice. A conscious *exercising* of faith is relying on religious laws and doctrines to feed our faith, in the same sense that the body, when ready to die, needs life-support to stay alive. Such a manner of living is artificial, temporarily keeping the *body* of our faith breathing when, in reality, there is no real life flowing through it.

12. Creation's law preaches killing the *body* of faith for the organs of our faith and mind to develop original and personal strength, and "wisdom strengtheneth."[1849] As the human body needs good blood to keep its physical and mental government in good shape, so the *body* of

---

1845 Romans 14:23
1846 Galatians 3:12
1847 Galatians 2:21
1848 Romans 3:21
1849 Ecclesiastes 7:19

our spiritual understanding needs the wisdom of the living God's Spirit flowing through it, which is why our conversation's conscience is "to be strengthened with might by his Spirit in the inner man."[1850]

13. Therefore, to be filled with the Spirit is according to the saying, "I will pour out my spirit unto you, I will make known my words unto you,"[1851] and, "I have filled him with the spirit of God, in wisdom, and in understanding, and in knowledge."[1852] The Word's wisdom and knowledge is to rest within the inwards of our conversation's character, and this is the beginning of creation's present science, which is not without "the washing of water by the word."[1853]

14. Again, whatever interferes with the conversation's mind soberly and wholeheartedly retaining the Spirit's wisdom within its inward parts is "sin," for then the Spirit's will is disturbed, which will is to "purge your conscience from dead works to serve the living God."[1854] "Dead works" are of a manner of worship and service supported by the philosophy of the religious law, wherefore it is well to remember that "the sting of death is sin; and the strength of sin is the law."[1855]

15. The "death" spoken of is not literal, but is according to the saying, "He hath shut their eyes, that they cannot see; and their hearts, that they cannot understand."[1856] The religious law forwards "death's" conversation to "the eyes of your understanding,"[1857] for if all I must do is adhere to a handwritten commandment or doctrine for *righteousness*, then my eyes become centered on what halts faith for knowledge, distorting my perception of the living God's religious character. It is this religious distortion that is spoken of through the saying, "As by one man sin entered into the world, and death by sin,"[1858] "for until this day

---

1850 Ephesians 3:16
1851 Proverbs 1:23
1852 Exodus 31:3
1853 Ephesians 5:26
1854 Hebrews 9:14
1855 1 Corinthians 15:56
1856 Isaiah 44:18
1857 Ephesians 1:18
1858 Romans 5:12

remaineth the same vail untaken away in the reading of the old testament; which vail is done away in Christ."[1859]

16. Because this "vail" is in reference to the fact that "their minds were blinded,"[1860] we cannot take "Christ," as Paul here uses the term, as being a reference to a man. For this cause, in right context of language, "the Lord Jesus Christ our Saviour"[1861] is "the commandment of God our Saviour."[1862]

17. What defines to the mind "the transgressions that were under the first testament,"[1863] and the redemption to occur from those transgressions, is the Word's commandment living within the spirit of the mind, which is why we are counseled, "Live according to God in the spirit."[1864] While the wisdom of "sin" preaches a creed that "sanctifieth to the purifying of the flesh";[1865] that is, that *blesses* the conversation's outward appearance above the conversation's conscience; the Word's Faith preaches the creation of a perfect personal faith, and "perfect, as pertaining to the conscience."[1866] The issue at hand is the estate of our faith's mind and temper: if it will come under the rule of the spirit and philosophy of the serpent by "the law of commandments contained in ordinances,"[1867] or if it will embrace the liberty of the Spirit's will to learn that "we through the Spirit wait for the hope of righteousness by faith."[1868]

18. The spirit of religious error preaches that "you are justified by the law";[1869] that your conversation is sanctified by "the tradition of the elders"[1870] "according to the perfect manner of the law of the

---

1859 2 Corinthians 3:14
1860 2 Corinthians 3:14
1861 Titus 1:4
1862 Titus 1:3
1863 Hebrews 9:15
1864 1 Peter 4:6
1865 Hebrews 9:13
1866 Hebrews 9:9
1867 Ephesians 2:15
1868 Galatians 5:5
1869 Galatians 5:4
1870 Matthew 15:2

fathers";[1871] but this doctrine is contrary to the living God's spiritual understanding, whose ministry is ordained "to redeem them that were under the law."[1872] Herein we may understand why the Spirit's man would not give a sign, or work a religious law or commandment, of his *righteousness*, for he would be a hypocrite, seeing as how it is him that says, "Except your righteousness shall exceed the righteousness of the scribes and Pharisees, ye shall in no case enter into the kingdom of heaven."[1873]

19. The *righteousness* of the religious world is a conversation supported by the philosophy of the religious law, but the righteousness of the Spirit says, "Be not conformed to this world: but be ye transformed by the renewing of your mind, that ye may prove what is that good, and acceptable, and perfect, will of God."[1874] With the LORD's man annihilating, by his flesh on the tree, the conversation upholding the religious law, it is become an indisputable fact that "the strength of sin is the law."[1875]

20. Jewish priests and elders pressed this man to get him to speak falsely against his God, hoping to tempt him to utter a religious law that they could discern as being of their "God's" voice. But this man spoke no thing to these men, and has never, whether in that age or at this present time, spoken any thing to ministers of their spirit.

21. Another *Christ* is therefore demanded if a sign should be given from *heaven*. This other *Christ* is not that doctrine of creation, for his counsel is against creation, being an'tichrist. Isn't this what we are told? Isn't it written, "Every spirit that confesseth not that Jesus Christ is come in the flesh is not of God: and this is that spirit of an'tichrist, whereof ye have heard that it should come; and even now already is it in the world"?[1876]

1871 Acts 22:3
1872 Galatians 4:5
1873 Matthew 5:20
1874 Romans 12:2
1875 1 Corinthians 15:56
1876 1 John 4:3

22. Again, the "flesh" is figurative language denoting the *body* of faith, the conversation of the personal religion; "the Lord Jesus Christ our Saviour"[1877] is a term denoting "the commandment of God our Saviour."[1878] To possess a spirit confessing that "Jesus Christ" is come in to the flesh is to possess a mind confessing that the Spirit's commandment lives within the conversation's conscience. The spirit and philosophy of the religious world is against this confession because its "God" or wisdom is against this understanding. One who is "an'tichrist" is a mind refusing to bring creation's law in to its conversation's inwards to experience creation's higher education for creation's science. Such a mind is against "Christ," or is stout against the Word's law of regeneration, seeing as how "the carnal mind is enmity against God: for it is not subject to the law of God, neither indeed can be."[1879]

23. Such a mind is against creation's commandment because its "God" is "the enmity, even the law of commandments contained in ordinances,"[1880] therefore it cannot think straight, even as it says, "The flesh lusteth against the Spirit, and the Spirit against the flesh: and these are contrary the one to the other: so that ye cannot do the things that ye would. But if ye be led of the Spirit, ye are not under the law."[1881] It is therefore evident that any *Christ* preaching, "You are justified by the law,"[1882] is a spirit absolutely contrary to the Faith of the living God's man, which doctrine "hath redeemed us from the curse of the law."[1883]

24. If the living God's chief ambassador had consented to decree any religious law from his mouth, he would have violated his mission to heap honor on the Word's law and judgment of creation, even as it says of him, "He will magnify the law, and make it honourable."[1884] Such a law speaks against the use of religious laws and traditions for any thing, going so far as to report, by the passing, regenerating, and

---

1877   Titus 1:4
1878   Titus 1:3
1879   Romans 8:7
1880   Ephesians 2:25
1881   Galatians 5:17,18
1882   Galatians 5:4
1883   Galatians 3:13
1884   Isaiah 42:21

high priestly consecration of its ambassador's conversation, that "the strength of sin is the law."[1885] Thus, when we hear a *Christ* ordaining a ceremony, a church manual, a baptism, or a *sabbath* for his own name, we may understand that this creed, while wearing the face of *heaven*; even as Esau wore Jacob's face but was not Jacob; is an'tichrist, and is a practice of the religious world "through philosophy and vain deceit, after the tradition of men."[1886]

25. Therefore if the living God's chief apostle would not submit to be tempted to utter a religious law in his own name, must we today think that the present doctrine of the living God's Faith would utter any thing against its Father? Isn't it written, "Thy will be done in earth, as it is in heaven"?[1887] Isn't it written of His man's conversation, "Who is gone into heaven, and is on the right hand of God"?[1888]

26. Blessed revelation! To hear, "He was parted from them, and carried up into heaven,"[1889] is to hear that "we have such an high priest, who is set on the right hand of the throne of the Majesty in the heavens,"[1890] whose office is in regulating the laws and judgments of that Majesty's throne, and not that of flesh. This is crucial to understand because, as a high priest, this man's spiritual understanding is bound to the voice of the living God's religious character, to be a mediator between the Spirit of its intercession and the spirit of *man*. Therefore, "when he saith all things are put under him, it is manifest that he is excepted, which did put all things under him,"[1891] meaning that this man's name is ordained to bring us to the Word of his counsel to learn the name of that counsel's LORD, to sincerely love that name, "and this is love, that we walk after his commandments."[1892]

27. Therefore, with this man possessing a spirit confessing "Jesus Christ" within his conversation, and being anointed as "a merciful and

---

1885 1 Corinthians 15:56
1886 Colossians 2:8
1887 Matthew 6:10
1888 1 Peter 3:22
1889 Luke 24:51
1890 Hebrews 8:1
1891 1 Corinthians 15:27
1892 2 John 1:6

faithful high priest in things pertaining to God,"[1893] we have confidence that what the Spirit has uttered concerning the religious law is indisputable fact, allowing us to understand that our conversation, through the offering of the LORD's man, is bound to his LORD's Faith and Ten Commandments. Herein is the reason why we are counseled, "Keep the commandments of God, and the faith of Jesus."[1894]

28. The Word is, and always will be, God, and to keep the commandments of God is to keep the commandments of the Word. Now, if "in the beginning was the Word, and the Word was with God, and the Word was God,"[1895] then there is no arguing the fact that this same Word of the heavenly Sanctuary is that same God who "blessed the seventh day, and sanctified it."[1896]

29. The Jews tempted the LORD's man to give them a sign or work of *righteousness* testifying to his service to their "God"; which "God" preaches religious dominion by "the handwriting of ordinances";[1897] but he would not. This Christ, understanding that "the strength of sin is the law,"[1898] would not commit religious error against creation's wisdom, saying, "There shall no sign be given unto this generation."[1899]

30. It is not the LORD's man speaking against any one of the living God's commandments, and especially that commandment of His seventh day. It is therefore well for us to know where, and in what spirit, our confidence rests.

1893 Hebrews 2:17
1894 Revelation 14:12
1895 John 1:1
1896 Genesis 2:3
1897 Colossians 2:14
1898 1 Corinthians 15:56
1899 Mark 8:12

23

That Reasonable Refreshing

1. Why did those women return to the tomb of the LORD's man? It says that they "bought sweet spices, that they might come and anoint him,"[1900] but why? Didn't one of these women already anoint him? Isn't it written, "In that she hath poured this ointment on my body, she did it for my burial"?[1901]

2. Are these women appearing the second time to anoint the Word's man for a burial? Isn't it again written, "Then took they the body of Jesus, and wound it in linen clothes with the spices, as the manner of the Jews is to bury"?[1902]

3. This man's body, before their arrival at the sepulcher, had already been anointed for death twice, so must we believe that these

---

1900 Mark 16:1
1901 Matthew 26:12
1902 John 19:40

women are appearing to again anoint for death? If they are here to anoint, for the third time, this body for death, then why are they coming with sweet spices?

4. What is sweet spice used for? It says, "He put the golden altar in the tent of the congregation before the vail: and he burnt sweet incense thereon,"[1903] and, "Oil for the light, spices for anointing oil, and for sweet incense."[1904] Herein we are made to understand that sweet spices are used by one in charge of the temple, and are used to anoint one in charge of the temple. These women are coming to anoint the LORD's *man* as the living God's Chief Priest, even as it says, "Moses took of the anointing oil, and of the blood which was upon the altar, and sprinkled it upon Aaron, and upon his garments...and sanctified Aaron, and his garments."[1905]

5. These women came to consecrate the LORD's man as that High Priest over their LORD's name and will, but why? How did they know to do such a thing?

6. What these women brought with them "in the end of the Sabbath, as it began to dawn toward the first day of the week,"[1906] is very specific. What they carried with them was no accident, but how did they know to bring what they brought? The answer is not hidden from us, for it says, "They returned, and prepared spices and ointments; and rested the Sabbath day according to the commandment."[1907]

7. Between the time when the Sabbath began and when it ended, these women received an incredible amount of knowledge and understanding on what the LORD's Spirit was preparing to accomplish through His man. The only reason they cared to return to the tomb; for there "came Mary Magdale'ne and the other Mary to see the sepulchre";[1908] was to observe the revelation they had received during the Sabbath. These women kept the Sabbath commandment according to

---

1903 Exodus 40:26,27
1904 Exodus 25:6
1905 Leviticus 8:30
1906 Matthew 28:1
1907 Luke 23:56
1908 Matthew 28:1

how it was given and intended, and through them, we may learn the intelligent consolation contained within that Sabbath of the seventh day, and why "God blessed the seventh day, and sanctified it."[1909]

8. These women are not Roman Christians; they are not Greek Jews; they are not American Christians; these women are Jews, and being of that natural religion, there is no other fact to these women than that "the seventh day is the Sabbath."[1910] This is crucial to understand because the "rest" kept and experienced by these women is that refreshing of the living God's seventh day; there is no other *sabbath* for this "rest" of the living God in existence. These women kept His Sabbath according to the commandment, allowing us to understand that the Sabbath is a very complex institution created by the LORD's Word at creation.

9. There is a commandment for the seventh day, and that commandment is to "rest," and this "rest" is as it says, "Precept must be upon precept, precept upon precept; line upon line, line upon line...To whom he said, This is the rest wherewith ye may cause the weary to rest."[1911] The "rest" of the Sabbath, according to Scripture, is a commandment to edify the mind of the conversation by "comparing spiritual things with spiritual."[1912] During the hours of the Sabbath, what matters is "not in the words which man's wisdom teacheth, but which the Holy Ghost teacheth,"[1913] because, concerning *heaven's* words, "they are spiritually discerned."[1914]

10. The Word's Sabbath is a full twenty-four hours of receiving, from taxing the mind on His words, "knowledge of his will in all wisdom and spiritual understanding."[1915] The Spirit's "rest" is "the spirit of wisdom and revelation in the knowledge of him."[1916] "Rest," in simple terms, means spiritual learning and correction by the direct

---

1909 Genesis 2:3
1910 Exodus 20:10
1911 Isaiah 28:10-12
1912 1 Corinthians 2:13
1913 1 Corinthians 2:13
1914 1 Corinthians 2:14
1915 Colossians 1:9
1916 Ephesians 1:17

impression of the LORD's new covenant counsel on the mind of the spiritual understanding, as it says, "Then had the churches rest...and were edified; and walking in the fear of the Lord, and in the comfort of the Holy Ghost, were multiplied."[1917]

11. He or she partaking of the Sabbath's "rest" and "refreshing" is not one lazily asleep all day; is not inactive both mentally and spiritually; but is one willingly setting aside common mental and religious distractions to honor the charge, "Seek ye out of the book of the LORD, and read."[1918] With common noise; both personal and devotional; removed from the person on the seventh day, allowing full attention to be given to the living God's Bible, an open channel will be presented to the conversation's conscience, allowing the heart to embrace free and unadulterated communion with His face, and with the face of His religious character.

12. To hear that these women "rested" on the Sabbath, and according to the commandment, is to hear that they did pass in to the refreshing of the seventh day to have their faith's intelligence strengthened by the wisdom of the living God's new covenant law. These women spent the Word's Sabbath diligently examining the events that transpired against His man with what Scripture had to say on the matter, for they had witnessed all things, but the prophecy concerning him was not yet complete.

13. These women left the site of that tomb and, returning home, were gathered together for the entire Sabbath, reviewing how it says, "Seventy weeks are determined upon thy people and upon thy holy city, to finish the transgression, and to make an end of sins, and to make reconciliation for iniquity, and to bring in everlasting righteousness, and to seal up the vision and prophecy, and to anoint the most Holy."[1919]

14. The seventy weeks begin "from the going forth of the commandment to restore and to build Jerusalem";[1920] from 457BC by the decreed given Ezra; and they end 34AD, when Stephen fell *asleep*. Sixty-nine of

---

1917 Acts 9:31
1918 Isaiah 34:16
1919 Daniel 9:24
1920 Daniel 9:25

the seventy weeks, beginning at 457BC, end 27AD, at the coronation of the ministry of the LORD's man by His Spirit, as it says, "From the going forth of the commandment to restore and to build Jerusalem unto the Messi'ah the Prince shall be seven weeks, and threescore and two weeks."[1921]

15. The LORD's man spent that last week; these are weeks of years; preaching *heaven's* new covenant commandment. He preached for three and a half years and then was then cut off from the *earth*, but that preaching, for another three and a half years, was continued by them that first heard it, even as it says, "Which at the first began to be spoken by the Lord, and was confirmed unto us by them that heard him."[1922] By the time it was fulfilled, "And he shall confirm the covenant with many for one week";[1923] which final week was that week after the sixty-ninth week, for the vision is of seventy weeks; the women that observed the doctrine of *heaven's* chief apostle had seen all things fulfilled except the anointing of that most Holy *one*.

16. The Sabbath after the crucifixion was an important Sabbath, for by their communion with *heaven's* throne, they learned that "transgression" and "sin" was finished and came to an end, understanding that, with this minister "having abolished in his flesh the enmity, even the law of commandments contained in ordinances,"[1924] "the strength of sin is the law."[1925] Thus, this man, being found on the tree, not only defined "sin" as the philosophy of the religious law, but made reconciliation for "sin" by "blotting out the handwriting of ordinances"[1926] for "the law of the Spirit of life."[1927]

17. By annihilating "sin's" spirit and philosophy from the Word's Faith, ever-lasting righteousness is become the end and intention of the Word's law and course of learning, which righteousness is not "of

---

1921 Daniel 9:25
1922 Hebrews 2:3
1923 Daniel 9:27
1924 Ephesians 2:15
1925 1 Corinthians 15:56
1926 Colossians 2:14
1927 Romans 8:2

the law, but that which is through the faith of Christ, the righteousness which is of God by faith."[1928]

18. The *righteousness* nailed to the tree is one where I dawn "mine own righteousness, which is of the law,"[1929] meaning that my religious conversation is become an outward show of *piety* "having a form of godliness, but denying the power thereof."[1930] The righteousness of the living God is contrary to a sensual or flesh-stimulating craft, seeing as how "God is a Spirit."[1931] Because "a spirit hath not flesh and bones,"[1932] the Spirit's righteousness is above a conversation that is pleasant to the eyes, for the aim is to create a new and more benevolent conversation, even one that is "perfect, as pertaining to the conscience."[1933]

19. Paul's language is very important. He doesn't say, "That which is through faith on Christ," or, "That which is through Christ," but he says, "That which is through the faith of Christ."[1934] Heaven's righteousness is through the spiritual understanding OF the LORD's man, meaning that in order to experience that righteousness, knowledge of His man's doctrine is an inarguable prerequisite.

20. Learn the knowledge of this man's Faith, to do it, and the promise will be fulfilled, "If the Spirit of him that raised up Jesus from the dead dwell in you, he that raised up Christ from the dead shall also quicken your mortal bodies by his Spirit."[1935]

21. As these women studied Scripture, they began to understand that a major change in personal manners of worship and service had begun, for they learned that the former spirit had "stood only in meats and drinks, and divers washings, and carnal ordinances, imposed on them until the time of reformation."[1936] The time of reform had commenced with the passing of the LORD's man on the tree, for by

---

1928 Philippians 3:9
1929 Philippians 3:9
1930 2 Timothy 3:5
1931 John 4:24
1932 Luke 24:39
1933 Hebrews 9:9
1934 Philippians 3:9
1935 Romans 8:11
1936 Hebrews 9:9

cursing religious "philosophy and vain deceit, after the tradition of men,"[1937] the Spirit's sacrifice eternally blessed faith's higher education, counseling every one joined to its learning, "Keep the commandments of God, and the faith of Jesus."[1938]

22. A new spiritual age had dawned, and with the passing of the former religious age, questions concerning the new arose. If "sin" has been defined, abolished, and purged from the living God's religious character, this means that the conversation is still naturally wrong in its devotion to His Faith. The prophecy concerning His man speaks no thing of removing "sin" from the natural estate of the conversation, but only from the Word's will, name, and course of learning, thereby personally affecting the doer of that will. This means that, if the Word's Faith is liberated from the serpent's spirit and persuasion, then a greater Sanctuary with a greater priesthood, and fastened by a greater covenant, rules this great time of reformation.

23. With the salvation's chief minister "having abolished in his flesh the enmity, even the law of commandments contained in ordinances,"[1939] it is that with "the priesthood being changed, there is made of necessity a change also of the law,"[1940] for the will of *heaven* is now become a living intention "made, not after the law of a carnal commandment, but after the power of an endless life."[1941] With the earthy mission of the LORD's man finished, "sin" is become highlighted to help the person comprehend that "divine nature, having escaped the corruption that is in the world through lust,"[1942] and seeing as how the purging or pardoning of "sin" against the living God did not occur without a priesthood, it is that these women learned the office that the LORD's spiritual wisdom should pick up after its resurrection, which is why they came to the sepulcher with the same spices used to anoint Aaron.

1937 Colossians 2:8
1938 Revelation 14:12
1939 Ephesians 2:15
1940 Hebrews 7:12
1941 Hebrews 7:16
1942 2 Peter 1:4

24. But although they learned much during the Sabbath, their appearing with instruments for anointing reveals that they did not know the manner in which this consecration was to occur. It was not their assignment to bless this man, but rather the Spirit of his LORD and Father personally performs this consecration, even as it says, "I will declare the decree: the LORD hath said unto me, Thou art my Son; this day have I begotten thee,"[1943] and, "No man taketh this honour unto himself, but he that is called of God, as was Aaron. So also Christ glorified not himself to be made an high priest; but he that said unto him, Thou art my Son, to day have I begotten thee."[1944]

25. It was "God the Father, who raised him from the dead,"[1945] therefore it cannot be flesh that anoints *him* for any priestly consecration. If this man were around for the coronation of these women, the ministry of the LORD's man would be one that is carnal, resembling the very course blotted out by his passing flesh on the tree. If this man were anointed of these women, this man would be a high priest over a sensual conversation by the philosophy of the religious law and doctrine, fully admitting that it is a lie to believe that "Christ hath redeemed us from the curse of the law."[1946] But it is important to understand that, not only was this man not there for their anointing, but that when *he* saw them, he said, "Touch me not."[1947]

26. This man's mind of devotion had a ceremony to attend, and if his mediation is today for a "circumcision made without hands,"[1948] then his office must exist "by a greater and more perfect tabernacle, not made with hands."[1949] This man's resurrected conversation is that "merciful and faithful high priest in things pertaining to God, to make reconciliation for the sins of the people,"[1950] therefore being brought up by his LORD's Spirit in to His heavenly Sanctuary; as it says, "Who

---

1943 Psalm 2:7
1944 Hebrews 5:4,5
1945 Galatians 1:1
1946 Galatians 3:13
1947 John 20:27
1948 Colossians 2:11
1949 Hebrews 9:11
1950 Hebrews 2:17

is gone into heaven, and is on the right hand of God";[1951] it is that flesh cannot bless this ministry, but only the hand of the One that resurrected it to His self.

27. If anointed of flesh, this man would not have it said of his office, "Angels and authorities and powers being made subject unto him."[1952] Thus, although comprehending his priestly appointment, these women did not understand that "Christ is not entered into the holy places made with hands, which are the figures of the true; but into heaven itself, now to appear in the presence of God for us."[1953] They were right in their findings; the LORD's man should be anointed as that Chief Governor over the living God's heavenly Temple and assembly; but they didn't know that this office and Temple is not fleshy, and that his "name" should be "a minister of the sanctuary, and of the true tabernacle, which the Lord pitched, and not man."[1954]

28. And their knowledge would not be left to disappoint them, for when they didn't see him, to perform for him what Moses did for Aaron, they were perplexed. But after he opened "their understanding, that they might understand the scriptures,"[1955] "he was parted from them, and carried up into heaven."[1956] Hereafter the first apostles would learn that "we have such an high priest, who is set on the right hand of the throne of the Majesty in the heavens,"[1957] and it all began with these women that had first "seen a vision of angels, which said that he was alive."[1958]

29. This great revelation would not have been imparted to these women if they had not "rested" on the Sabbath according to the commandment. Because they remained within the Spirit's edification on the seventh day, being taught of His wisdom by diligently examining Scripture, it would have never been understood what the rising from

---

1951 1 Peter 3:22
1952 1 Peter 3:22
1953 Hebrews 9:24
1954 Hebrews 8:2
1955 Luke 24:45
1956 Luke 24:51
1957 Hebrews 8:1
1958 Luke 24:23

the dead should mean, and what ministry, and new covenant, should find itself ratified by that High Priest brought up and anointed by the LORD's Spirit.

30. The record of these things is left for our example to shed light on the importance of the living God's Sabbath, and on why "God blessed the seventh day, and sanctified it."[1959] If these women had failed to honor the Sabbath's "rest," we today would not have any knowledge that the LORD's man has fulfilled the saying, "He shall stand and feed in the strength of the LORD, in the majesty of the name of the LORD his God."[1960] This is that conversation who, because it is not anointed of *men*, is a High Priest over the LORD God's religion, making it, due to the service of its offering, our assignment to "fear God, and keep his commandments."[1961]

31. The key word in the previously mentioned verse is "HIS," when hearing about *heaven's* commandments. With His man perpetually annihilating the philosophy of the religious law from the living God's spiritual understanding, it is that our conversation is to be "written not with ink, but with the Spirit of the living God."[1962] With this man's course of learning presently consecrated as creation's Chief Priest, every commandment of the living God's Spirit is become a binding joy and responsibility to the one joined to His mediation's hope and service, allowing us to understand that "we do know that we know him, if we keep his commandments."[1963]

32. It is therefore a privilege to reverence the living God's Sabbath, and through these women we clearly discern the reason why He made it for His church. The hours of this day are for adding consciousness to the eyes of our understanding, and we should never miss this great appointment of His wisdom's benevolence if we care to increase our faith in the living God's will and wisdom.

1959 Genesis 2:3
1960 Micah 5:4
1961 Ecclesiastes 12:13
1962 2 Corinthians 3:3
1963 1 John 2:3

24

Creation's Body

1. What is it that the LORD's man sacrificed on the tree? Isn't it written, "Thou that destroyest the temple, and buildest it in three days, save thyself"?[1964]

2. Although observing a man on the tree, it is evident that, above the man, a key part of that man was put to a perpetual slumber. When speaking on this act of destroying and rebuilding, "he spake of the temple of his body,"[1965] allowing us to understand that what suffered annihilation by the tree was not ultimately a man bound to the tree, but rather the temple of this man's *body*. It is this temple, and all belonging to it, that suffered a "death," and concerning this "temple," the LORD's man says, "I was shapen in iniquity; and in sin did my mother conceive me."[1966]

1964 Mark 15:29,30
1965 John 2:21
1966 Psalm 51:5

3. This temple formed in "sin" rested within the body of the LORD's man as that "body of the sins of the flesh."[1967] Two worlds were constrained to one personal religious conversation within this man, but with him "having abolished in his flesh the enmity, even the law of commandments contained in ordinances,"[1968] only one mind exists within his conversation, and it is that spirit confessing, "Keep the commandments of God, and the faith of Jesus."[1969]

4. That temple destroyed was that foundation strengthened by "sin" against the Word's Faith, "and the strength of sin is the law."[1970] To therefore hear of this man's resurrection, it is to hear of a temple restructured under a new spiritual rule, which rule is a conversation exercising faith on the Word's voice for knowledge of its benevolence.

5. Again, if "he spake of the temple of his body,"[1971] then the LORD's man accomplished "blotting out the handwriting of ordinances"[1972] by suffering the tree. His original religious nature was "sin's" spiritual philosophy, and with this sacrifice proving that "the strength of sin is the law,"[1973] it is become evident that "whatsoever is not of faith is sin,"[1974] and that "the law is not of faith."[1975]

6. Paul therefore correctly pronounces this man's original form by saying, "And was made in the likeness of men: and being found in fashion as a man,"[1976] for he was "made under the law."[1977] To be found in fashion as a "man" is to be found dawning the "body" of men, which "body" is not that literal human form, but rather the *body* of the religious conversation's confidence.

1967 Colossians 2:11
1968 Ephesians 2:15
1969 Revelation 14:12
1970 1 Corinthians 15:56
1971 John 2:21
1972 Colossians 2:14
1973 1 Corinthians 15:56
1974 Romans 14:23
1975 Galatians 3:12
1976 Philippians 2:7,8
1977 Galatians 4:4

7. This "body" is a temple made under the rule of "the tradition of the elders,"[1978] and is a persuasion fulfilling the saying, "Full well ye reject the commandment of God, that ye may keep your own tradition."[1979] The fashion of men; or rather the form of priests and ministers; is a religious conversation maintained by handwritten religious laws and doctrines, which is why the LORD's man tells us that his conception was in "sin," for "the strength of sin is the law."[1980] He knew only devotion by the religious bill, but he spoke a mystery to the people, preaching the destruction of his natural form for its perfect regeneration, and "perfect, as pertaining to the conscience."[1981]

8. This is why the Word's man taught, "That which is born of the flesh is flesh; and that which is born of the Spirit is spirit."[1982] The "flesh" mentioned is the "body" spoken of, which "body" is, again, the conversation of the personal religion. A clear change since his youth, by him saying this, has occurred in his spiritual understanding, for, although conceived in "sin"; in devotion to a conversation by the pen of flesh; a new understanding is spoken of, in that a more beneficial baptism for the spirit of the mind is the means whereby newness and resurrection is to remove the "body" from *earth* in to the heavenly Sanctuary, as it says, "They have escaped the pollutions of the world through the knowledge of the Lord and Saviour Jesus Christ."[1983]

9. As opposed to a conversation bound to the law and tradition of priests and elders, the LORD's man preached the living God's new covenant will, that it is His intention to "purge your conscience from dead works to serve the living God."[1984] This allows us to understand that to the natural conversation, that practice of the flesh is its reward, but to the creation of the living God's religious character, that course of His mind is their delight, which is why they confess resurrection from

---

1978 Matthew 15:2
1979 Mark 7:9
1980 1 Corinthians 15:56
1981 Hebrews 9:9
1982 John 3:6
1983 2 Peter 2:20
1984 Hebrews 9:14

the estate of the religious world by saying, "The law of the Spirit of life in Christ Jesus hath made me free from the law of sin and death."[1985]

10. Liberty from the religious law is the aim of *heaven's* Faith for knowledge of heaven's kindness, to forever experience that kindness. The LORD's man proved and executed this knowledge, saying, for our comfort and consolation, "I know him, and keep his saying,"[1986] thus, by his sacrifice, fulfilling the saying, "By his knowledge shall my righteous servant justify many."[1987]

11. This revelation opens us up to question, "Just what was exactly sacrificed?"

12. It is evident that if "he spake of the temple of his body,"[1988] that the literal flesh and blood of the man is of no true value to the living God's plain spiritual intention. This man, holding within himself two religious forms or natures, when passed away on the tree, condemned one form to utter condemnation while magnifying the other as a perpetual law and covenant.

13. If the temple of this man's body is become accursed; for it says, "He that is hanged is accursed of God";[1989] then his naturally "sinful" religious mind was exchanged for that spirit regenerated by creation's knowledge and saying, which is why He said, "Father, into thy hands I commend my spirit."[1990] This sacrificed temple had a ghost, but by giving up that temple's ghost to death, and by securing that spirit edified by the Spirit to his LORD and Father's hands, it is that this spirit baptized of the Spirit should retake that temple of his "body," thereby sharing with every spirit the same "death" and "resurrection" by this one act unto the same LORD and Father.

14. Just as the first Adam, by one sacrifice, bound the conversation of every minister to "sin's" spirit and philosophy, so by the last Adam an offering is given whereby the spirit of the mind may be trained to

---

1985 Romans 8:2
1986 John 8:55
1987 Isaiah 53:11
1988 John 2:21
1989 Deuteronomy 21:23
1990 Luke 23:46

put that routine of the first Adam to sleep. "Whatsoever God doeth, it shall be for ever,"[1991] therefore it is an everlasting fact that "he that is hanged is accursed of God,"[1992] that His "Christ hath redeemed us from the curse of the law,"[1993] and "that we might be justified by the faith of Christ, and not by the works of the law."[1994]

15. What is accursed of the Word is no man, but the religious ideology represented by the flesh of the man, which philosophy is a conversation supported by "sin," "and the strength of sin is the law."[1995] That "temple" accursed by the tree is a philosophy preaching that "righteousness come by the law,"[1996] condemning that persuasion nailed to the tree as "sin" to *heaven's* new covenant charge. But a wonderful mystery occurred after the condemnation of this man's flesh. A new temple was not only found separated from the tree, but it was taken by the Spirit into the heavenly Sanctuary and blessed to be shared with whoever should incline their heart to know the living God by it. Today, that conversation nailed to the tree is not that conversation of *heaven*, but that course of learning educating the conversation's conscience on the living God's name and praise is the intention of creation's present science.

16. We are therefore confronted with a question that we need to personally ask our self: "Is the likeness of my conversation after that temple conceived in "sin," or is it in likeness to that conversation "who is holy, harmless, undefiled, separate from sinners, and made higher than the heavens"?[1997]

17. "Having abolished in his flesh the enmity, even the law of commandments contained in ordinances,"[1998] the saying is fulfilled, "I will put enmity between thee and the woman."[1999] With the religious

---

1991 Ecclesiastes 3:14
1992 Deuteronomy 21:23
1993 Galatians 3:13
1994 Galatians 2:16
1995 1 Corinthians 15:56
1996 Galatians 2:21
1997 Hebrews 7:26
1998 Ephesians 2:15
1999 Genesis 3:15

law today separated from the Word's Faith, we understand a "sinful" religious conversation by its friendship with enmity, and if in bond to enmity, then the conversation is subject to "philosophy and vain deceit, after the tradition of men, after the rudiments of the world."[2000]

18. The religious world adheres to that spirit nailed to the tree, which spirit preaches, "You are justified by the law,"[2001] when it is ultimately written, "By his knowledge shall my righteous servant justify many."[2002] We therefore understand that our conversation is formed after that perverse conversation nailed to the tree by our open consent to religious laws and commandments contrary to the Spirit's words, seeing as how "we do know that we know him, if we keep his commandments."[2003]

19. That religious nature nailed to the tree is a mind devoutly against the LORD God's voice, claiming *righteousness* by obedience to the pen of flesh above the counsel, "Worship God in the spirit."[2004] But in order to bless creation's saying in the spirit of the mind, it is that the mind needs knowledge to examine and do, which is why we are counseled, "Worship him that made heaven, and earth, and the sea, and the fountains of waters."[2005]

20. In such a commandment is revealed the name and praise of the living God, for He who created is the Word of this wisdom, as it says, "In the beginning was the Word, and the Word was with God, and the Word was God."[2006] Although the temple of His man's "body" was destroyed and rebuilt, we cannot forget that, when firstly a natural minister, within that temple dwelt the same Word of creation's LORD and Spirit, for "the Word was made flesh."[2007]

2000 Colossians 2:8
2001 Galatians 5:4
2002 Isaiah 53:11
2003 1 John 2:3
2004 Philippians 3:3
2005 Revelation 14:7
2006 John 1:1
2007 John 1:14

21. Because "the Spirit of life"[2008] is "the Word of life,"[2009] and because "that which is born of the Spirit is spirit,"[2010] it is that the knowledge of the Spirit dwelt within the mind of this man's conversation. By abolishing, through his passing flesh on the tree, that naturally erroneous religious mind from his conversation, what is become elevated is that Faith and course of learning by the Word of creation, which conversation, since blessed of the living God's mind, is not without that same seventh-day Sabbath blessed by the same Word.

22. With righteousness entirely by an experimental faith on the living God's new covenant saying, creation is become *heaven's* assignment, and if the Word, in the beginning, blessed the seventh day, then whosoever is today created by this same wisdom will understand why and how "the seventh day is the Sabbath."[2011] Again, "whatsoever God doeth, it shall be for ever: nothing can be put to it, nor any thing taken from it,"[2012] and if it says, "He that is hanged is accursed of God,"[2013] then that "old" temple and philosophy is for ever accursed of the Word.

23. This means that the saying, "Righteousness come by the law,"[2014] is, by the act of the LORD's man suffering the tree, religious error, making it true that "the strength of sin is the law."[2015] Our adherence to religious laws crafted after the tradition and judgment of priests and elders makes our profession false before creation's new covenant commandment, for we violate the indisputable fact that "Christ hath redeemed us from the curse of the law."[2016] For this cause, we may plainly recognize the sign of our conversation drowning in "sin" when discerning that our confidence is strengthened by "the enmity, even the law of commandments contained in ordinances."[2017]

2008 Revelation 11:11
2009 1 John 1:1
2010 John 3:6
2011 Exodus 20:10
2012 Ecclesiastes 3:14
2013 Deuteronomy 21:23
2014 Galatians 2:21
2015 1 Corinthians 15:56
2016 Galatians 3:13
2017 Ephesians 2:15

24. All such religious laws and commandments by the pen of flesh are therefore according to that spirit nailed to the tree, for the tree is become a symbol of utter division from the living God's Word, making the conversation a routine without creation's Faith, and if so, without the sign of our fellowship in that learning. Every conversation involved with redemption's higher education will accordingly know "the sign of circumcision, a seal of the righteousness of the faith,"[2018] even as it says, "Thou hast given a banner to them that fear thee, that it may be displayed because of the truth."[2019]

25. Because the Spirit's Faith counsels its student to "worship him that made heaven, and earth, and the sea, and the fountains of waters,"[2020] knowledge of the Creator's authority over regeneration allows the doer of creation's law to hear how it written, "In six days the LORD made heaven and earth, the sea, and all that in them is, and rested the seventh day: wherefore the LORD blessed the Sabbath day, and hallowed it."[2021]

26. Because of His man's offering, the commandment of the seventh day is become that brilliant link to heaven's new covenant will, shedding light on the other nine commandments of creation. Creation's Sabbath is set; creation's Sabbath is immutable; and with it understood that "the strength of sin is the law,"[2022] any religious law contradicting any one of the Word's Ten Commandments is become religious "sin," and our consent to that contradiction making our conversation "sinful."

2018 Romans 4:11
2019 Psalm 60:4
2020 Revelation 14:7
2021 Exodus 20:11
2022 1 Corinthians 15:56

25

An Abolished Ghost

1. There is a direct connection between how it says, "And Jesus cried with a loud voice, and gave up the ghost. And the veil of the temple was rent in twain from the top to the bottom,"[2023] and, "The spirit cried, and rent him sore, and came out of him: and he was as one dead; insomuch that many said, He is dead."[2024]

2. This spirit that cried and rent this young man is equivalent to that ghost coming out of the LORD's man, which exit caused a rent to occur within that temple being destroyed. When the Word's man cried out, that *ghost* coming up out of that "temple" rent him sore, so much so that "Pilate marvelled if he were already dead."[2025] Seeing as how, concerning this destruction and resurrection, "he spake of the

---

2023 Mark 15:37,38
2024 Mark 9:36
2025 Mark 15:44

temple of his body,"[2026] it is evident that, when observing the events surrounding the last act of His man, this scene embraces a higher spiritual understanding.

3. The ghost this man gave up was that natural spirit of his religious conversation, or that veil shrouding creation's new covenant commandment, as it says, "Before faith came, we were kept under the law, shut up unto the faith which should afterwards be revealed."[2027] That "ghost" of this man's personal temple of faith was "the law of commandments contained in ordinances,"[2028] and to hear, "Jesus cried with a loud voice, and gave up the ghost,"[2029] is to hear that the spirit of religious error departed from the heart of a religious conversation, causing a rent within that conversation to establish a new mind of devotion.

4. The "veil" is language referencing the religion of the tabernacle, for it says, "The vail that is by the ark of the testimony, before the mercy seat that is over the testimony."[2030] The "veil" represents the religious standard and philosophy of "the Jews' religion,"[2031] which practice is "according to the perfect manner of the law of the fathers."[2032] This "veil" of religious laws "after the commandments and doctrines of men"[2033] covered the face of the doctrine of the living God's man, but with this man abolishing the ghost of the religious law from the living God's spiritual understanding, it is that the will and doctrine of that commandment is without "the handwriting of ordinances."[2034]

5. The "veil" that is rent is therefore according to the saying, "The veil, that is to say, his flesh,"[2035] for what suffered crucifixion was that "body of the sins of the flesh,"[2036] which is why, "having abolished in his flesh the enmity, even the law of commandments contained in ordi-

---

2026 John 2:21
2027 Galatians 3:23
2028 Ephesians 2:15
2029 Mark 15:37
2030 Exodus 30:6
2031 Galatians 1:13
2032 Acts 22:3
2033 Colossians 2:22
2034 Colossians 2:14
2035 Hebrews 10:20
2036 Colossians 2:11

nances,"[2037] it is become an indisputable fact that "the strength of sin is the law."[2038] Like as it says, "The spirit cried, and rent him sore, and came out of him,"[2039] it is that as "Jesus" cried, the mind within the temple of his "body" came out of that *body*, allowing us to understand that, because a certain mind of devotion quit his *body*, "Jesus" is a term or name used to denote that mind formed by the living God's spiritual wisdom within the mind of His man.

6. It is herein well to understand that "though we have known Christ after the flesh, yet now henceforth know we him no more,"[2040] for according to the language and context of Scripture, "the Lord Jesus Christ our Saviour"[2041] is, in reality, "the commandment of God our Saviour."[2042]

7. If "before faith came, we were kept under the law, shut up unto the faith which should afterwards be revealed,"[2043] when that Faith is fully revealed, it is that the religious law is become shut up unto perpetual darkness by the exercising of faith on that revealed spiritual confidence. "Jesus" crying out is the Spirit's commandment crying out, for over the face of this commandment, like as "Moses, which put a vail over his face, that the children of Israel could not stedfastly look to the end of that which is abolished,"[2044] so the Word's Faith had a veil over its face, and when that commandment cried out, that veil was finally destroyed, exposing the face of creation's science and abolishing that philosophy to be rent, to the end no one should steadfastly look to what is become abolished, even to "the law of commandments contained in ordinances."[2045]

2037 Ephesians 2:15
2038 1 Corinthians 15:56
2039 Mark 9:26
2040 2 Corinthians 5:16
2041 Titus 1:4
2042 Titus 1:3
2043 Galatians 3:23
2044 2 Corinthians 3:13
2045 Ephesians 2:15

8. The "flesh" of the LORD's man is what suffered crucifixion, and concerning how the "flesh" is defined, we read, "My heart and my flesh crieth,"[2046] and, "My flesh and my heart faileth."[2047]

9. Being formed in the fashion of *men* and having the Word within the heart of his conversation, it is that the LORD's man carried within his faith's *body* two minds conflicting with on another. This man's *body* had within it the spirit of righteousness and the spirit of unrighteousness, and if "all unrighteousness is sin,"[2048] and if "the strength of sin is the law,"[2049] then all righteousness is a conversation strictly based upon an experimental faith without the philosophy of the religious law.

10. Within one conversation sat the knowledge of good and evil with the wisdom of righteousness and creation, but at the time appointed, it would be that one mind would suffer utter condemnation while the other perpetual blessing. If it is that "before faith came, we were kept under the law, shut up unto the faith which should afterwards be revealed,"[2050] then it is that what must come under condemnation is what speaks against faith's exercise, and since "whatsoever is not of faith is sin,"[2051] it is that "the law is not of faith."[2052]

11. It is therefore evident that the illustration of the LORD's man suffering the tree preaches the exchanging of one religious conversation for another, for ever cursing that spirit and philosophy preaching that "righteousness come by the law,"[2053] and exalting that rule preaching, "Through the Spirit wait for the hope of righteousness by faith."[2054] Paul is therefore correct to say that, in reference to our approaching the living God's will, that it is "by a new and living way, which he hath consecrated for us, through the veil, that is to say, his flesh."[2055]

2046 Psalm 84:2
2047 Psalm 73:26
2048 1 John 5:17
2049 1 Corinthians 15:56
2050 Galatians 3:23
2051 Romans 14:23
2052 Galatians 3:12
2053 Galatians 2:21
2054 Galatians 5:5
2055 Hebrews 10:20

12. With the "flesh," or the religious conversation of His man broken, it is that the new covenant's conversation is born, and this is what meant by the saying, "Take, eat: this is my body, which is broken for you."[2056] That broken *body* is that sacrificed "flesh," which "flesh" is that conversation fashioned after the likeness of priests and elders, which religious form is according to the saying, "Full well ye reject the commandment of God, that ye may keep your own tradition."[2057] A conversation ruled by "the law of commandments contained in ordinances"[2058] is the "nature" or fashion of *men*, and with this man dawning the fashion of men and breaking the *body* of that fashion, what is preached is "the time of reformation,"[2059] in that the religious conversation is to be "written not with ink, but with the Spirit of the living God."[2060]

13. This man, being born as *men*; that is, being "made under the law";[2061] sacrificed that natural conversation to an eternal *burning* by willingly nailing that natural conversation to the tree, and in so doing, opened up to the conscience of every conversation the opportunity to receive that new nature he himself experienced when in that *body* when it was not yet broken, which is why it is important that he says, "Father, into thy hands I commend my spirit."[2062] Before passing, this man secured the spirit of his mind in to the hands of the living God's spiritual understanding, and after passing, that original ghost of his *body* expired in to nothingness, leaving that spirit preserved by the Word as that new governor over his conversation, rebuilding that *body's* temple "by the law of faith."[2063]

14. Thus, when hearing that "Jesus" cried and gave up the ghost, it is that we are hearing of the spirit or mind of this man's conversation giving up that veil over its face, for he "took it out of the way, nailing it

---

2056 1 Corinthians 11:24
2057 Mark 7:9
2058 Ephesians 2:15
2059 Hebrews 9:10
2060 2 Corinthians 3:3
2061 Galatians 4:4
2062 Luke 23:46
2063 Romans 3:27

to his cross."[2064] To pick up that rent veil is to therefore transgress the doctrine and revelation of creation's new covenant science, that this "Christ hath redeemed us from the curse of the law, being made a curse for us: for it is written, Cursed is every one that hangeth on a tree."[2065]

15. What is on the tree is not to be regarded as a man, but, according to the Bible's speech, is s religious spirit and philosophy. The illustration of this man's flesh on the tree is the complete condemnation of the fashion of men, and the illustration of this man's flesh, being passed away on the tree, is the giving up of that ghost distorting the face of that conversation formed by creation's new covenant commandment within his faith's body.

16. To hear that "Jesus cried with a loud voice, and gave up the ghost,"[2066] is to observe a record stating the liberty of the Spirit's will and commandment from the religious law of any and every *Moses* "not only in this world, but also in that which is to come."[2067] That former "body" is broken; it is "as water spilt on the ground, which cannot be gathered up again";[2068] wherefore to pick up that which is abolished is to violate the present charge of the heavenly Sanctuary, "for if I build again the things which I destroyed, I make myself a transgressor."[2069]

17. If the LORD's man destroyed the rule of the religious law from the Bible's spiritual understanding, by our dressing our conversation with the religious law, are we become doers of His doctrine's present will and commandment? What is preached through the LORD's man is our conversation's resurrection from a mind subject to the pen of flesh, which is why every faithful spirit of creation's higher education states, "The law of the Spirit of life in Christ Jesus hath made me free from the law of sin and death."[2070]

18. This statement of faith is that statement of the Faith uttered by the LORD's man on the tree, wherefore we understand that this

---

2064 Colossians 2:14
2065 Galatians 3:13
2066 Mark 16:37
2067 Ephesians 1:21
2068 2 Samuel 14:14
2069 Galatians 2:18
2070 Romans 8:2

is not our declaration if honoring a *Christ* preaching that it is well to believe that "righteousness come by the law."[2071] This is today a plain lie to preach, and it is evident religious delusion to accept *righteousness* by a religious law and doctrine, for this spirit conflicts with that spirit teaching that "Christ hath redeemed us from the curse of the law."[2072]

19. The LORD's man still possesses a ministry ordained "to redeem them that were under the law,"[2073] and if our confidence is in a *Christ* preaching that "you are justified by the law,"[2074] it is evident that our conversation is come under the possession of an unclean disposition, "for if righteousness come by the law, then Christ is dead in vain."[2075] Thus, it is well to analyze and question our own conversation, for if it holds dear to handwritten religious laws without plain and unforced scriptural citation, it is that "your faith is vain; ye are yet in your sins."[2076]

20. To pick up what the LORD's man abolished by his passing is to, in essence, confess that, not only did this man not pass away on the tree, but also that no minister fulfilling the prophecy of the LORD's man has ever existed, or is yet to appear. This means that every delineation given by the first apostles concerning the LORD's chief prophet is fraudulent, and that the LORD's man is just another *Christ*, therefore "if Christ be not raised, your faith is vain; ye are yet in your sins."[2077]

21. With the LORD's man neither passed away or risen, the dynamic of the Word's Faith changes, for the spiritual speech of His man is become vanity, turning the doctrine of His face upside down and inside out. Thus, with our conversation entertaining the lore of such "philosophy and vain deceit, after the tradition of men,"[2078] it is that our conversation, being without that risen knowledge of His Spirit's will and wisdom, will remain in and forward "sin," "and the strength

---

2071 Galatians 2:21
2072 Galatians 3:13
2073 Galatians 4:5
2074 Galatians 5:4
2075 Galatians 2:21
2076 1 Corinthians 15:17
2077 1 Corinthians 15:17
2078 Colossians 2:8

of sin is the law."[2079] A *sabbath*, and ceremonies, and doctrines, and traditions, and baptisms, and degrees, are now become a credible revelation of *favor* and *righteousness*, for "in works they deny him, being abominable, and disobedient, and unto every good work reprobate."[2080]

22. Blatant atheism is herein understood to be through acts contradicting the plain revelation of the living God's doctrine. If the Spirit's man is sent "to redeem them that were under the law,"[2081] yet our conversation is not redeemed or purged from subjection under the religious law, but is in support of it, and is even *covered* by it, then our conversation is possessed by "that spirit of an'tichrist."[2082] Again, it is well to remember that "the Lord Jesus Christ our Saviour"[2083] is, in right context of language, "the commandment of God our Saviour."[2084]

23. To own that spirit of an'tichrist is to own a mind willingly ignorant to the fact that it is *heaven's* intention to "purge your conscience from dead works to serve the living God."[2085] How is this "purging" accomplished? Because it is a cleansing of the conversation's conscience, it can only commence when once the mind and *body* of faith examine and prove creation's present commandment, which is why it says, "Be renewed in the spirit of your mind,"[2086] and, "Ye are clean through the word which I have spoken."[2087]

24. He or she nursing that spirit of an'tichrist will not draw out their thoughts and feelings to creation's science, for an issue perverts their heart, which issue would find rest if they would exercise faith on its commandment. But because faith's course is willingly halted, the conversation embraces "sin," "and the strength of sin is the law."[2088]

2079 1 Corinthians 15:56
2080 Titus 1.16
2081 Galatians 4:5
2082 1 John 4:3
2083 Titus 1:4
2084 Titus 1:3
2085 Hebrews 9:14
2086 Ephesians 4:23
2087 John 15:3
2088 1 Corinthians 15:56

25. For this cause, must we think that the spirit of an'tichrist is a fit condition? The Spirit's Faith explains the living God's name, and the mediation of His spiritual wisdom preaches the aim of that name, which aim is creation. If an'tichrist, then the mind is against the commandment of creation, and must we believe that that spirit of an'tichrist will reverence creation's Sabbath if it will not hear creation's kind science?

26. That spirit of religious error is stout because it has not experienced redemption from that sensual nature and philosophy abolished and wounded by the passing flesh of the LORD's man, seeing as how "the carnal mind is enmity against God: for it is not subject to the law of God, neither indeed can be."[2089] The "law of God" mentioned by Paul is "the law of the Spirit,"[2090] for the Spirit of creation is the God of creation. That conversation possessing a mind contrary to the Word's law will pick up that spirit and ideology nailed to the tree, and in so doing, will base its religious confidence on the religious bill.

27. If possessing a mind similar to creation's law, the Word of creation would be understood, and every word proceeding out of that Spirit's mouth would be a delight to hear. But since the mind of the conversation will not bring the Word's voice in to it, creation's new covenant manner of redemption cannot commence, drawing the conversation further from *heaven* and plunging it in to the religious world.

28. Now, the spirit of the religious world is that spirit nailed to the tree, yet it is mysteriously still said, "Every spirit that confesseth not that Jesus Christ is come in the flesh is not of God: and this is that spirit of an'tichrist, whereof ye have heard that it should come; and even now already is it in the world."[2091] The entire point of heaven's new covenant commandment is to engrave the confession of "Jesus Christ" within the conversation's conscience, and given the language used in Scripture to pronounce this commandment, we must not think that "Jesus Christ" is a term used to denote a man.

2089 Romans 8:7
2090 Romans 8:2
2091 1 John 4:3

29. How do we dawn a mind confessing "the Lord Jesus Christ our Saviour";[2092] which "Lord" and "Savior" is "the doctrine of God our Saviour";[2093] living within the spirit of our mind? We are counseled, "Be ye transformed by the renewing of your mind,"[2094] and, "If a man love me, he will keep my words."[2095]

30. Words are not firstly physical. To keep words, the mind must be transformed by those words. The spirit of the mind is to confess its service to the Spirit's Faith, and although that confession is through benevolently performing the Spirit's heart; as it says, "Let every one of us please his neighbour for his good to edification";[2096] a conscience in service to creation's law references creation's Sabbath, for the same Word of salvation's science is the same Word who, in the beginning, "blessed the seventh day, and sanctified it."[2097]

31. The spirit of an'tichrist, being opposed to creation's law, does not know creation's Word or LORD, and is therefore ignorant of redemption's Sabbath. Being a mind of religious error, he or she of that mind of an'tichrist cannot know the Word's Sabbath "rest," for they are faithless towards creation's present act, for "to whom sware he that they should not enter into his rest, but to them that believed not? So we see that they could not enter in because of unbelief."[2098]

32. Having no belief in creation's record by the tree, must we think their temper will quiet their conscience to keep the Word's seventh day in remembrance? That spirit of an'tichrist will magnify a *sabbath* of a contrary *Christ* to forward the spirit of its philosophy, making it a lie, to such a mind, to trust that "Christ hath redeemed us from the curse of the law."[2099]

33. If the "body" of this man had not become a curse for our conversation, then this man is absolutely pointless. The illustration of

---

2092 Titus 1:4
2093 Titus 2:10
2094 Romans 12:2
2095 John 14:23
2096 Romans 15:2
2097 Genesis 2:3
2098 Hebrews 3:18,19
2099 Galatians 3:13

this man preaches the putting away of that *body* of religious error for a new mind to live by. If the LORD's man has suffered for this revelation, only to have what is abolished exist for continued use, then this man has wasted his and our time, even as it says, "If Righteousness come by the law, then Christ is dead in vain."[2100]

34. By adhering to that *Christ* preaching devotion to the religious law, we are, in essence, honoring a nonexistent policy made to exist by the force of our own hand, inventing a creed "by works of righteousness which we have done."[2101] Therefore, being against creation, and against creation's Spirit and God, handwritten laws of *righteousness* will delude personal faith, and that delusion clearly witnessed by a law contradicting creation's seventh-day Sabbath.

35. Any law speaking against that Sabbath of creation is, by the passing flesh of the LORD's man, "sin," and to consciously take hold of it, especially after right knowledge has dawned upon the conscience, is to accept our conversation as "sinful." Our hearing the record say, "And Jesus cried with a loud voice, and gave up the ghost,"[2102] is a witness to the fact that "the strength of sin is the law."[2103] "The Lord Jesus Christ our Saviour";[2104] which "Lord" and "Savior" is "the commandment of God our Saviour";[2105] is, by the record of Scripture, without "the law of commandments contained in ordinances,"[2106] which is why it says, "In him is no sin. Whosoever abideth in him sinneth not: whosoever sinneth hath not seen him, neither known him."[2107]

36. It is therefore a fact that the handwritten law or doctrine of priests and elders is religious error, and to hear of any *sabbath* speaking against that Sabbath of creation is to hear of another *Christ* perverting the living God's name. The Faith of the heavenly Sanctuary is without the philosophy of the religious bill, for with that broken "body" of the

---

2100 Galatians 2:21
2101 Titus 3:5
2102 Mark 15:37
2103 1 Corinthians 15:56
2104 Titus 1:4
2105 Titus 1:3
2106 Ephesians 2:15
2107 1 John 3:5,6

LORD's man, there is a reform in manners of devotion, which reform, when soberly executed, will move the person to confess, "The law of the Spirit of life in Christ Jesus hath made me free from the law of sin and death."[2108]

37. This confession is that speech saying, "Jesus cried with a loud voice, and gave up the ghost,"[2109] wherefore it is well to know where our heart is, if it is with this LORD's spiritual understanding, or with *another*.

2108 Romans 8:2
2109 Mark 15:37

26

An Eternal Substitute

1. Although there are various lessons given through that scene recalling Abraham offering Isaac, there is a hidden message in hearing the man say, "God will provide himself a lamb,"[2110] and then reading how "Abraham lifted up his eyes, and looked, and behold behind him a ram caught in a thicket by his horns."[2111]

2. What is interesting to note is that the "lamb" found is not, in reality, a lamb, but is a ram, signifying not only what Isaac represented to the sacrifice when bound to the wood, but also what the LORD's man should later represent when found on the tree. The "lamb" to be offered for sacrifice is a ram; for Abraham to sacrifice Isaac, it is that Abraham must slay the ram of his son's figure.

2110 Genesis 22:8
2111 Genesis 22:13

3. When Abraham turned, he saw a ram and not a lamb because the ram is, in Scripture, specifically defined as an animal that is stout, self-centered, disobedient, and unwilling to listen, even as it says, "I saw the ram pushing."[2112] The illustration of what pushes against the LORD God's name is maintained by the vision of the ram, which is why, when "among the sons of the priests there were found that had taken strange wives,"[2113] "being guilty, they offered a ram of the flock for their trespass."[2114] The ram represents a criminal religious conversation, and to offer the ram for sacrifice is to admit to a false religious obedience, and to for ever condemn that manner of service as accursed.

4. Abraham offering Isaac is but an illustration of the LORD's Word suffering the LORD's man to experience the tree, but what is most important to this illustration is what this man represents to the offering. When found on the tree, this man is the Word's lamb in the same sense of what Isaac was to that "lamb" of Abraham. By finding a ram to offer, it is that Isaac's substitute was found, allowing us to understand that although the flesh of the LORD's man passed away on the tree, the LORD God would provide a substitute for that slain "flesh."

5. The "flesh" of the LORD's man is that sacrificed "ram"; is that religious conversation pushing against *heaven's* new covenant will; which is why it says, "Having abolished in his flesh the enmity, even the law of commandments contained in ordinances."[2115] The "ram" nailed to the tree is the religious conversation of priests and elders; even a *spiritual* course bound by religious laws and traditions; making it a fact that, by this man's passing, "the strength of sin is the law."[2116]

6. That "ram" put to sleep by the Word's Spirit is "the handwriting of ordinances"[2117] by the pen of any and every *Moses* "not only in this world, but also in that which is to come."[2118] With this man's flesh

---

2112 Daniel 8:4
2113 Ezra 10:18
2114 Ezra 10:19
2115 Ephesians 2:15
2116 1 Corinthians 15:56
2117 Colossians 2:14
2118 Ephesians 1:21

representing that spirit and philosophy of the serpent, it is that we now understand, through his passing flesh, what "sin" is, and that "whatsoever is not of faith is sin,"[2119] and that "the law is not of faith."[2120]

7. Seeing as how this man was "made under the law";[2121] "for verily he took not on him the nature of angels; but he took on him the seed of Abraham";[2122] this man's flesh represents the religious law and commandment of priests and elders. It is today an inarguable fact, by the testimony of the LORD's man on the tree, that "the strength of sin is the law,"[2123] and that because Isaac, being of Abraham's seed or mind, was not slain, but rather that ram, that the LORD's man offered a better conversation to the religious world than that held to his flesh.

8. And this is important to understand, for, the "world" that is blessed by the LORD's man is clearly understood by how it says, "Get thee into the land of Mori'ah; and offer him there for a burnt offering upon one of the mountains which I will tell thee of."[2124] As Isaac was called to a specific mountain, so also the LORD's man was called to a specific mountain, even as it says, "The mountain of the house of the LORD,"[2125] and, "My holy mountain Jerusalem."[2126]

9. A "mountain" is language denoting a "house," and a "house" is language denoting a church, as it says, "The house of God, which is the church of the living God."[2127] The conversation of the LORD's man is that Savior for a particular church of people, and he tells us which *mountain* his ministry claims by saying, "I spake openly to the world; I ever taught in the synagogue, and in the temple, whither the Jews always resort."[2128]

2119 Romans 14:23
2120 Galatians 3:12
2121 Galatians 4:4
2122 Hebrews 2:16
2123 1 Corinthians 15:56
2124 Genesis 22:2
2125 Micah 4:1
2126 Isaiah 66:20
2127 1 Timothy 3:15
2128 John 18:20

10. The sacrifice of the LORD's man is held to the church and synagogue of the *Jews*, which church claims a branch on the tree of Eden, whose Architect is the LORD and Word of creation. This doctrine of this LORD's man is that Deliverer of the "world" of the Jewish religion; this man's spiritual saying is that Liberator of that religious world born in Eden. There is no other spiritual understanding in existence than that born to slay the ram of Eden, and this condemnation occurring by suffering the tree, for with that contrary spirit and philosophy nailed to the tree, the tree is actually become blotted out of existence, even as it says, "The fig tree which thou cursedst is withered away."[2129]

11. Is not the tree of this man's passing cursed? Isn't it written, "Christ hath redeemed us from the curse of the law, being made a curse for us: for it is written, Cursed is every one that hangeth on a tree"?[2130] What is cursed is not the man on the tree, but what the flesh of the man represents. "Having abolished in his flesh the enmity, even the law of commandments contained in ordinances,"[2131] it is become a living fact that the will and doctrine of Eden is restored to ordered, and not by "the handwriting of ordinances,"[2132] that is, not "through the law, but through the righteousness of faith."[2133]

12. The issue at hand, through that scene in Mori'ah, is the perpetual slumber of the ram and the ever-lasting continuation of Isaac's conversation. The LORD's man, by appearing "in the likeness of sinful flesh,"[2134] it is that he, being "made under the law,"[2135] is one possessing the religious persuasion of priests and elders. The "flesh" of the man is a figurative illustration of that spirit and philosophy naturally covering the face of the conversation's conscience, but with that mind and religion nailed to the tree, it is that the tree is become entirely withered and passed away from observation.

2129 Mark 11:21
2130 Galatians 3:13
2131 Ephesians 2:15
2132 Colossians 2:14
2133 Romans 4:13
2134 Romans 8:3
2135 Galatians 4:4

13. This man purged the religious world of his LORD and Father's name of all unrighteousness against His Word and Spirit, and "all unrighteousness is sin,"[2136] "and the strength of sin is the law."[2137] Thus, the pen and judgment of priest and elder is officially removed from the living God's religious character, leaving only the inspiration of His voice, which inspiration is "the commandments of God, and the faith of Jesus."[2138]

14. Like as the LORD's man cursed that fruitless tree, and surely it withered away, so this man also nailed to the tree that mind and practice of religious error, and as soon as he said, "It is finished,"[2139] "he bowed his head, and gave up the ghost"[2140] of the ram. This ram is nailed to the tree, making this religious service "sin" to entertain, therefore to unlawfully pick up this tree is to unlawfully adhere to religious error, seeing as how, by this act on the tree, "in him is no sin."[2141]

15. There is no "sin" in His man's spiritual confidence, and, again, "the strength of sin is the law."[2142] This means that any *Christ* preaching a ceremony, a baptism, a feast, and a *sabbath* pushing against the Faith and Sabbath of the living God, is blatant religious error.

16. If His man took it upon himself to curse a tree for its lack of productivity, must we think the Spirit tells a lie when saying, "He that is hanged is accursed of God"?[2143] By this man saying, when on the tree and not yet passed away, "Father, into thy hands I commend my spirit,"[2144] a clear condemnation of that *ghost* then within his *body* is evident.

17. What hangs on the tree is the flesh of this man's faith, the *body* of his religious conversation. This man's flesh had two minds living within it: the first and natural taught, "Righteousness come by the

---

2136　1 John 5:17
2137　1 Corinthians 15:56
2138　Revelation 14:12
2139　John 19:30
2140　John 19:30
2141　1 John 3:5
2142　1 Corinthians 15:56
2143　Deuteronomy 21:23
2144　Luke 23:46

law";[2145] the second and spiritual taught, "Through the Spirit wait for the hope of righteousness by faith."[2146] These two cannot continue with one another; one has to be sacrificed to *death* and the other offered for *life*. Seeing as how "the flesh lusteth against the Spirit, and the Spirit against the flesh,"[2147] and that "if ye be led of the Spirit, ye are not under the law,"[2148] remembering that "the Spirit of life"[2149] is "the Word of life,"[2150] since "the Word was made flesh"[2151] within this man's spirit, it is that the ghost of that flesh should halt, but the spirit of that flesh should continue.

18. The religious law is contrary to the Spirit's will and doctrine, therefore with error's ghost given up, only the spirit of the conscience's liberty remains, which is why we are counseled, "Stand fast therefore in the liberty wherewith Christ hath made us free, and be not entangled again with the yoke of bondage."[2152] That "yoke" is "bondage under the elements of the world";[2153] even subjection to that accursed religious world nailed to the tree and put to sleep by his passing flesh; which "world" is possessed by a "God" preaching *righteousness* through "the law of commandments contained in ordinances."[2154]

19. The substituted spirit of His man liberates the religious world from error against *heaven's* throne, for with one mind passed away, a new mind is needed to fill the vacancy. This new spirit entered in to the religious world is a "spirit that confesseth that Jesus Christ is come in the flesh,"[2155] allowing us to understand that since the Word made flesh is "Jesus Christ" come in to the flesh, "Jesus Christ," being the Word's spiritual law, is no physical or literal man. In reality, and according

---

2145 Galatians 2:21
2146 Galatians 5:5
2147 Galatians 3:17
2148 Galatians 5:18
2149 Revelation 11:11
2150 1 John 1:1
2151 John 1:14
2152 Galatians 5:1
2153 Galatians 4:3
2154 Ephesians 2:15
2155 1 John 4:2

to Scripture's tongue, "the Lord Jesus Christ our Saviour"[2156] is "the commandment of God our Saviour."[2157] Because "a spirit hath not flesh and bones,"[2158] it is that "Jesus Christ" is not flesh and bones, for what word or commandment is flesh and bones?

20. Because "that which is born of the Spirit is spirit,"[2159] it is that the Word is come in to the spirit of the mind for directing, correcting, educating, and sealing the flesh of our faith. "Jesus Christ" made flesh is the Spirit's commandment entered in to the heart of our conversation for sanctifying the conscience of our conversation; this is that new mind given in to the Father's hands before the ghost of religious error passed away from creation's will and course of learning. Thus, by this man, our higher education is set, teaching us that there should be a passing away from that conversation bound to the spirit and philosophy of the religious law for picking up a conversation blessed by that mind offered for the ram, which is why we are counseled, "Put off concerning the former conversation the old man, which is corrupt according to the deceitful lusts; and be renewed in the spirit of your mind; and that ye put on the new man."[2160]

21. That "old" man is the old mind of that *ghost* encouraging subjection of the conscience to "the law of commandments contained in ordinances,"[2161] but that "new" man is that renewed mind encouraging the conversation to "live according to God in the spirit."[2162] Herein we may understand that false *Christ* from the Word's Savior, for where we see a *Christ* preaching obedience to the religious law and doctrine, we may understand that this *Christ* is not that "Christ," which "Christ hath redeemed us from the curse of the law."[2163]

22. By this "Christ" of the Word's Spirit, we may clearly comprehend the living God's intention, that His intention is for the creation of

---

2156 Titus 1:4
2157 Titus 1:3
2158 Luke 24:39
2159 John 3:6
2160 Ephesians 4:22-24
2161 Ephesians 2:15
2162 1 Peter 4:6
2163 Galatians 3:13

a new mind of personal and devotional government. With the LORD's man slaying that contrary spirit by his passing flesh, what remains for our observation is creation's science by faith on creation's commandment, and because it is of creation by faith, creation's Sabbath of faith's righteousness is assigned to this knowledge and experience.

23. The doctrine of the LORD's man is that Savior of His commandment's *mountain*; there is no other Savior or *mountain* in existence. This mountain is that synagogue of the Jews, and by this man's sacrifice, that ram within the Jewish religion hiding the Word's face is withered away, allowing every eye to clearly perceive "the fellowship of the mystery, which from the beginning of the world hath been hid in God,"[2164] "which is Christ in you, the hope of glory."[2165]

24. Again, "the Lord Jesus Christ our Saviour"[2166] is, in all actuality, "the commandment of God our Saviour."[2167] This commandment within the conversation's inwards performs the glory hoped for and taught through the passing and regenerating of the LORD's man. That hope promised of the Spirit is that "if the Spirit of him that raised up Jesus from the dead dwell in you, he that raised up Christ from the dead shall also quicken your mortal bodies by his Spirit,"[2168] which is why it says, "If ye through the Spirit do mortify the deeds of the body, ye shall live."[2169]

25. The "body" of our faith, and the "bodies" or members of our faith's mind, are to experience regeneration and reformation, which experience is taught by the passing ghost and secured spirit of the LORD's man. The hope of this Spirit's glory is to "purge your conscience from dead works to serve the living God";[2170] this is the kingdom and righteousness of God. Because "whatsoever is not of faith

---

2164 Ephesians 3:9
2165 Colossians 1:27
2166 Titus 1:4
2167 Titus 1:3
2168 Romans 8:11
2169 Romans 8:13
2170 Hebrews 9:14

is sin,"²¹⁷¹ and that "the law is not of faith,"²¹⁷² it must be taken out of the Word's Faith, for it halts the name of Abraham, which name is chosen above the name of Moses for blessing. Being first chosen for blessing, "the scripture, foreseeing that God would justify the heathen through faith, preached before the gospel unto Abraham, saying, In thee shall all nations be blessed."²¹⁷³

26. The spirit of Moses came after Abraham, and this spirit is not that Spirit of the living God, and this we understand because that "which was four hundred and thirty years after, cannot disannul, that it should make the promise of none effect. For if the inheritance be of the law, it is no more of promise: but God gave it to Abraham by promise."²¹⁷⁴ This is why "they which are the children of the flesh, these are not the children of God: but the children of the promise are counted for the seed."²¹⁷⁵

27. With Isaac's flesh or conversation representing that course of learning by and through faith, it is not that such a conversation should be put to death, but that a substitute wholly contrary to this course of learning should find itself withered away. As Isaac was saved, so the spirit of the LORD's man was preserved, and as Isaac continued to live, but that ram suffered to die on the wood, so also the spirit of the LORD's man must live, meaning that the natural conversation of this man's flesh must suffer perpetual condemnation on the tree. Herein creation's science is pronounced to us, and that confession sealed by the declaration, "The law of the Spirit of life in Christ Jesus hath made me free from the law of sin and death."²¹⁷⁶

28. Blessed revelation! With newness of spiritual understanding occurring through the Spirit's present voice, all subjection to a "vain conversation received by tradition"²¹⁷⁷ is come to an end. If it is then

---

2171 Romans 14:23
2172 Galatians 3:12
2173 Galatians 3:8
2174 Galatians 17:18
2175 Romans 9:8
2176 Romans 8:2
2177 1 Peter 1:18

that "of his own will begat he us with the word of truth,"[2178] then it is that the celebration of conception is blessed to the Word's doer, even as it says, "Thou hast given a banner to them that fear thee, that it may be displayed because of the truth."[2179]

29. This same Word, in the beginning, is that God of creation, and if that promise made with Abraham outweighs that formed by Moses, must not the Word's Sabbath continue to outweigh any other *sabbath* invented by any other *Moses*? It does outweigh, for this Sabbath is creation's celebration, and seeing as how creation occurred by faith on the Spirit's Word, the same manner of creation occurring within man's inwards unseals the same Sabbath of the same LORD and Word to the conversation's character.

30. With the LORD's man abolishing the serpent's spirit to magnify "the spirit of wisdom and understanding, the spirit of counsel and might, the spirit of knowledge and of the fear of the LORD,"[2180] what remains for our learning is the religious character of his LORD, which character is revealed on those "two tables of testimony, tables of stone, written with the finger of God."[2181] Thus, by this LORD's man, the Word's finger is become eternally superior to the pen of flesh, and we may sincerely know this by that commandment stating the authority of this finger, which counsel says, "In six days the LORD made heaven and earth, the sea, and all that in them is, and rested the seventh day: wherefore the LORD blessed the Sabbath day, and hallowed it."[2182]

31. "God blessed the seventh day, and sanctified it,"[2183] because of the wisdom and power contained within His voice, and by the act of the LORD's chief apostle, that voice is become *life's* new song, and the seventh day of that song, the Sabbath for every mind created by that voice.

2178 James 1:18
2179 Psalm 60:4
2180 Isaiah 11:2
2181 Exodus 31:18
2182 Exodus 20:11
2183 Genesis 2:3

27

That Alpha And Omega

1. Why is it important that the living God's Spirit said to John, "I am Alpha and Omega, the first and the last: and, What thou seest, write in a book, and send it unto the seven churches which are in Asia; unto Eph'esus, and unto Smyrna, and unto Per'gamos, and unto Thyati'ra, and unto Sar'dis, and unto Philadelphia, and unto Laodice'a"?[2184]

2. We find the answer to our question through John, who writes, "I was in the Spirit on the Lord's day, and heard behind me a great voice, as of a trumpet, saying, I am Alpha and Omega, the first and the last."[2185]

3. The "Lord" that John references is that One from verse eight, saying, "I am Alpha and Omega, the beginning and the ending, saith the Lord, which is, and which was, and which is to come, the Almighty."[2186]

2184 Revelation 1:11
2185 Revelation 1:10,11
2186 Revelation 1:8

This "Lord" is the same "Almighty" that John speaks of when saying, "A throne was set in heaven, and one sat on the throne";[2187] this is "the LORD sitting upon his throne."[2188] Therefore, there can only be one "day" of this Almighty LORD, and it is the "day" of His Spirit.

4. Remembering that "the Spirit of life"[2189] is "the Word of life,"[2190] it is that John received this vision of the Revelation on the Word's day, and, seeing as how in "the beginning was the Word, and the Word was with God, and the Word was God,"[2191] it is that John is in the day of God when receiving this revelation. Because the Word is God, and because "God blessed the seventh day,"[2192] this message to the churches is born during the Word's Sabbath.

5. We may understand the purpose of the Revelation through the period of time in which it is given. The reason why the churches of Asia must know that this LORD's Word is that first and last Spirit is because the spirit of Asia is possessing those churches professing His Spirit's Faith.

6. "Asia" is no literal location, but is a term pointing the mind in the direction of a religious persuasion, seeing as how all of Asia, and every assembly joined to Asia, "is a worshipper of the great goddess Diana, and of the image which fell down from Jupiter."[2193] The Spirit's first message is directed to Eph'esus because the spirit of Eph'esus is a service and philosophy to *Jupiter's* son and mother. Certain Jewish ministers of *heaven's Faith* began picking up the religion of the pagan Roman churches of Asia, moving the Spirit to say of them, "Thou canst not bear them which are evil: and thou hast tried them which say they are apostles, and are not, and hast found them liars."[2194]

7. Christian ministers found their conversation in this condition because they practiced Cain's evil works, which works were labors of

---

2187 Revelation 4:2
2188 2 Chronicles 18:18
2189 Revelation 11:11
2190 1 John 1:1
2191 John 1:1
2192 Genesis 2:3
2193 Acts 19:35
2194 Revelation 2:2

"sin" for *righteousness*. By believing on the saying, "Righteousness come by the law,"[2195] especially when "Christ hath redeemed us from the curse of the law,"[2196] spiritual negligence held the eyes of Jewish ministers in "death's" prison. Because "the sting of death is sin; and the strength of sin is the law";[2197] and that "all unrighteousness is sin";[2198] by picking up what the passing flesh of the LORD's man condemns as abominable, Christian ministers began to fulfill the rebuke, "And for this cause God shall send them strong delusion, that they should believe a lie: that they all might be damned who believed not the truth, but had pleasure in unrighteousness."[2199]

8. Religious delusion retarded the spiritual understanding of Christian ministers because they violated the Spirit's doctrine. By treating an accursed religious spirit and philosophy as though it was not accursed, because such a course is abolished from creation's reality, whosoever is joined to it must also find their faith's consciousness abolished from the same realm of existence. Thus, as time passed, Christian ministers had erred so greatly in their understanding that the Spirit was moved to say of them, "I know thy works, and where thou dwellest, even where Satan's seat is."[2200]

9. Satan's seat is no literal throne, but is a spiritual ambition fulfilling the saying, "Thou hast there them that hold the doctrine of Ba'laam, who taught Ba'lac to cast a stumblingblock."[2201]

10. The figures presented to John are not literal figures, but are character illustrations fulfilling particular roles against the living God's name and doctrine. To comprehend these names, it is well to think on the person of their figure, and when we hear of Ba'laam and Ba'lac, we are, in reality, hearing of a false church coming together with a pagan religious State to execute a mission against the Spirit's host and doctrine.

2195 Galatians 2:21
2196 Galatians 3:13
2197 1 Corinthians 15:56
2198 1 John 5:17
2199 2 Thessalonians 2:11,12
2200 Revelation 2:13
2201 Revelation 2:14

11. We are, when entered in to the age of Per'gamos, observing the movements of the Christian church through Constantine. This message of the Revelation is given to John for the churches of Asia because Constantine would re-invent the religion of Asia; calling it Christianity; and would move that religion to Asia Minor, to a place he would call, "Constantinople."

12. Every church of the Revelation is no literal church, but is a specific age of the Christian church, which church is an institution devoutly stout to the Spirit's Faith, which is why, to them, the Spirit comes to John, and on His seventh-day Sabbath, saying, "I am Alpha and Omega, the first and the last."[2202] Such a confession is needed because that church abandoning "the apostles' doctrine and fellowship,"[2203] and inventing to her self a creed of her own spirit, has lost sight of the Spirit's present science.

13. Jewish and Gentile Jewish ministers strayed from the first apostles' Faith due to their violating the illustration taught by the LORD's man suffering the tree. Such error moved the Spirit to say of them, "I know the blasphemy of them which say they are Jews, and are not, but are the synagogue of Satan,"[2204] for, at this time, they had put off *heaven's* heritage to become one denomination with "the people of the prince."[2205]

14. This "people" prophesied to destroy Jerusalem are the same people the LORD's man references when saying, "When ye shall see Jerusalem compassed with armies, then know that the desolation thereof is nigh."[2206] This prophecy was fulfilled 70AD by Rome, led by Titus, who savagely destroyed the temple and city of Jerusalem. This "people" of the prince are Romans, and for Christian ministers to take on the spirit of this people; which mind is "the course of this world, according to the prince of the power of the air, the spirit that now

---

2202 Revelation 1:11
2203 Acts 2:42
2204 Revelation 2:9
2205 Daniel 9:26
2206 Luke 21:20

worketh in the children of disobedience";[2207] is to abandon the heavenly Sanctuary's wisdom for the *Lord* and *God* of the sun, even for that chief religious image of the Greek and Roman religion.

15. The LORD's Spirit must approach the churches of Asia; who are the sun-worshipping churches of the Christian religion; by saying, "I am Alpha and Omega, the first and the last,"[2208] because her ministers have forgotten how it is written, "I am the first, and I am the last; and beside me there is no God."[2209] For the Spirit to bring up the subject of Alpha and Omega, and of the first and the last, is for the Spirit to stir up the conscience of Christian ministers to the fact that they are worshipping a nonexistent force through "sin" and "transgression." Christian ministers, seeing as how "the strength of sin is the law,"[2210] by harkening to the "God" of "sin," had formed a religion through that spirit and persuasion nailed to the tree.

16. "Strength" is another term for "God," as it says, "Save me, O God, by thy name, and judge me by thy strength,"[2211] and, "My God, my strength."[2212] One's "strength" is the "name" of one's confidence, and "name" means "doctrine" or spiritual "knowledge," as it says, "And hast kept my word, and hast not denied my name,"[2213] and, "Thou holdest fast my name, and hast not denied my faith."[2214]

17. "Having abolished in his flesh the enmity, even the law of commandments contained in ordinances,"[2215] it is that the LORD's man blotted "sin's" name and doctrine out of the Word's Faith, making it an open fact that, hereafter, "the strength of sin is the law."[2216] By adhering to spiritual government by the philosophy of the religious

---

2207 Ephesians 2:2
2208 Revelation 1:11
2209 Isaiah 44:6
2210 1 Corinthians 15:56
2211 Isaiah 54:1
2212 Psalm 18:2
2213 Revelation 3:8
2214 Revelation 2:13
2215 Ephesians 2:15
2216 1 Corinthians 15:56

law, Christian ministers began transgressing the Spirit's counsel for creation, "for he that is hanged is accursed of God."[2217]

18. The illustration of the LORD's man on the tree is not our observing an accursed man, but rather the condemnation of what the flesh of that man represents. This man's flesh represents the philosophy of the religious law, and "not only in this world, but also in that which is to come,"[2218] seeing as how "whatsoever God doeth, it shall be for ever."[2219] The perpetual and eternal condemnation of that spirit and philosophy nailed to the tree is sealed by the blood of the man, making our handling that spirit a very great mocking of that crucifixion, especially since this man's shed blood illustrates the dawn of a new will to learn of and do, and the utter annihilation of that former one.

19. The spirit nailed to the tree is a routine speaking against faith's free exercise for *heaven's* manner of righteousness, and by this LORD's man, we today may know that "whatsoever is not of faith is sin,"[2220] and that "the law is not of faith."[2221] It was therefore inevitable that Christian ministers professing *the LORD* and *Word* of *the Bible* should fulfill the saying, "They went out, that they might be made manifest that they were not all of us."[2222]

20. The Revelation is given to Asia's household because they pervert heaven's manners, and by honoring the charge, "Strengthen the things which remain, that are ready to die,"[2223] and, "Remember therefore from whence thou art fallen, and repent, and do the first works,"[2224] her men may avoid the end promised to her through the Revelation. Because Asia's ministers; then and now; have no knowledge of creation's Spirit, a hard slumber rests on her host, and worse, "ye bring more wrath upon Israel by profaning the Sabbath."[2225]

2217 Deuteronomy 21:23
2218 Ephesians 1:21
2219 Ecclesiastes 3:14
2220 Romans 14:23
2221 Galatians 3:12
2222 1 John 2:19
2223 Revelation 3:2
2224 Revelation 2:5
2225 Nehemiah 13:18

21. There is only one Sabbath of the Word's Spirit, and to come as One who is first and last, and who is Alpha and Omega, is to testify of creation's God, that this wisdom and saying is an everlasting wisdom and saying pointing the doer of it to their place before this wisdom's heavenly throne, as it says, "Therefore are they before the throne of God, and serve him day and night in his temple: and he that sitteth on the throne shall dwell among them."[2226] The Spirit of that Almighty One on heaven's throne inspires this wisdom of creation, and if it is that our conversation's conscience is brought up in this throne's will and knowledge, then our conversation will function according to this wisdom's love, and "this is the love of God, that we keep his commandments."[2227]

22. The "love" of God is the Spirit's manner of righteousness or benevolence. It is the Spirit's righteousness to "purge your conscience from dead works to serve the living God,"[2228] and if "the sting of death is sin; and the strength of sin is the law";[2229] then every "dead work" is according to "the law of commandments contained in ordinances."[2230] "The kindness and love of God our Saviour"[2231] is a conversation resurrected from "death's" tradition to know a sober reform in spiritual thought and feeling, which is why it says, "Put off concerning the former conversation the old man...and be renewed in the spirit of your mind."[2232]

23. With the LORD's man "having abolished in his flesh the enmity, even the law of commandments contained in ordinances,"[2233] all that remains is to "keep the commandments of God, and the faith of Jesus."[2234] Where we find a religious conversation deviating from any one of the Spirit's Ten Commandments, or from any one of His Faith's principles, it is that religious error against the illustration of the

---

2226 Revelation 7:15
2227 1 John 5:3
2228 Hebrews 9:14
2229 1 Corinthians 15:56
2230 Ephesians 2:15
2231 Titus 3:4
2232 Ephesians 4:22,23
2233 Ephesians 2:15
2234 Revelation 14:12

LORD's man has taken the mind and *body* of faith away, seeing as how their *eyes* observe that *ghost* taken away from the living God's religious character.

24. The Spirit's Faith is ordained for our conversation's blessing through the saying of His voice, to the end our conversation may reverence every word of this same Spirit. To hear the Spirit continually approach John by mentioning His wisdom's perpetual sovereignty is to hear the Spirit putting Christian ministers in remembrance of just what "God" to honor. With the Spirit's wisdom being the first, the last, and the only body of knowledge to examine and do, it is that the conscience proving this wisdom is returned to the beginning of all things for learning why this Word is the end of all heavenly things.

25. What distinguishes this Spirit from every other "God" is creation, and the authority of His voice to create. There is no other Spirit of creation in existence other than this Spirit of creation, and we know that this is true because of this Spirit's present science, which redemption moves its student-patient to say, "The law of the Spirit of life in Christ Jesus hath made me free from the law of sin and death."[2235]

26. Being made free from the pen and judgment of flesh; whether ancient or modern; means liberty of the conscience to learn the Spirit's name and law for the Spirit's benevolence. That benevolence is witnessed through this confession recorded in the eighth chapter of the book of Romans, in verse two,[2236] which is a statement of creation away from a former religious thought process to a more sober manner of devotion.

27. The imprint of creation's Spirit is within the will of its LORD's new covenant, opening up the doer of that new covenant will to the fact that "the seventh day is the Sabbath,"[2237] and that their communion with this Sabbath is that "sign of circumcision, a seal of the righteousness of the faith."[2238] The Spirit must come to Asia's host in the manner that He does because they have fallen away from heaven's manner of

---

2235 Romans 8:2
2236 Romans 8:2
2237 Exodus 20:10
2238 Romans 4:11

righteousness, making it necessary for them to hear, "Christ is become of no effect unto you, whosoever of you are justified by the law; ye are fallen from grace."[2239]

28. "Grace" is creation's present aid for the Spirit's righteousness, as it says, "Abundance of grace and of the gift of righteousness."[2240] We receive grace as our conversation takes in and proves the Spirit's law and knowledge of creation, which is why it says, "Grow in grace, and in the knowledge of our Lord and Saviour Jesus Christ."[2241] This allows us to understand that it is "the grace of God that bringeth salvation,"[2242] and that this salvation, because it is through mental and spiritual discernment, is for the conversation's conscience, to "purge your conscience from dead works to serve the living God."[2243]

29. He or she failing to bring the Spirit's wisdom in to their faith's *body* has disqualified their faith's mind from this Spirit's righteousness, thereby disqualifying them from grace for that benevolence, which disqualification only appears when once the heart believes that "righteousness come by the law,"[2244] when it is that, in reality, His "Christ hath redeemed us from the curse of the law, being made a curse for us: for it is written, Cursed is every one that hangeth on a tree."[2245]

30. Asia's host is in a very deplorable condition when approached by the Spirit, for they have put off *heaven's* righteousness for the serpent's spirit and persuasion, growing hard in their heart against His doctrine's reign over their inward parts. And indeed she remains stout against His throne's will, for the Spirit says of her and her ministers, "I gave her space to repent of her fornication; and she repented not."[2246] To appear as that first and last, and as that Alpha and Omega, is to appear by a counsel sending the mind to the beginning of all things,

---

2239 Galatians 5:4
2240 Romans 5:17
2241 2 Peter 3:18
2242 Titus 2:11
2243 Hebrews 9:14
2244 Galatians 2:21
2245 Galatians 3:13
2246 Revelation 2:21

where only the LORD God's Word is that supreme authority over the conversation of His stewards.

31. The Revelation is addressed to every conversation deviating from that practice formed during creation and blessed to Eden, which religion the LORD's man has officially reinstated by the passing of his flesh on the tree, and by the regeneration and priestly appointment of that conversation within the heavenly Sanctuary. Thus, by one sacrifice, the living God has created one *body* of Faith through His man's conversation, for the saying is today fulfilled, "Thou wert cut out of the olive tree which is wild by nature, and wert graffed contrary to nature into a good olive tree."[2247]

32. The natural conversation, which is wild, is one that functions through "the handwriting of ordinances"[2248] according to "the tradition of the elders."[2249] But with the LORD's man "having abolished in his flesh the enmity, even the law of commandments contained in ordinances,"[2250] "your vain conversation received by tradition"[2251] is become useless, for it is written, "To him that ordereth his conversation aright will I shew the salvation of God."[2252]

33. The fact that the conversation must be "ordered" informs us of a change in mind and operation. The illustration of the LORD's man on the tree preaches the reform of the conversation's mind on heavenly things, and the regeneration of that mind through that reform. By learning of and doing the Spirit's wisdom, we will find our naturally wild conversation edified and welcomed in to heaven's right manner, and this creation sealed with His wisdom's seventh day Sabbath.

34. It is necessary for the Spirit to approach the churches by His full name because their minds have deviated from His will and science. This is why He openly tells them, "I have somewhat against thee, because thou hast left thy first love."[2253] As much good as this first

---

2247 Romans 11:24
2248 Colossians 2:14
2249 Matthew 15:2
2250 Ephesians 2:15
2251 1 Peter 1:18
2252 Psalm 50:23
2253 Revelation 2:4

Christian generation did for heaven's Faith, Eph'esus was an age of secret violence against creation's new covenant commandment, which also won supporters according to its spiritual fraudulence.

35. The Revelation is a key document for Asia's present ministers and supporters, for the Word still comes to us as that first and last wisdom, and as that Alpha and Omega spiritual understanding. We therefore understand our sincere devotion to this Spirit by our love for His name, "and this is love, that we walk after his commandments."[2254]

36. The passing flesh of the LORD's man on the tree means that there exists only one denomination of this Spirit's Faith, and this one body is bound to one LORD and Father by the priestly mediation of His ascended and anointed counsel on creation. The mind of this one body exists within His heavenly Sanctuary; "our conversation is in heaven";[2255] where we, again, "have a great high priest, that is passed into the heavens."[2256] Thus, as that Chief Priest over the living God's name and science, it is that our conversation is one honoring the counsel, "Fear God, and keep his commandments,"[2257] for we do know what is of His spiritual understanding.

2254 2 John 1:6
2255 Philippians 3:20
2256 Hebrews 4:14
2257 Ecclesiastes 12:13

28

Every Jew Of Shu'shan

1. The record given us in the book of Esther tells of two very interesting Jewish denominations. We understand their spirit by how it says, "The other Jews that were in the king's provinces gathered themselves together, and stood for their lives, and had rest from their enemies, and slew of their foes seventy and five thousand, but they laid not their hands on the prey, on the thirteenth day of the month Adar; and on the fourteenth day of the same rested they, and made it a day of feasting and gladness. But the Jews that were at Shu'shan assembled together on the thirteenth day thereof, and on the fourteenth thereof; and on the fifteenth day of the same they rested, and made it a day of feasting and gladness."[2258]

2. The days and months of the Jewish calendar are very simple to understand, as they are pronounced to us through the periods of time

---

2258 Esther 9:16-18

referenced in Genesis concerning the stay of Noah's ark on the waters. The Jewish calendar is made up of twelve months and with thirty days per month. The first day of the month is always the same, along with the seventh day of the month, which is the last day of the week.

3. The king's commandment, through Mor'decai's hand, commenced the thirteenth day of the twelfth month, a Friday. After this day, "the king said unto Esther the queen, The Jews have slain and destroyed five hundred men in Shu'shan the palace, and the ten sons of Ha'man; what have they done in the rest of the king's provinces? now what is thy petition? and it shall be granted thee: or what is thy request further? and it shall be done. Then said Esther, If it please the king, let it be granted to the Jews which are in Shu'shan to do to morrow also according unto this day's decree, and let Ha'man's ten sons be hanged upon the gallows. And the king commanded it so to be done."[2259]

4. Thus, on the fourteenth day; Saturday; the Jews did what they had done on the thirteenth day; Friday; wherefore "on the thirteenth day of the month A'dar; and on the fourteenth day of the same rested they, and made it a day of feasting and gladness."[2260]

5. This should appear quite odd to us, for if we add seven days to seven days, we arrive at the fourteenth day of the month, which day falls on the Sabbath. It is during the Sabbath of the seventh day that Mor'decai, along with Jewish ministers, chose "to gather themselves together, and to stand for their life, to destroy, to slay, and to cause to perish, all the power of the people and province that would assault them, both little ones and women, and to take the spoil of them for a prey."[2261]

6. Such a labor, we should think, is contrary to the Sabbath, whose primary rule states: "To morrow is the rest of the holy Sabbath unto the LORD: bake that which ye will bake to day, and seethe that ye will seethe; and that which remaineth over lay up for you to be kept until the morning."[2262]

2259 Esther 9:12-14
2260 Esther 9:17
2261 Esther 8:11
2262 Exodus 16:23

7. The preparation day, which is Friday, is used as a day to prepare for the next day's mental and spiritual stillness, which day is the Sabbath. By doing what ought to be done for the next day on Friday, the Jews hoped to make the Sabbath's communion easier to maintain, for the majority of the day's responsibilities were taken care of the day before. It is therefore quite odd to hear that the Jews kept the thirteenth day of the month for executing the king's commandment, especially since the king's scribes were called in nine months before the actual commandment commenced, allowing us to understand that the Jews could have chosen a date that did not conflict with the Sabbath.

8. And this we can confirm by how "the king Ahasue'rus said unto Esther the queen and to Mor'decai the Jew, Behold, I have given Esther the house of Ha'man, and him they have hanged upon the gallows, because he laid his hand upon the Jews. Write ye also for the Jews, as it liketh you, in the king's name, and seal it with the king's ring: for the writing which is written in the king's name, and sealed with the king's ring, may no man reverse."[2263]

9. Both Esther and Mor'decai had control over the date of their gathering and defense, and both chose to execute the written and sealed judgment on the thirteenth day, and when that day came, they decreed another day, the fourteenth day, for doing the same.

10. It would be one thing to hear that the Jews were locked in to a date, but to hear that, according to their own judgment, they could and should freely act, and chose to act on the Sabbath, raises many flags about the world's then Jew. And as if it was no thing at all to execute a movement on the Sabbath contrary to the Sabbath's intention, the Jewish ministers of the city Shu'shan did as the other Jews, but went a step further, for "the Jews that were at Shu'shan assembled together on the thirteenth day thereof, and on the fourteenth thereof; and on the fifteenth day of the same they rested, and made it a day of feasting and gladness."[2264]

11. The thirteenth day of the month; Friday; and the fourteenth day; Saturday; were days of warfare, and we should expect the celebration to

---

2263 Esther 8:7,8
2264 Esther 9:18

end the fourteenth day, but the Jews of Shu'shan were not like the Jews outside of Shu'shan, for while "the Jews of the villages, that dwelt in the unwalled towns, made the fourteenth day of the month A'dar a day of gladness and feasting, and a good day, and of sending portions one to another,"[2265] the Jews of Shu'shan made the fifteenth day; Sunday; a day of celebration also.

12. These Jews of Shu'shan, whose head or chief representative was Mor'decai, were instructed by him "to stablish this among them, that they should keep the fourteenth day of the month A'dar, and the fifteenth day of the same, yearly."[2266] And why should Mor'decai do this? The acts ended the fourteenth day, and with that, it should be expected to honor the *God* of the fourteenth day for the deliverance procured to them through *Him*. But their taking "rest" on the fifteenth day reveals just where their perceived deliverance came from, for, concerning this commandment, Mor'decai "wrote in the king Ahasue'rus' name, and sealed it with the king's ring."[2267]

13. It was not the *God* of the fourteenth day that these Jews were celebrating by their feast, but the *God* of Shu'shan, which *God* is not recognized on the thirteenth or the fourteenth day of the month, but on the fifteenth. This is that *God* worshipped by pagan tribes, and he is honored on the fifteenth day, Sunday, because it is the ancient day or celebration of the sun.

14. Mor'decai could have enlisted any day to act, but he chose the thirteenth, and Esther consented to the fourteenth, and they together established the fifteenth, because the *God* of this people, at this time in their history, the *God* that warred on their behalf on the thirteenth and fourteenth day, was not that Spirit or God of the Bible. We may understand what *God* ruled this people by how it says, "The Jews ordained, and took upon them, and upon their seed, and upon all such as joined themselves unto them, so as it should not fail, that they would

---

2265 Esther 9:19
2266 Esther 9:21
2267 Esther 8:10

keep these two days according to their writing, and according to their appointed time every year."[2268]

15. "Mor'decai wrote these things, and sent letters unto all the Jews that were in all the provinces of the king Ahasue'rus, both nigh and far, to stablish this among them, that they should keep the fourteenth day of the month A'dar, and the fifteenth day of the same, yearly";[2269] the spirit behind this act is according to "the handwriting of ordinances."[2270]

16. With the LORD's man "having abolished in his flesh the enmity, even the law of commandments contained in ordinances,"[2271] it is that, whether anciently or modernly, the religious law and tradition concocted by priests and elders has always, to the living God's mind, been looked at as "sin" against His will and voice, for "the strength of sin is the law."[2272] Thus, if Moses constrained the people, even before that covenant had bound them to the LORD God, to reverence the seventh day, what spirit is moving Mor'decai to disregard that seventh day, or to add on to it, after and while bound to the LORD God by covenant? This inspiration of Mor'decai's hand is the same inspiration of Moses' hand, which inspiration the LORD's man's perpetually silenced by his passing on the tree.

17. To hear how it says, "The Jews ordained,"[2273] is to hear of ministers whose conversation is actuated by that spirit and philosophy nailed to the tree. And to further hear that the fourteenth day and the fifteenth day were seasons of a particular feast and celebration is to observe a Jewish people professing *the LORD God's name* while subscribing to Ba'al's impression.

18. We should think their days of "joy" should end by the fourteenth day, but, being Jews of Shu'shan, and being afforded this opportunity by the king's good and kind hand, the *God* of the fifteenth day is become the prime subject of worship for all three days; the thirteenth

---

2268 Esther 9:27
2269 Esther 9:20,21
2270 Colossians 2:14
2271 Ephesians 2:15
2272 1 Corinthians 15:56
2273 Esther 9:27

to the fifteenth. No act occurred on the fifteenth day, and the Jew is not bound to any thing concerning pagan holidays, but it is evident that these Jews honored the god of the sun while professing *the living God's name*, and so out of respect for the king's *God*, which *God* is the means whereby the king's heart was softened, a celebration was decreed for both the Sabbath and Sunday.

19. This would appear to be a harmless decree, for, why should days matter? The Bible's record and perspective is no accident, and if a thing is left for us to investigate, and if that thing speaks against the Bible's counsel, then all things matter, and all things are for our edification.

20. The time that we have entered in to is one where, some time before, Cyrus has liberated the Jews from Babylon, bringing the Jews under subjection to the new empire of the then world. It is evident, from Mor'decai's stance on the fifteenth day, and from the consent of the fifteenth day by his fellow Jewish leaders, that Babylon greatly impacted the spiritual understanding of this people.

21. The *God* of Babylon is the *God* of the Medes and Persians, and this *God* is the same *God* of the Egyptians and Romans, whose name is originally called Ba'al. The Jews worshipped Ba'al quite openly, so much so that the LORD's Spirit says of their ministers, "Their fathers have forgotten my name for Ba'al,"[2274] and, "According to the number of thy cities were thy gods, O Judah; and according to the number of the streets of Jerusalem have ye set up altars to that shameful thing, even altars to burn incense unto Ba'al."[2275]

22. Ba'al, to pagan cults, is that *Lord* of light, healing, war, revelation, and prosperity, which is why Ba'al's day is called the *Lord's* day, for the mysterious *Lord* and *God* of the sun owns the fifteenth day. Jewish ministers welcomed Ba'al worship into the Word's doctrine, further perverting the living God's Faith by the superstitions of a spiritually anxious pagan people. Again, with the LORD's man suffering

---

2274 Jeremiah 23:27
2275 Jeremiah 11:13

the tree, the philosophy of Ba'al is become as extinct as the spirit of Moses' hand.

23. These Jews under the reign of Cyrus, and then Ahasue'rus, kept the tradition of their fathers above the impression of the LORD's Spirit, for they not only *blessed* their religion by Moses' spirit, but they, in addition to honoring *the LORD* through that spirit, kept the Babylonian gods in their worship, along with their chief *Lord*, Ba'al. With the gods of Ahasue'rus being the gods of Nebuchadnez'zar, and with both kings subscribing to Ba'al, these Jewish ministers at the center of Ba'al worship; which center is the city Shu'shan; operate differently than them without paganism's cultural center.

24. The record in Scripture is very specific, for the Jews that assembled together at Shu'shan, in addition to the thirteenth and fourteenth day, also held the fifteenth as a season of "rest." Mor'decai is quite adamant about the fourteenth and fifteenth in his letters, when we should think that the thirteenth and the fourteenth should consume his thoughts. But Mor'decai's mind is quite different from Moses', who would have the people do what ought to be done on the sixth day to avoid breaking that channel of blessing on the seventh. This decree of Mor'decai therefore reveals just where his heart is at, for if he is not concerned with that Sabbath of the living God, but is content holding it in a context not originally intended, and wiling to call the fifteenth day a season of "rest," then we have before us the history of the Christian church before it ever took place.

25. The God and Word of the Sabbath is not that *God* of the fifteenth day. Mor'decai blesses Ba'al on his day because this is the only *God* without any living "rest," and who, by war against flesh, conquers for his congregation. This feast drawn up by Mor'decai's mind is not in any form or way devoted to the living God of the Bible; the inclusion of the fifteenth day allows us to understand this. The *God* of this triumph, in essence, because it was the king's name and seal that granted the Jews their deliverance and defense, is that *God* of the king, which *God* is *Lord* of the sun.

26. This *God* fought for them, and they through *him*, on the thirteenth and fourteenth day, making it reasonable to take the fifteenth day as a season of "rest," for the *God* of the fifteenth day wrought a

victory for them. This is not the living God's battle because it is entirely addressed to and issuing from flesh. Therefore if, for example, the Spirit instructed Moses, "On the first day of the first month shalt thou set up the tabernacle of the tent of the congregation,"[2276] it is become blatantly clear that the first day of the week; Sunday; is no time of "rest" to the living God's Spirit, but is a day like any other from Sunday to Friday. To hear that the fifteenth day; the first day of the week; is set aside as some thing, is to hear of a handwritten religious law and ordinance, letting us know that it is "sin," seeing as how "the strength of sin is the law."[2277]

27. Mor'decai tried to appease those Jews honoring the LORD's Sabbath and those Jews, while also honoring the seventh day, honored Ba'al's feast. The structure of this tradition of Mor'decai is forced, for if it was of the LORD's Spirit, all acknowledgment of His hand on their fortune would have been given, but this feast for the fourteenth and fifteenth is not of His wisdom or power. If this LORD's Spirit moved Moses to build on the first day of the week, and not on the seventh, it is plain to see that this Spirit would have His assembly sincerely honor His Sabbath. But with Mor'decai, the decision to act on the seventh day is no issue because tradition has, in his mind, blended paganism with the *Word's Faith*. To Mor'decai, "the LORD is a man of war,"[2278] and religious delusion has so perverted his spiritual understanding that he does not comprehend the LORD's Spirit didn't overthrow Pharaoh by violating the Sabbath.

28. The issue at hand between Pharaoh and Moses is revealed in how it says, "Ye make them rest from their burdens."[2279] The Sabbath was actually an issue within Egypt, for, according to the Egyptian, the Spirit's Sabbath is foolishness.

29. Pharaoh overworked the Jews, and especially on the seventh day, preventing them from passing in to the refreshing of the seventh day's hours. For, what was Moses' plea to Pharaoh? Didn't he say,

---

2276 Exodus 40:2
2277 1 Corinthians 15:56
2278 Exodus 15:3
2279 Exodus 5:5

"The LORD God of the Hebrews hath met with us: and now let us go, we beseech thee, three days' journey into the wilderness, that we may sacrifice to the LORD our God"?[2280] And when in the wilderness, what was the very first thing the LORD God tried to educate them on? He tried to teach them about His Sabbath through a lesson on diet, to the end they may never fail of His Sabbath "rest," and that the generations after them should never find themselves in the condition their fathers experienced when in Egypt.

30. This LORD labored for His people to remember the day that He Himself blessed for their spiritual renewal, and here is Mor'decai, moved by the spirit of Moses, uttering a thing not only contrary to the LORD's Word, but in devotion to that spirit and *Lord* who stripped Eden's heritage from her LORD and Creator.

31. It is therefore no surprise that a later figure should do for the Christian church what Mor'decai performed for the Jews through the consent of Ahasue'rus. These two men; Mor'decai and Ahasue'rus; when combined, are Pharaoh, even "the son of perdition; who opposeth and exalteth himself above all that is called God, or that is worshipped; so that he as God sitteth in the temple of God, shewing himself that he is God."[2281]

32. Them that should fill this role would be those ministers who quit the doctrine of the first apostles, only to have this seat legally filled by Constantine, and every other pope thereafter, who should write against the living God for a memorial to their offspring. This places us in remembrance that such as subscribe to "the handwriting of ordinances"[2282] are in communion with the "God" of "sin," seeing as how "the strength of sin is the law."[2283]

33. This record is left for us in the book of Esther that we may thoroughly examine the ancient spirit of error and measure it with that Spirit within the living God's religious character. These people called themselves Jews, and were outwardly known as Jews, but to the Spirit,

---

2280 Exodus 3:18
2281 2 Thessalonians 2:4
2282 Colossians 2:14
2283 1 Corinthians 15:56

they fulfill the saying, "I know the blasphemy of them which say they are Jews, and are not, but are the synagogue of Satan."[2284]

34. It is our responsibility to learn from past spiritual error, wherefore if we are joined to a tradition and ordinance singling out the fifteenth day as any thing, it is well to know that it is today, being of the pen of priests and elders, "sin" to the Word's Faith, for "the strength of sin is the law."[2285] Such an ancient record confesses to the fact that a church of religious error should find itself devoted to both the fourteenth day and the fifteenth day, and we may understand our affiliation with any synagogue of the serpent by it dawning the image of the tree, for it is written, "He that is hanged is accursed of God."[2286]

2284 Revelation 2:9
2285 1 Corinthians 15:56
2286 Deuteronomy 21:23

29

One Present Manner

1. When hearing, "And Jesus cried with a loud voice, and gave up the ghost. And the veil of the temple was rent in twain,"[2287] it is as if we are made to think on how, after weighing Saul's ignorance, "as Samuel turned about to go away, he laid hold upon the skirt of his mantle, and it rent. And Samuel said unto him, The LORD hath rent the kingdom of Israel from thee this day, and hath given it to a neighbour of thine, that is better than thou."[2288]

2. What rent when the Spirit's Christ gave up the *ghost* was that veil "of the temple of his body,"[2289] even that covering distorting the face of the *body* of His conversation's knowledge. Like as when Samuel rent his mantle and confessed the separation of the kingdom from Saul into the

---

2287 Mark 25:37,38
2288 1 Samuel 15:27,28
2289 John 2:21

possession of one better, so when the veil of the doctrine of the Word's man found itself rent, a spirit better than that *ghost* previously occupying that *body* of knowledge found itself possessing the conversation of that knowledge. A mind of devotion better than that former mind is herein become the Ruler and Governor over the living God's kingdom and righteousness, and it is our responsibility to know the certainty of this new and greatly benevolent doctrine that our conversation may never fail of a perfect devotion, to the end we may "serve him with a perfect heart and with a willing mind."[2290]

3. That ghost the Spirit's man gave up was the ghost of Saul, which ghost is innately rebellious against the living God's voice for self's uneducated and unsanctified impression. "Thou hast rejected the word of the LORD,"[2291] is the rebuke against Saul's ghost, and it is uttered for a reason, which reason the LORD's man states by saying, "Full well ye reject the commandment of God, that ye may keep your own tradition."[2292]

4. Saul's ghost favors religious "philosophy and vain deceit, after the tradition of men, after the rudiments of the world,"[2293] above "the commandments of God, and the faith of Jesus."[2294] Such a *ghost* preaches subjection of the conversation's conscience to "the tradition of the elders"[2295] by "the handwriting of ordinances."[2296] The appearance of the conversation in the sight of priests and ministers is of greater importance to this ghost, which is why this ghost says to the Spirit's messenger, "Honour me now, I pray thee, before the elders of my people, and before Israel."[2297]

5. What about the living God's honor? What about reverencing the living God before the *people*? Isn't His man's spirit a mind confessing,

---

2290 1 Chronicles 28:9
2291 1 Samuel 15:23
2292 Mark 7:9
2293 Colossians 2:8
2294 Revelation 14:12
2295 Matthew 15:2
2296 Colossians 2:14
2297 1 Samuel 15:30

"I will declare thy name unto my brethren, in the midst of the church will I sing praise unto thee"?[2298]

6. The fact of the living God's voice, to this man's mind, is above self's religious concoction, which is why this man, "having abolished in his flesh the enmity, even the law of commandments contained in ordinances,"[2299] denounced the handwritten law and tradition of priests and elders as "sin" to heaven's will and wisdom; it is herein well to know that, today, "the strength of sin is the law."[2300]

7. Saul's ghost; the religious course of priests and ministers; is that spirit and philosophy the Word's man gave up when on the tree; this "Christ hath redeemed us from the curse of the law, being made a curse for us: for it is written, Cursed is every one that hangeth on a tree."[2301] By giving up this religious ghost from the temple of his faith's *body* to utter separation from the living God's religious character, and by securing that spirit blessed of His God's Spirit into the hands of that Spirit, a better spiritual mind than that former mind is given sway over the conversation's conscience to better bless the reign of the Spirit's will and wisdom. With that ghost of rebellion silenced, and with that new mind sanctified by the Spirit's voice regenerating and carrying the temple of that *body's* faith, there is become only one Spirit and Word to learn of and do, and only one rule and commandment from one Word and Spirit to execute.

8. By this Spirit's man, every word of his spiritual understanding is become the responsibility of every conversation, thereby fulfilling the saying, "One law shall be to him that is homeborn, and unto the stranger that sojourneth among you."[2302]

9. This Spirit's chief messenger, by suffering the tree, utters the witness for only one LORD and Father, for with this man "having abolished in his flesh the enmity, even the law of commandments contained

---

2298   Hebrews 2:12
2299   Ephesians 2:15
2300   1 Corinthians 15:56
2301   Galatians 3:13
2302   Exodus 12:49

in ordinances,"[2303] what remains for accomplishment is every commandment of the living God.

10. Since "whatsoever God doeth, it shall be for ever,"[2304] to hear, "He that is hanged is accursed of God,"[2305] is to hear of an eternal rebuke placed upon the flesh of the Spirit's man. What is accursed is not the literal flesh of the man, but what the flesh of the man represents, which is "the handwriting of ordinances."[2306] The pen of priests and elders; and "not only in this world, but also in that which is to come";[2307] is perpetually accursed by the living God's man suffering the tree. Being "made under the law"[2308] and found on the tree means the condemnation of what this man was made under, which is "the law of commandments contained in ordinances."[2309]

11. And it makes no sense to condemn a thing and not supply a better thing for what is condemned, which is why "he taketh away the first, that he may establish the second."[2310] That "first" *thing* taken away is the former covenant and its promise, which covenant taught, "Righteousness come by the law."[2311] But with the LORD's man made under the religious law and found on the tree, a change in manners of personal worship and service is evident; in essence, a new priesthood is preached, and with "the priesthood being changed, there is made of necessity a change also of the law."[2312] This change is the new or second covenant, which covenant promises "the time of reformation,"[2313] in that the conversation is to be "perfect, as pertaining to the conscience."[2314]

2303   Ephesians 2:15
2304   Ecclesiastes 3:14
2305   Deuteronomy 21:23
2306   Colossians 2:14
2307   Ephesians 1:21
2308   Galatians 4:4
2309   Ephesians 2:15
2310   Hebrews 10:9
2311   Galatians 2:21
2312   Hebrews 7:12
2313   Hebrews 9:10
2314   Hebrews 9:9

12. No longer can that which "sanctifieth to the purifying of the flesh";[2315] namely, religious laws and traditions "after the commandments and doctrines of men";[2316] represent any *thing* any longer, for the conversation is to be "written not with ink, but with the Spirit of the living God."[2317] This is indeed a great reform in worship and service, for if "God is a Spirit,"[2318] and if "that which is born of the Spirit is spirit,"[2319] then *heaven's* present promise demands that you are "transformed by the renewing of your mind."[2320]

13. The former manner taught, "You are justified by the law,"[2321] wherefore it was lawful to hear and do the counsel, "Hearken, O Israel, unto the statutes and unto the judgments, which I teach you, for to do them."[2322] This counsel was given to the people through Moses, to receive *righteousness* by their obedience to the pen of his inspiration, but with His man "blotting out the handwriting of ordinances"[2323] from Moses' hand; whether that Moses be a *Moses* of that day or ours; the definition of "sin" is become blatantly plain, for "the strength of sin is the law."[2324]

14. By silencing the first will and covenant, the LORD's man, through suffering the tree, has opened up every one to the same heavenly congregation. There is, by this man suffering the tree, only one LORD God and Commandment of that God, for by nailing error's ghost to the tree, and by replacing that ghost with that spirit preserved within the Spirit's hands, every mind found where this man's mind of devotion is will obtain the same privilege of preservation by the same hands that keep his *body* and *temple*.

15. This is why "we have such an high priest, who is set on the right hand of the throne of the Majesty in the heavens."[2325] The present

---

2315 Hebrews 9:13
2316 Colossians 2:22
2317 2 Corinthians 3:3
2318 John 4:24
2319 John 3:6
2320 Romans 12:2
2321 Galatians 5:4
2322 Deuteronomy 4:1
2323 Colossians 2:14
2324 1 Corinthians 15:56
2325 Hebrews 8:1

covenant is a promise of creation, and this creation occurring within the conversation's inwards, seeing as how *they* are "to be strengthened with might by his Spirit in the inner man."[2326]

16. This allows us to further understand the perpetuity of the counsel, "One law and one manner shall be for you, and for the stranger that sojourneth with you."[2327] Herein is revealed to us the fact that we, being naturally ignorant of the living God, "wert cut out of the olive tree which is wild by nature, and wert graffed contrary to nature into a good olive tree"[2328] through the act of His man on the tree. This Spirit's man, by suffering the tree, opened up every mind to the same foundation of the same tree, for his doctrine is that Savior of this tree and foundation, saying, "I spake openly to the world; I ever taught in the synagogue, and in the temple, whither the Jews always resort."[2329]

17. This man of the Bible is that man of the Jewish synagogue, or of the Jewish religion. As that man, his office is not to destroy the religion of the Jews, but to alleviate it, and that alleviation appearing by him "having abolished in his flesh the enmity, even the law of commandments contained in ordinances."[2330] With the ghost of that flesh nailed to the tree, and with this man's law of devotion not only separated from the tree, but preserved and resurrected from the tree, what is preached is the conversation's return to the living God's original will and wisdom, which will and wisdom is found in Eden and at creation, and which religion is sealed with the sign of His voice's righteousness, saying, "God blessed the seventh day, and sanctified it."[2331]

18. With the LORD's man suffering the tree, "the general assembly and church of the firstborn"[2332] is opened to every mind willing to enter into it "after they have escaped the pollutions of the world through the knowledge of the Lord and Saviour Jesus Christ."[2333]

2326 Ephesians 3:16
2327 Numbers 15:16
2328 Romans 11:24
2329 John 18:20
2330 Ephesians 2:15
2331 Genesis 2:3
2332 Hebrews 12:23
2333 2 Peter 2:20

19. He or she learning of and doing heaven's knowledge will quit the spirit and philosophy of the religious world. "Full well ye reject the commandment of God, that ye may keep your own tradition,"[2334] says the Bible's Spirit of them that trust their confidence to the spirit of religious error, for from such a spirit comes "uncleanness, lasciviousness, idolatry, witchcraft, hatred, variance, emulations, wrath, strife, seditions, heresies, envyings, murders, drunkenness,"[2335] for it is believed that "you are justified by the law."[2336] But this is blatant religious error, for it is written, "By his knowledge shall my righteous servant justify many."[2337]

20. Justification; which is another term for sanctification; occurs as the mind is edified by the knowledge of creation's present will and wisdom. The conversation beautified "with the washing of water by the word"[2338] is become a creation of that wisdom; the statement of faith is become, "The law of the Spirit of life in Christ Jesus hath made me free from the law of sin and death."[2339]

21. Herein is witnessed the Spirit's righteousness, and that conversation sanctified by this Spirit's ministry will receive the privilege of passing in to this Spirit's sanctified seventh day; this is fact. A conflict occurs against the Spirit's Faith when the conversation is filled with that abolished ghost, and this is a great mystery, for isn't it written, "Whatsoever God doeth, it shall be for ever: nothing can be put to it, nor any thing taken from it"?[2340]

22. It is impossible for any thing done by the living God to find its self retarded, but this is "the mystery of iniquity,"[2341] wherein willing rebellion is chosen above humble obedience, and where humble obedience to rebellion is seen to be admirable among them that do "not like

---

2334 Mark 7:9
2335 Galatians 5:19-21
2336 Galatians 5:4
2337 Isaiah 53:11
2338 Ephesians 5:26
2339 Romans 8:2
2340 Ecclesiastes 3:14
2341 2 Thessalonians 2:7

to retain God in their knowledge."[2342] And what is "rebellion" today? If the LORD's "Christ hath redeemed us from the curse of the law,"[2343] our rebellion is understood by our willingness to stubbornly commit self to the philosophy of the religious law.

23. The *ghost* of Saul naturally rules the temple of our faith's *body*, and this government is contrary to the testimony of the Spirit's man, who "abolished in his flesh the enmity, even the law of commandments contained in ordinances."[2344] But if we are free of the religious law, we may know that our conversation stands in the liberty purchased for its conscience to be sanctified. It is this sanctification that will inform us of the fact that only one law and counsel for creation exists, and that where a contrary is found, it is not of the Godhead's intention. For it makes no sense that a house stands united while divided; there is no intelligent doctrinal togetherness wrought by a separation of opinion.

24. Isn't it written, "If a house be divided against itself, that house cannot stand"?[2345] Through the LORD's man, that Church within the heavenly Sanctuary is eternally established, and every other household of *earth* annihilated and made to experience division.

25. Unity is born as the mind is edified, which is why it says, "Stand fast in one spirit, with one mind striving together,"[2346] and, "That ye may with one mind and one mouth glorify God."[2347] Without heaven's manner of sanctification, disagreement and dissimulation will occur, for what is uttered is not proven to be the heavenly Sanctuary's science. But where sanctification prevails, faith's benevolent bond will be found, for heaven's educational course is one that only the doers of it can respect, and that respect awakening a gentle fondness for every mind traveling the same course of learning.

2342 Romans 1:28
2343 Galatians 3:13
2344 Ephesians 2:15
2345 Mark 3:25
2346 Philippians 1:27
2347 Romans 15:6

26. Creation is the end of heaven's Faith, and that Faith is ordained to bless the conversation with unfeigned love for creation's Spirit, "and this is love, that we walk after his commandments."[2348]

27. We really comprehend our fondness for the blessing of other conversations by our fondness for the living God's words. And is not this the example His man set?

28. By one act on the tree, we are made to see ultimate love for every word of the living God, and a benevolent kindness to the spirit of every conscience. This man suffered the tree to magnify the law of the living God's spiritual understanding, opening up to every mind the opportunity his spirit received, which opportunity is "the washing of regeneration, and renewing of the Holy Ghost."[2349] It is by this mental and spiritual baptism that every word of the LORD God's throne will become delightful, which is why His man says, "I have kept my Father's commandments, and abide in his love."[2350] Such a course of learning will open up the ear to hear, "Turn away thy foot from the Sabbath, from doing thy pleasure on my holy day; and call the Sabbath a delight, the holy of the LORD, honourable,"[2351] for by becoming a creation, the conversation is blessed to enter into creation's Sabbath.

29. Truly "God blessed the seventh day, and sanctified it,"[2352] but we can only know this when giving up the ghost of religious error to preserve the spirit of our mind by the mind of the heavenly Sanctuary's chief apostle.

2348 2 John 1:6
2349 Titus 3:5
2350 John 15:10
2351 Isaiah 58:13
2352 Genesis 2:3